The
Search
for
Self-Sovereignty

Elizabeth Cady Stanton. *Photo courtesy of Seneca Falls Historical Society.*

The
Search
for
Self-Sovereignty

The Oratory of Elizabeth Cady Stanton

Beth M. Waggenspack

Foreword by
Halford R. Ryan

Great American Orators, Number 4
Bernard K. Duffy and Halford R. Ryan, Series Advisers

Greenwood Press
New York • Westport, Connecticut • London

Library of Congress Cataloging-in-Publication Data

Waggenspack, Beth Marie.
   The search for self-sovereignty : the oratory of Elizabeth Cady
Stanton / Beth M. Waggenspack ; foreword by Halford R. Ryan.
      p.   cm. — (Great American orators, ISSN 0898-8277 ; no. 4)
   Bibliography: p.
   Includes index.
   ISBN 0-313-25978-X (lib. bdg. : alk. paper)
   1. Feminism—United States—History—Sources. 2. Stanton,
Elizabeth Cady, 1815-1902—Oratory. 3. Women's rights—United
States—History. 4. Political oratory—United States—History.
5. Rhetoric—Political aspects—United States—History.
6. Rhetoric—Social aspects—United States—History. 7. Speeches,
addresses, etc., American—Women authors—History and criticism.
8. Women orators—United States—History. I. Stanton, Elizabeth
Cady, 1815-1902. Speeches. Selection.   1989. II. Title.
III. Series.
HQ1426.W33   1989
305.42'0973—dc20   89-7519

British Library Cataloguing in Publication Data is available.

Library of Congress Catalog Card Number: 89-7519
ISBN: 0-313-25978-X
ISSN: 0898-8277

First published in 1989

Greenwood Press, Inc.
88 Post Road West, Westport, Connecticut 06881

Printed in the United States of America

The paper used in this book complies with the
Permanent Paper Standard issued by the National
Information Standards Organization (Z39.48-1984).

10 9 8 7 6 5 4 3 2 1

Copyright Acknowledgment

The author and publisher are grateful to Harper and Row, Pub-
lishers, Inc. for permission to use extracts from *Elizabeth Cady
Stanton as Revealed in Her Letters, Diary, and Reminiscences*,
volumes 1 and 2, by Theodore Stanton and Harriot Stanton
Blatch.

Contents

PART II: COLLECTED SPEECHES

Series Foreword

The idea for a series of books on great American orators grew out of the recognition that there is a paucity of book-length studies on individual speakers and their craft. Apart from a few notable exceptions, the study of American public address has been pursued in scores of articles published in professional journals. Yet, no matter how insightful their intellectual forebears, each generation of rhetorical critics must reexamine its universe of discourse, expand the compass of its researches, and redefine its purpose and methods. To avoid intellectual torpor, scholars and students cannot be content simply to see through the eyes of those who have gone before them. As helpful as article-length studies have been none has or can provide a complete analysis of a speaker's rhetoric. Book-length studies, such as those in this series, will help fill the void that has existed in the study of American public address. In books, more than in articles, the critic can explicate a speaker's persuasive discourse that ranges over politics and history, theology and sociology, communication and law. The comprehensive research and sustained reflection that books require will undoubtedly yield telling examinations and enduring insights for the nation's most important voices.

This series chronicles the role of public discourse in the United States. American speakers shaped the destiny of the colonies, the young republic, and the mature nation. During each stage of the intellectual, political, and religious development of the United States, great orators, standing at the rostrum, on the stump, and in the pulpit, persuaded their audiences with word and gesture. Usually striving for the noble, sometimes achieving the base, they urged their fellow citizens toward a more perfect Union.

Each book is organized to meet the needs of scholars and students who would evaluate the effects of American public address. Previously, if one desired to assess the impact of a speaker or a speech upon history, the path was, at best, not well marked and, at worst, littered with obstacles. To be sure, one might turn to biographies to learn about an orator, but for the public address scholar these sources often prove unhelpful. Rhetorical topics, such as speech invention, disposition, style, delivery, and persuasive effect, are often treated in passing, if at all. Authoritative speech texts are often difficult to locate and the problem of textual accuracy is frequently encountered. This is especially true for early figures, or for those whose persuasive role, though significant, was secondary to other leading lights of the age.

Part I is a critical analysis of the orator and his or her speeches. Within the format of a case study, one may expect considerable latitude. For instance, in a given chapter an author might explicate a single speech or a group of related speeches, or examine orations that comprise a genre of rhetoric such as forensic speaking. But the critic's focus remains on the rhetorical considerations of speaker and speech, purpose and effect.

Part II contains the texts of the important addresses that are discussed in the critical analysis that precedes it. To the extent possible, each author has endeavored to collect definitive speech texts, which have often been found through original research in historical materials. In a few instances, because of the extreme length of a speech, texts have been edited, but the authors have carefully deleted material that is least important to the speech, and these deletions have been held to a minimum.

Each book contains a chronology of major speeches that serves several purposes. Pragmatically, it lists all of the orator's know addresses. Places and dates of the speeches are also given, although this information is sometimes difficult to determine precisely. But in a wider sense, the chronology attests to the scope of rhetoric in the United States. Certainly in quantity, if not always in quality, Americans are historically talkers and listeners.

Because of the disparate nature of the speakers examined in the series, there is some latitude in the nature of the bibliographical materials that have been included in each book. But in every instance, authors have carefully described historical collections, and have gathered primary and secondary sources that bear on the speaker and the oratory. By combining in each book critical chapters with bibliographical materials and speech texts, this series notes that textual and research sources are interwoven in the act of rhetorical criticism.

May the books in this series serve as a fitting memorial to the nation's greatest orators as students and scholars study anew the history and criticism of American public address.

Bernard K. Duffy
Halford R. Ryan

Foreword

As an orator, Elizabeth Cady Stanton faced constraints her male counterparts did not confront. Free to devote themselves to their chosen paths, men could initiate their careers through oratory, develop their ethos on the stump, rostrum, or pulpit, and sustain their fame with the spoken word. Nor did they have to contend with presumption in the minds of many that males should not speak in public. As a wife and then a mother, Elizabeth Cady Stanton had to balance home and hearth with the public platform. And some males and females would have been content for Cady Stanton to remain in the home. Her oratorical career amidst the nineteenth century was not as varied in prestigious genres as Daniel Webster's, nor as long or uninterrupted as the Reverend Henry Ward Beecher's, nor as sublimely presidential as Abraham Lincoln's, but the lacunae in her speech making, although she admittedly addressed less august audiences than the United States Senate or Plymouth Church or the White House, were compensated by the exigencies she addressed. For if Webster was the voice of the Senate, and Beecher, the *vox Dei*, and Lincoln the *vox populi*, then surely Elizabeth Cady Stanton was the *prima vox feminarum* (the first voice of women).

Unfortunately, Elizabeth Cady Stanton has not been accorded the rhetorical attention she so richly deserves. This scholarly oversight in the history and criticism of American public address is hereby addressed by Professor Beth Waggenspack. Professor Waggenspack has based her study of Cady Stanton's speaking on original research that she conducted in the Elizabeth Cady Stanton Papers in the Library of Congress. One of the scholarly consequences of her research, which should facilitate the study of feminist rhetoric, is that some of Cady Stanton's significant persuasions are gathered in the "Collected Speeches." Hitherto, many of these canonical communications were practically inaccessible. Another result is a speech chronology, which has not been published before, that details all of Cady Stanton's known addresses. Moreover, Waggenspack has carefully annotated biographies on Cady Stanton, and has detailed the contents of the Elizabeth Cady Stanton Papers in the Library of Congress.

Yet, Waggenspack has not in her book created a paean to feminist rhetoric or an encomium to Elizabeth Cady Stanton. To be sure, Waggenspack details the feminine topics that Cady Stanton characteristically developed in her public orations, and admittedly these issues affected women more than men. But the efficacy of Waggenspack's critical exegesis of Cady Stanton's speeches is her insight that Cady Stanton really cast her rhetoric in the best humanistic tradition of American public address. That is to say, whether excoriating males for their unwarranted dominance over women or scolding women for their passive dependence on men, Cady Stanton spoke to develop the best humane qualities in both sexes. After reading Waggenspack's critical exegisis of Cady Stanton's rhetoric, many will probably select a favorite speech, but surely most can agree that Cady Stanton's "Solitude of Self" engages men and women today even as it addressed Americans of both sexes a century ago.

Halford Ryan

Preface

My "friendship" with Elizabeth Cady Stanton began in a doctoral class at Ohio State University; she has been with me for several years now, and her wit, skilled articulation of arguments, and logic still serve to amaze and delight. As far as I am concerned, she set a standard for all people to follow: speak your mind, hold fast to your convictions, and argue for what is right.

For Courtney and Stephen, who someday will read this work and marvel that equality of the sexes was ever a divisive issue, I hope that they can learn from Elizabeth Cady Stanton that SELF-DEVELOPMENT IS A HIGHER DUTY THAN SELF-SACRIFICE.

Acknowledgments

This work has benefited from the critical reading of Halford Ryan of Washington and Lee University, who nurtured both the manuscript and its author. Edward Sewell and Jean Speer of Virginia Polytechnic Institute and State University also helped me to cultivate the writer's craft, and their eagle eyes and encouragment are much appreciated.

I am also indebted to Sylvia Farrer-Bornarth, Executive Director of the Seneca Falls Historical Society for her help in securing photographs; Mildred Vasan, Editor, Politics and Law, and Catherine A. Lyons, Production Editor, of Greenwood Press for putting up with endless questions about manuscript details; Ruth Adkins, the copyeditor whose fine eye helped me to gain insight into my own writing; and Kenneth F. Rystrom and Robert E. Denton, Jr., department heads who enthusiastically encouraged me to undertake and complete this project.

I

ELIZABETH CADY STANTON

Introduction

Elizabeth Cady Stanton has received acclaim as one of the founders and leaders of the woman's rights movement, yet her impact on American customs, traditions, and laws went beyond the concerns of rights for women. In fact, her decades-long public support for various reform causes touched all parts of daily living. Because of her advocacy of such a breadth of issues, including divorce, suffrage, abortion, work laws, property rights, and education, some detractors accused her of lacking direction. Others charged her with radicalism and the destruction of any hopes women had of gaining ground. However, more than most other reformers of her times, Elizabeth Cady Stanton charged ahead, confronting society's perceptions of women's duties and roles. She believed that change could only come through total self-dependence and self-reliance; once women and men were freed from encumbering social, moral, legal, and religious traditions, then they could achieve their true potential. Her native curiosity, audacious thinking, and bold advocacy on various fronts combined with the galvanized spirit of reform to create a larger-than-life figure whose impact on society is still being felt.

It is ironic that Cady Stanton is often referred to as the silent partner of the much better known Susan B. Anthony; their decades-long partnership was marked by anything but Cady Stanton's silence. Indeed, Cady Stanton was one of the most conspicuous women's rights advocates of her century. As the philosopher-founder of the movement, she devised its charter, set its agenda, and helped create its organizations; as one of its most recognized national leaders, she chronicled its history, participated in and survived its split and restructuring, and became its "grand old woman." In addition, as an agitator within the movement, she served to decry its eventual conservative turn, and she became a thorn and embarassment to the new leaders who emerged as the movement entered its third and fourth decades. It is all of these roles that this book intends to investigate; indeed, by examining her rhetoric on various topics and in various stages, Elizabeth Cady Stanton's leadership role within the movement can be fully chronicled and analyzed. Cady Stanton was a prolific writer and speaker, newspaper editor and contributing columnist, and her words shaped a nation's destiny.

One of the recurrent stylistic problems facing the modern author is what to call Elizabeth Cady Stanton. I have chosen to refer to her in childhood as Elizabeth or Elizabeth Cady. Beginning with her 1840 marriage, I refer to her as Cady Stanton or Elizabeth Cady Stanton, which is how she always signed her name. While newspapers tended to call her Mrs. Stanton, I have chosen not to use that style. One of the essential aspects of Cady Stanton's self-sovereignty was her insistence that she be called by the name that represented her own self; this early emphasis on independence was a hallmark of her feminist ideology. Although she never referred to her beliefs as feminist thinking (for the term had not been coined yet), it is appropriate to use the word feminist when referring to Cady Stanton. The advocacy of equal rights for women is the essence of what we now call feminism.

Elizabeth Cady Stanton recognized that custom and prejudice carry more power than logic or rational arguments. Because she saw that the perception of woman's sphere and capabilities was based on traditions of irrationality, she realized that the tactics used to refute such illogical misrepresentations had to shift the way people viewed the truth. This work attempts to bring light to the arguments Cady Stanton utilized in creating, developing, and articulating her feminist philosophy throughout her various roles in the first fifty years of the women's movement.

Hers was an unconventional upbringing that supported a keen intelligence and outspoken views, so she was able to develop the advocacy skills necessary to present a revolutionary vision for societal change. Because she was fortunate enough to encounter several role models who, in varying turns and times, encouraged her political, religious, social, intellectual, and physical development, she was able to develop a sense of self-sovereignty throughout her lifetime. Her father's tolerance of her desire for education; Simon Hosack and Edward Bayard's encouragement of her critical skills; Lucretia Mott's tutelage in the ways of religion, politics, and equality; Henry B. Stanton's radical ideals and tolerance of a wife who went beyond woman's sphere; and Susan B. Anthony's complementary partnership in many reform issues: each in turn would play an important reinforcing aspect in her personal development, public acclaim, and success in attaining self-sovereignty.

Each of these role models supplied the means for Cady Stanton to achieve independence. Most of them encouraged her intellectual skepticism and activity; all gave her affection and approval. At the same time, each mentor's role was more developmental than lasting; as Cady Stanton learned from them, she tended to move on, and often her role models became her adversaries, or at least her doubters. For example, although she found in Lucretia Mott the first woman who could articulate woman's social ills, she later discounted Mott's admonitions that arguing for suffrage would make Cady Stanton appear ridiculous. Although Henry Stanton was at first a dashing, eloquent abolitionist, his impact on her burgeoning public career was minimal, as they lived in separate households and led independent lives. Susan B. Anthony may have spurred Cady Stanton to work, keeping her intimately involved in the women's rights movement despite Cady Stanton's domestic responsibilities, but Anthony's influence evolved into an equal partnership, including tension and differences of opinion. As she aged, Cady Stanton lost the need for these mentors' approval, and as she became more sure of her own self-worth, she became her own model of authority. She achieved the self-sovereignty that her oratory had long demanded.

From these mentors and other secondary figures, Cady Stanton gradually developed an ideal vision of the heroic woman she wanted to be. She was disciplined in her intellectual pursuits, reading voraciously and writing constantly on a breadth of subjects. Thus, she developed a scope and a tolerance for a wide variety of new ideas. She possessed argumentative skills for public and private debate, which she developed and exploited as a lyceum speaker, social reform critic, and women's rights advocate. At the 1869 Woman Suffrage Convention, Grace Greenwood in the *Philadelphia Press* described Cady Stanton:

> Of all their speakers, she seemed to me to
> have the most weight. Her speeches are
> models of composition, clear, compact, elegant
> and logical. She makes her points with
> perculiar sharpness and certainty, and there
> is no denying or dodging her conclusions . . . .
> (She is) now impassioned, now playful, now
> witty, now pathetic . . . . Mrs. Stanton has the
> best arts of the politician and the training of
> the jurist, added to the fiery, unresting spirit
> of the reformer. She has a rare talent for
> affairs, management, and mastership. Yet she
> is in an eminent degree womanly, having an
> almost regal pride of sex."[1]

Her ability to run a large household smoothly, successfully raise seven children without much help from her abolitionist husband, and her pride in housekeeping skills added to the matronly image of motherhood she wanted to foster. Cloaked in the mantle of motherhood, she shrewdly depicted herself as a respectable, congenial matron. Cady Stanton knew the powers of images, and she exploited desirable ones to her public advantage.

In learning about Elizabeth Cady Stanton, it might help the reader to have a physical picture of her. She is often shown in pictures dressed in black silk with a touch of lace, possessing a halo of white curls which contributed to a matronly or queenly look. Journalists often compared her to Queen Victoria or Martha Washington, and she played upon the grandmotherly image. As she aged, she suffered physical ailments of obesity (a combination of seven childbirths and uncontrollable eating) and blindness, but her wit and intellect remained sharp.

This work attempts to provide some insight into the origins, arguments, and logic of Elizabeth Cady Stanton's oratory. I have selected several speech texts, many of which have not been published elsewhere, to illuminate her style, tone, and logic. Although the sheer volume of speeches and essays, both published and unpublished, is enormous, I have attempted to choose texts that give the reader a sense of the breadth of her concerns, along with her ideology and intellectual strategies as she played various advocacy roles (leader and internal agitator) within the movement.

The addresses covering her suffrage arguments demonstrate the essential nature of her use of logical argument and extensive proof in her arguments against woman's legal and political wrongs. The first, her 1854 Address before the New York State Legislature's Joint Judiciary Committee, attempts to clarify the actual position of woman in society as contrasted with the public's false perception of those roles. The second, her 1860 Address before the New York State Legislature, illuminates Cady Stanton's extensive use of extended metaphors and attempts at dissociation of false images from reality. Both addresses rely upon a wealth of legal evidence combined with liberal uses of arguments using the Golden Rule. She sensed that if she could make men realize that they were treating women as less than equal to the negro slaves who were being given citizen's rights, then perhaps the legislators would recognize the need for change.

The discontent and reform addresses that present her positions on other reform issues display the vexation Cady Stanton felt with woman's position in society. In addition to an excerpt from her presidential remarks on religion given at the Seventeenth National Suffrage Convention of 1885, I analyze two speeches on divorce and marriage. The first, "Speech on Marriage and Divorce" was delivered in 1869 with no description of setting or audience; it attempted to clarify the true meaning of the term marriage. The second address was delivered on October 20, 1870 at the Decade Meeting on Marriage and Divorce. As another indication of her frustration with woman's position in society, I analyze one of her lyceum addresses, entitled "Co-Education," in which she called for equality in all educational opportunities. Finally, the two addresses that demonstrate Cady Stanton's image of woman include one of her most popular lyceum addresses, "Our Girls," and her most famous and well-received speech, "The Solitude of Self." These two addresses not only revealed Cady Stanton's feminist self-image but also exhibited the depth of her skills as a rhetor: use of clear arguments, illustrative supporting materials, and expressive language.

The scope of this book is designed to provide the reader with some insights into the formation of Cady Stanton's character, philosophy, leadership, and spoken rhetoric. In addition, a selected bibliography reviews the major research collections, primary and secondary materials, and books and articles written about Elizabeth Cady Stanton in order to provide a framework for further research. Little rhetorical analysis has been completed on the extensive amount of essays, speeches, and drafts that Cady Stanton left for history to analyze. Her public career spanned over fifty years, and she rarely left unspoken her views on social, political, moral, religious, or legal issues. She was responsible for many of the profound changes in the conditions of women; her vision of self-sovereignty became both a personal creed as well as the basis for all reform.

1

From Defect of Sex
to Self-Sovereignty

Elizabeth Cady Stanton lived during an era that maintained women's inferior status due to a supposed defect of sex, which affected legal conditions concerning women's property, children, employment, and marriage. This supposed defect was to be the source of much of her life's arguments and fame. Born November 12, 1815, in Johnstown, New York, Elizabeth Cady was the daughter of Margaret Livingston, whose father, Colonel James Livingston, fought in the Revolution under General Washington; and Daniel Cady, a distinguished lawyer, New York State judge and congressman. Of her birth, Cady Stanton noted in her autobiography:

> With several generations of vigorous, enterprising ancestors behind me, I commenced the struggle of life under favorable circumstances . . . the same year . . . that my father was elected to Congress. Perhaps the excitement of a political campaign, in which my mother took the deepest interest, may have had an influence on my life and given me the strong desire that I have always felt to participate in the rights and duties of government.[1]

Margaret Livingston Cady (1785-1871), of Scottish and Dutch descent, was said by Cady Stanton to have the "military idea of government," which translated into childraising with the use of fear rather than love and compassion.[2] Daniel Cady (1773-1859), the earliest influential figure in Elizabeth's life, was both loved and feared by his family. She recalled him as "a man of firm character and unimpeachable integrity, and yet sensitive and modest to a painful degree."[3] He was conservative and self-made; in fact, he became one of the wealthiest landowners in New York. He was elected to the state legislature (1808-1814), to Congress (1814-1816), and served as a circuit court judge. In 1847, he was elected associate justice of the New York Supreme Court (Fourth District), where he served until 1855. Cady Stanton portrayed her father in a much kinder light in her autobiography, but it is apparent that he opposed much of what she came to stand for: he did not care for higher education for women, forbade her marriage, and opposed her public activities on reform. Much of her rhetoric would appear to be in direct rebuttal to his beliefs.

As fitting a family of moderate wealth, the Cadys' home was a two-story white frame house, whose grounds joined those of a Presbyterian minister, Simon Hosack. The Cadys had eleven children, six girls and five boys. Four of the sons died before becoming adults; only Eleazar lived until he was twenty. Elizabeth was the seventh child and middle daughter: her sisters were Harriot (1802-1810), Tryphena (1804-1891), Harriet (1810-?), Margaret (1817-1912), and Catherine (1819-?). Daniel's wealth and the family's social position ensured that the children had opportunities for education, holidays, and physical activity. Elizabeth recalled Johnstown as an intellectual center that also provided much outdoor activity. She most clearly remembered the Johnstown Academy and churches, each of which owned bells that "seemed to be forever tolling for school, funerals, church, or prayer meetings."[4] Perhaps part of the mature Cady Stanton's rebukes against organized religion had their roots in these early admonitions against sin.

This early resistance to established and expected custom was enhanced by Elizabeth's ability to use words effectively in expressing her thoughts and arousing action in others. She recalled arguing about the constant restrictions placed in a child's life with her sister Margaret, noting, "I have a confused memory of being often under punishment for what was in those days were called 'tantrums.' I suppose they were really justifiable acts of rebellion against the tyranny of those in authority."[5]

MILESTONES

Two events served as important milestones in Elizabeth's childhood; these stirred her early feminist thought and would also become recurring illustrations in her speeches on the wrongs done to women. The first event, the 1819 birth of her sister Catherine, elicited youthful compassion for the new stranger. Having heard many visitors regretfully remark that it was a pity the child was a girl, Elizabeth could not see where pity was deserved. The second event occurred when she was eleven and her only brother, Eleazar, who had just graduated from Union College, died of an illness resulting from an accident. Elizabeth went to her father's study to seek and provide comfort.

> We both sat in silence, he thinking of the
> wreck of all his hopes in the loss of a dear
> son, and I wondering what could be said or
> done to fill the void in his breast. At length
> he heaved a deep sigh and said, "Oh, my
> daughter, would that you were a boy!"[6]

This statement was repeated by Daniel Cady several more times in Elizabeth's youth; it was then that she resolved to dedicate her life to study in order to be the best in her father's eyes, even though she was a member of the wrong sex. This tale plays a leading role in many of Cady Stanton's reminiscences, letters, and addresses. At a vulnerable time in her youth, when she wanted to comfort a grieving father, circumstances and his unthinking remarks caused her to strengthen a resolve to do everything she could to be manly. It was as though her character were given a new feminist direction.

Eleven-year-old Elizabeth Cady was enrolled at the Johnstown Academy, where she studied Latin, Greek, and mathematics with boys. She received class honors in Greek, but when she informed her father of her prize, beyond a look of pleasure and some questions about her class and teachers, Daniel's only comment was the sigh, "Ah, you should have been a boy!"[7] She learned to be physically active, became a skilled and artful debater, and fostered a strong intellect with wide-ranging reading and analytical skills. Judge Cady indulged these academic and athletic achievements, for he allowed her to spend hours in the library and law office, let her attend court sessions, and encouraged her to compete and perform. However, he did not provide much approval of her activities; and as she grew older and wanted to do more, Daniel Cady eventually voiced absolute disapproval of the unseemly behavior which he had condoned.

At about the same time of her youthful vow to achieve, a Presbyterian pastor named Simon Hosack became Elizabeth's new intellectual influence. As their gardens shared common boundaries, she was Hosack's frequent visitor; he seemed never too weary to answer her endless questions. Elizabeth Cady became Hosack's companion on his parish rounds, and they rode endless miles together, talking for hours. Elizabeth called her discussions the earliest influences on her intellectual development: "Some of the rare phrases with which he besprinkled his conversation have always abided with me and did not a little to awaken in my young and receptive brain a taste for rhetoric."[8] Hosack also sensitized the young girl to respond with compassion to her surroundings, creating in her an openness and liberal view that was beyond her youthful years.

Elizabeth turned to Hosack for tutelage in horseback riding, Greek, and grammar. He also provided comfort for her feelings of suffering, sorrow, and inferiority at her "defect of sex." Hosack encouraged her self-confidence, as he admonished:

> It is your mission to help mold the world anew. May good angels give you thoughts and move you to do the work which they want done on earth. You must promise me one thing, and that is that you will always say what you think. Your thoughts are given to you to utter, not to conceal; and if you are true to yourself, and give to others all you see and know, God will pour more light and truth into your soul. [9]

Since her father's law office adjoined the house, Elizabeth spent much of her time there listening to clients' cases, talking with law students, and becoming familiar with laws affecting women. She remembered: "The tears and complaints of the women who came to my father for legal advice touched my heart, and early drew my attention to the injustice and cruelty of the laws."[10] Such experiences were to form the foundation for most of her life's work and public address toward changing statutes unfair to women. Judge Cady eventually acknowledged her interests and told her: "When you are grown up, and able to prepare a speech, you must go down to Albany and talk to the legislators; tell them all you have seen in this office . . . and, if you can persuade them to pass new laws, the old ones will be a dead letter."[11] In fact, most of her adult rhetoric was liberally sprinkled with legal cases and precedent, which she had learned in her father's office.

Until age 15, Elizabeth studied at the Johnstown Academy. In the winter of 1830, Elizabeth Cady was enrolled at the fashionable Willard's Troy Seminary, which was considered an intellectual Mecca, albeit entirely female. Here she came into contact with girls from Europe, Canada, and all parts of the United States. Emma Hart Willard (1787-1870) was the first educator to replace the traditional offerings of finishing schools with a comprehensive curriculum and education for domestic usefulness. Students were graduated with a breadth of intellectual interests along with a hearty dose of "womanly arts"; the purpose of education was ultimately to create better mothers. Willard gave her students a thorough grounding in physiology (a shocking topic for the times), geography (from her own text), higher mathematics, Greek and Latin, French, music, criticism, religious and moral instruction, chemistry, domestic science, and elocution (utilizing Blair's *Lectures on Rhetoric and Belles Lettres*).[12] Another event at Troy influential in molding Elizabeth Cady's character and rhetoric was the public preaching of the fiery pulpit orator, the Reverend Charles G. Finney (1792-1875), whom she termed "a terrifier of human soul."[13] The Great Troy Revival of 1831, six weeks of revival sessions, daily prayer, and experience meetings, had a terrifying effect on the young girl. While she had been raised as a Presbyterian, Elizabeth had a morose view of a punishing, wrathful God. Finney was able to exhort his audience into a state of total humility, which had only one source of salvation: turning their hearts over to Jesus. The spellbound young listeners were warned of their assured eternal damnation due to the total depravity of humanity and God's hatred of sin. Elizabeth noted the results in her diary, "Owing to my gloomy Calvinistic training in the old scotch Presbyterian Church, and my vivid imagination, I was one of the first victims."[14] Although many had imagined themselves converted and saved rather than among the sinful outcasts, Finney's oratory and theatrics shortened their hopes. Elizabeth found herself prostrated from her mental anguish and visions of hell; the resultant nervous condition endangered her health. Conversion thus shook her self-esteem and caused her to become ill. Returning home, she often awoke her family to pray for her immortal soul.

In order to ease her religious anguish, a family trip to Niagara Falls was planned. This six-week sojourn proved highly beneficial, and Elizabeth found her mind shifting from religious superstition to rational ideas whose basis existed in fact. Finney's ultimate influence on Elizabeth was that she came to question and reject all her Calvinistic training, and she chose skepticism. Theology became for her an analytic study, and eventually, she would reject religious authority of all kinds. A second result of the revival fervor was her introduction to the reform community, which was committed to perfecting humanity.

Elizabeth's childhood, which allowed her to experiment within the roles expected of men and of women, permitted her to attend legal hearings, and provided the chance for higher education, was not a typical one. She was given the opportunity to learn domestic arts along with intellectual, analytical skills. This early nontraditional grounding enhanced the independent spirit that was to triumph as she matured.

WOMANHOOD

After graduation in 1833, Elizabeth Cady returned home to Johnstown. Of particular importance was her eldest sister Tryphena's husband, homeopathic surgeon Edward Bayard. Elizabeth viewed Bayard as companion, counselor, and confidant because "in the pursuit of truth [he] was in no way trammeled by popular superstitions. He took nothing for granted, and, like Socrates, went about asking questions."[15] Bayard's discussions about law, philosophy, history, and literature sharpened the young girl's abilities in logic, analysis, and debate. His ideas became hers, and her adult rhetoric often mirrored these early conversations on topics from homeopathic health to religion. Elizabeth and Bayard were close friends and confidants for over ten years, yet his role as confidant eventually changed. According to biographer Elisabeth Griffith, Bayard proposed that Elizabeth run away with him; she refused and their relationship shifted. However, his impact on Elizabeth was strong, and in a family scrapbook, one daughter wrote under Bayard's photograph, "Perhaps the most formative influence in the life of Elizabeth Cady."[16] There was no divorce allowed in 1840; whether the Bayards' marriage was unhappy was irrelevant. Perhaps this early glimpse of an unfortunate marriage made its mark, for divorce reform was to become one of Cady Stanton's "scandalous" causes.

The Cady family paid yearly visits to the Peterboro, New York home of Margaret Livingston's nephew, Gerrit Smith (1797-1874). Smith, a leading orator, supported many reform causes, and his home was a central gathering place for discussion and action. Subjects as diverse as politics, temperance, religion, slavery, women's rights, and dress reform were freely discussed; Smith's generosity extended to guests from all walks of life. Oneida Indians enjoyed a long-established tradition of hospitality in his home. Escaped slaves knew the site as a station on the Underground Railroad; they often stopped there on their way north to Canada and freedom.The visits challenged her thinking about various issues, and she grew adept at arguing her points. As Elizabeth later noted, "These rousing arguments at Peterboro made social life seem tame and profitless elsewhere, and the youngest of us felt that the conclusions reached in this school of philosophy were not to be questioned." [17]

The Peterboro visits also provided a stimulus other than the intellectual, for it was here that Elizabeth fell in love with her husband. Henry Brewster Stanton (1805-1887) held a series of local antislavery meetings, making Gerrit Smith's home his base. The dynamic speaker was a well-known abolitionist who preached political action, saying the way to reform lay through the ballot. Stanton's impassioned oratory attracted the attention of Elizabeth Cady, who remarked on his power to make audiences cry and laugh. After knowing each other for less than one month, in October 1839 the two became engaged.

Despite family objections to Stanton's radicalism, her father's threat to disinherit her, their ten years' age difference, and the unlucky marriage day of a Friday, the two were wed on May 10, 1840. Stanton proved to be an apt partner for Elizabeth Cady, and their marriage lasted nearly half a century. He, too, acted upon strongly held beliefs. As Elizabeth remembered, "I felt a new inspiration in life and was enthused with new ideas of individual rights and the basic principles of government."[18] The tone for an equal marriage partnership was set when Elizabeth persuaded the Scotch clergyman to eliminate the word "obey" from the wedding vows; she declared that she wished to be known as Elizabeth Cady Stanton. She argued this belief by proclaiming:

> There is a great deal in a name. It often signifies much and may involve a great principle. Why are slaves nameless unless they take that of their master? Simply because they have no independent existence; even so with women. The custom of calling women Mrs. John This or Mrs. Tom That is founded on the principle that white men are the lords of us all. [19]

The two traveled on their honeymoon to the World's Anti-Slavery Convention, which met June 12, 1840, in London's Freemason's Hall, with international delegates from numerous antislavery societies. Though women were equal members of the American National Anti-Slavery Society, their representation was rejected by the dominating English factions who felt women were not fit to be delegates. The question was hotly debated, with the clerical delegates being the most violently opposed. With assurance by biblical clout, they argued woman's divinely decreed subjection. Cady Stanton remembered her disdain: "It was really pitiful to hear the narrow-minded bigots, pretending to be teachers and leaders of men, so cruelly remanding their own mothers, with the rest of womankind, to absolute subjection to the ordinary masculine type of humanity.[20] She was disgusted at the lack of justice promoted by those who, after eloquently decrying slavery, denied freedom to one-half of the human race.

Lucretia Mott (1793-1880), a 47-year-old Quaker intellectual on politics, religion, and social questions in general, was one of the convention delegates refused seating.[21] There, she met the young Elizabeth, who had largely lived outside of reform causes to any significant degree. Fortuitously, these two shared lodging in London, spending hours in each others' company. Cady Stanton found in the liberal Mott not only a companion, but a stimulating and willing mentor. She said:

> Mrs. Mott was to me an entire new revelation of womanhood. I sought every opportunity to be at her side, and continually plied her with questions . . . . When I first heard from her lips that I had the same right to think for myself that Luther, Calvin, and John Knox had, and the same right to be guided by my own convictions, I felt a born sense of dignity and freedom.[22]

In Mott, Elizabeth found a mentor who had sufficient confidence in herself to articulate an opinion in the face of opposition; she knew how to parry attacks and defend herself in public debates. Mott thus encouraged Cady Stanton's growing independence and self-confidence.

Many of the dinner-table discussions centered on the split in the American antislavery groups between those that allowed women as full members (the American Anti-Slavery Society) and those that didn't (the American and Foreign Anti-Slavery Society). Cady Stanton believed that the major issue of the day was not slavery but woman's rights. She later commented:

> The potent element which caused the division was the woman question, and as the Garrisonian branch (the American Anti-Slavery Society) maintained the right of women to speak and vote in the conventions, all my sympathies were with the Garrisonians, though Mr. Stanton and Mr. Birney belonged to the other Branch, called political abolitionists. To me there was no question so important as the emancipation of women from the dogmas of the past, political, religious, and social. It struck me as very remarkable that abolitionists who felt so keenly the wrongs of the slave, should be so oblivious to the equal wrongs of their own mothers, wives, and sisters. [23]

These discussions were a revelation to Elizabeth, who remembered: "These were the first women I had ever met who believed in the equality of the sexes. The acquaintance of Lucretia Mott . . . opened to me a new world of thought."[24] Long walks together and six weeks' time allowed the two to converse about social theories, religious issues, and reform programs of the day. Up to this point, Elizabeth had held strong opinions, but she had no framework through which to bind or articulate them. Her intellectual growth, coupled with her new-found independence from her family, allowed her to articulate questions about many of her previously held beliefs, motives, ideas, and religious precepts. Mott had been through a similar spiritual crisis, and she was able to help Cady Stanton understand the Quaker doctrine of "inner light" by giving her the sense that each individual had the right to interpret his or her experience with God, and that theology as the churches and clergy preached it often stopped people from experience this truth. Thus, through Lucretia Mott, Cady Stanton came to believe that questioning society's accepted truths was the way to find oneself. In Mott, Cady Stanton found a mentor whose intellectual curiosity stimulated and encouraged hers. These hours of discussions over topics of religion, politics, and custom culminated in an agreement between Mott and Cady Stanton to "hold a convention as soon as we returned home, and form a society to advocate the rights of women."[25]

What is the significance of this new state of intellectual being for Elizabeth Cady Stanton's rhetoric? Since she has been recognized as a founding mother and philosopher of the woman's movement, a brief departure from the narrative of her personal development is necessary. For a social movement (such as the one agitating for women's rights) to be born, certain conditions must exist. Society may be generally unaware of a problem, or it may give it low priority. The audience that may cause a change is often geographically scattered, making it necessary for a leader or prophet to come forward and dramatize an "imperfection" as the starting point for societal alteration. This early aspect of a movement is called "genesis;" for a movement to progress, leaders must achieve the next stage, called "social unrest."[26] These early leaders must attract members to the cause; their role is that of educator or prophet who persists in attempts to create interest, according to Lloyd Bitzer, because of the belief that "interest will increase insofar as the factual condition" becomes "known directly and sensibly, or through vivid representation."[27] It is the role of early leaders to discredit those in power and to set the stage for the rise of the movement. In London, the seeds of discontent were sown, and all it would take for the genesis stage to mature into social unrest would be a triggering event to bring the discontent into bloom. This would come eight years later in Seneca Falls, New York.

MOTHERHOOD

Upon their return to Johnstown, Henry Stanton began clerking for his father-in-law, hoping to soothe the family breach. Elizabeth's attention quickly shifted to a new concern: her first child, Daniel Cady Stanton, called Neil (1842-1891). An eagerness to raise her son in the best manner had her reading everything within reach; the lack of published information on such an important topic appalled her. Elizabeth's comments about the traditions and misconceptions perpetuated by the medical profession were characteristically biting: "I had been thinking, reading, observing, and had as little faith in the popular theories in regard to babies as on any other subject."[28] After disagreeing with a doctor's treatment of Daniel's bent collarbone, she provided her own successful treatment. She later observed:

> Thus, in the supreme moment of a young mother's life, when I needed tender care and support, the whole responsibility of my child's supervision fell upon me; but though uncertain at every step of my own knowledge, I learned another lesson in self-reliance. I trusted neither men nor books absolutely after this, either in regard to the heavens above or the earth beneath, but continued to use my "mother's instinct," if "reason" is too dignified a term to apply to a woman's thoughts.[29]

This concern over misinformation on babies was to become an another dimension of Cady Stanton's rhetoric, and she felt compelled to improve children's conditions in society. Many of her popular lyceum addresses would present her philosophies on childrearing, and her outspoken views were widely held in esteem.

In the autumn of 1843, Henry Stanton was admitted to the bar and entered legal practice with John Bowles in Boston. The city's stimulating intellectual climate opened an activity-filled life for Elizabeth, who attended antislavery conventions, temperance, peace, and prison reform fairs, and as many lectures, concerts, and theaters as possible. It was in Boston where she met John Pierpoint, John Greenleaf Whittier, Parker Pillsbury, Lydia Marie Child, Abby Kelly, and Stephen Foster. Her desire to find an understandable, logical religion found her encouraged by Theodore Parker's rejection of miracles and prayer to a God who was father and mother to all. Her frequent visits to William Lloyd Garrison's home allowed for lively, intriguing discussions. In addition, she spent time at the Brook Farm

Community at the height of its prosperity. At one local convention, she met and heard Frederick Douglass (1817-1895), whose friendship was to be fruitful and lasting. She became a woman in the center of an intellectual movement and her developing rhetorical talent was allowed to flourish, even though on an interpersonal rather than public basis.

During the winter of 1844, Elizabeth left the activity of Boston to retreat to the family home in Albany, awaiting the birth of Henry B. Stanton, Jr., nicknamed Kit (1844-1903). Elizabeth enjoyed housekeeping, which she saw as a new chapter in her book of experiences. She studied all aspects of running a household, including washing, planning meals, cleaning, and childrearing. She noted in her diary: "I felt the same ambition to excel in all departments of the culinary arts that I did at school in the different branches of learning. My love of order and cleanliness was carried throughout, from parlor to kitchen, from the front door to the back." [30]

Into this bustling regime Elizabeth's third son Gerrit, or Gat, (1845-1927) was born in September 1845. Due to the visit of her cousin Gerrit Smith, the child was named in his honor. Elizabeth's protests were ignored, for she didn't care for the practice of labeling children with family names. In addition, "I had a list of beautiful names for sons and daughters, from which to designate each newcomer; but, as yet, not one on my list had been used for my children." [31] Even though her ideas were accepted on the philosophical plane with her peers, in reality and in day-to-day matters, she was still treated as a lesser individual. These early slights would provide the springboard for her later calls for true equality between the sexes and for the legitimation of women's roles.

Henry's law practice grew, and he was considered to be a man of political promise; however, he claimed his delicate health was buffeted by Boston's fierce winters and that the family must move. Others suggested that the move was due more to the need to find a more comfortable political climate. On the advice of family and friends, the Stantons moved to Seneca Falls, New York, where Daniel Cady gave them a home on the outskirts of town. The next sixteen years there saw the birth of other Stanton children: Theodore (1851-1925), Margaret (1852-1938), Harriot (1856-1940), and Robert (1859-1920).

SENECA FALLS

The Stantons' 1847 move to Seneca Falls reawakened Elizabeth's restless spirit. Life in the small upstate town was less stimulating than in Boston or Albany; Elizabeth found her perspective narrowing to a small domestic focus. Running a household now held limited challenge, and there was a distinct lack of intellectual activity. Her diary reports: "My duties were too numerous and varied, and none sufficiently exhilarating or intellectual to bring into play my higher faculties. I suffered with mental hunger, which, like an empty stomach, is very depressing."[32] The isolated household, a frequently absent husband, and demanding children filled Cady Stanton with discontent:

> My experience at the World's Anti-Slavery Convention, all I had read of the legal status of women, and the oppression I saw everywhere, together swept across my soul, intensified now by many personal experiences. It seemed as if all the elements had conspired to impel me to some onward step. I could not see what to do or where to begin--my only thought was a public meeting for protest and discussion. [33]

At the same time that Cady Stanton's discontent was manifesting itself, momentous changes were occurring all over the nation. Gold was discovered at Sutter's Mill in California, and thousands of Americans swarmed westward. With the overthrow of the governments in France and Germany, immigrants by the hundreds fled to America' s promised freedom. Temperance and prison reforms came to dominate the headlines. In New York, the Married Woman's Property Act was passed, giving women control for the first time over the property they owned at the time of their marriage; what belonged to a wife could no longer be used to defray her husband's debts. Anesthesia was first used in childbirth, a blessed reform in medical care. But perhaps the most significant of these many milestones, as far as women were concerned, would be the first Woman's Rights Convention, held on July 19 and 20, 1848 at Seneca Falls.

The Seneca Falls Convention marks the triggering event to ending what Leland Griffin has called the "period of inception" or genesis stage of a social movement. This is a time when "the roots of a pre-existing sentiment, nourished by interested rhetoricians, begins to flower into public notice." [34] During this initial stage, early leaders serve as philosophers who see problems that others are ignorant of. They feel pain and visualize social ills that others do not. Because such a beginning requires an event that will advance the movement from philosophy to action, from unorganized and invisible entity into public fact, from genesis to social unrest, a social movement's leader must create some "happening" that will move ideals into actuality. Lloyd Bitzer suggests that during this stage, the most important rhetorical action will be the creation and apprehension of an exigence, an urgent situation, which will cultivate interest in change within an audience. [35] Without such a triggering event and recognition of an exigence, there will be no movement. The creation of the first women's rights convention and its resultant manifesto served these ends.

Although the idea for a convention had been conceived in 1840 at the Anti-Slavery Convention, it did not come to fruition for eight years. While Lucretia Mott and Elizabeth had continued their friendship via letters throughout the 1840s, Mott was preoccupied with illness, family responsibilities, and religious obligations. Cady Stanton was caught up in the start of her large family. Her life was rich, and she lived in relative ease. She remained interested in religious questions, becoming enthusiastic about Theodore Parker's theological visions, which blended Unitarianism with transcendentalism. Parker (1810-1860) freed Cady Stanton from her religious fears and made her realize that each individual could intuit God's will. Parker's emphasis on the individual thus directly affected Cady Stanton's self-concept and self-esteem. However, despite the various activities dominating their lives, neither woman lost sight of the disadvantages of being female.

An invitation for a reunion with Lucretia Mott at the home of Mrs. Jane Hunt in Waterloo, New York, offered Cady Stanton the chance to act. On July 13, Elizabeth Cady Stanton, Lucretia Mott, Mary Ann McClintock, Jane Hunt, and Martha C. Wright (Mott's sister) issued a call for a convention to discuss women's grievances. The call was published on July 14 in the *Seneca County Courier*, providing five days' notice for the convention to be held in Seneca Falls' Wesleyan Chapel on July 19-20. The first day's meeting was to be held exclusively for women, the second for the general public. There were to be several speakers, but only Lucretia Mott was named for the second day.

The five intervening days were hectic. The planners discussed women's wrongs and the means to make them apparent to the world, which up to then had called women's wrongs insignificant. What they felt was needed was some type of declaration, such as they were familiar with from antislavery experiences. Their ideas needed to be organized into one clear statement or manifesto that could guide future action. In considering an appeal to the basic philosophy of equal justice, Cady Stanton recognized that the Declaration of Independence appeared tailored to their needs. The planners held as many grievances against man's government and laws as the colonists had against King George; consequently, they drew up a "Declaration of Women's Rights and Sentiments."

The resulting document was presented by Cady Stanton on the first morning of the convention; its underlying thesis was that the rights declared by the forefathers in the Declaration of Independence must be extended to include women as well as men. She stated: "We hold these truths to be self-evident: that all men and women are created equal."[36] Using phrases from the 1776 declaration, the women's statement claimed that "the history of mankind is a history of repeated injuries and usurpations on the part of man to women, having in direct object the establishment of absolute tyranny over her."[37] Following this statement were a list of injuries to women perpetrated by men. Perhaps the most damaging claim was that man attempts to destroy woman's self-confidence and self-respect. The Declaration ended by insisting that women have "immediate admission to all the rights and privileges which belong to them as citizens of the United States."[38] The framers pledged to use all means possible to fight the ridicule and misrepresentations of their ideas that they knew would follow. And as foretold, the declaration did indeed arouse a storm of controversy.

Elizabeth Cady Stanton was charged with drafting the majority of the resolutions that would strengthen the declaration's demands. These resolutions attempted to improve woman's lot in two distinct ways: the legal one of removing barriers to political, educational, and professional equality; and the personal one of forcing men and women to acknowledge females' inferior position and to demand change. The ninth resolution, drafted by Cady Stanton alone, proved to be the most contentious. It read: "Resolved, that it is the duty of the women of this country to secure to themselves their sacred right to the elective franchise."[39] In creating the resolutions, Cady Stanton consulted her husband Henry, who insisted that the very mention of such a farfetched notion would make the entire project appear preposterous. While he willingly helped with the rest of the grievance list, Henry urged Elizabeth to give up such a revolutionary idea as woman suffrage. When his protests were ignored, Henry threatened to leave town and attend none of the meetings. He kept his word. [40]

Lucretia Mott, too, examined the resolutions with an approving eye until reaching the ninth. Elizabeth remembered, "When I spoke to Lucretia Mott about my intention to present this, she amazed me by objecting, 'Why Lizzie, thee will make us ridiculous.'"[41] Cady Stanton refused to remove the resolution, and she remained convinced that the ability to vote provided the power to make the laws. Cady Stanton believed that in order to overcome social and legal obstacles, one needed political actions and solutions; since women without voting rights had no independent access to this political power, she advocated suffrage. The right to vote was the means through which all other rights could legitimately be won.

July 19, 1848, dawned a fine summer morning. Carriages and wagons converged upon Seneca Falls from a radius of fifty miles, bringing a crowd of about 300 people. Although men were not supposed to attend the first day's session, about forty were admitted. And although this was to be a convention for and about women, it was still unthinkable for a woman to preside; James Mott was asked to serve as moderator. Lucretia Mott was given the floor to explain the convention's purpose; she was followed by Cady Stanton's reading of the Declaration of Sentiments and Resolutions.

Cady Stanton's maiden public speech was made despite a combination of her communication apprehension and the formidable undertaking of initiating radical action by and for women. The opening of the address admitted her strong feelings:

> I should feel exceedingly diffident to appear before you at this time, having never before spoken in public, were I not nerved by a sense of right and duty, did I not feel that the time had come for the question of woman's wrongs to be laid before the public, did I not believe that woman herself must do this work, for woman alone can understand the height, the depth, the length, and the breadth of her degradation.[42]

Day two found further discussions of the declaration and the resolutions. The ninth resolution was the only one not passed unanimously. Only after a heated discussion and with the support of Frederick Douglass was it carried by a small majority. He based his arguments on the need for oppressed people to be allowed to select their leaders and create their laws. Douglass's stirring speech claimed that suffrage was an indispensable basis for winning freedom and equality, whether it was for slaves or women. Both the declaration and resolutions were signed by sixty-eight women and thirty-two men.

Although participants considered the two days' meetings highly successful, there was so much more to be discussed that the sessions were scheduled to continue two weeks later in Rochester, New York. By itself, the initial convention did not physically reach many advocates, and a meeting of 300 people in a small New York town was not ordinarily a national event; but news of the two conventions spread. Reports were widely published and the proceedings were ridiculed by the press and denounced by the clergy. The venomous attacks gave the meetings a publicity boost that no one had dreamed of. Typical of press statements was one editorial that called the convention "the most shocking and unnatural incident ever recorded in the history of womanity."[43] Cady Stanton noted in her diary:

> No words could express our astonishment on finding that what seemed to us to timely, so rational, and so sacred, should be the subject for sarcasm and ridicule to the entire press of the nation . . . so pronounced was the popular voice against us, in the parlor, press, and pulpit, that most of the ladies who had attended the convention and signed the declaration, one by one, withdrew their names and influence, and joined our persecutors.[44]

Nevertheless, a strong core of instigators reassembled at Rochester to find growing numbers in attendance.

In identifying the Seneca Falls Convention with the birth of the women's rights movement, it must be noted that this was only one step in the growth process, for many of the stated grievances had been articulated years earlier. The Rochester convention raised the issue of whether men and women were really equal mentally and physically; if women were in any sense inferior, did that not mean that they needed men's protection? This issue would haunt the movement for decades. As news of the two conventions spread, people were aroused to convene their own local meetings. Although no formal ones took place for a year and a half, the first of four Ohio conventions took place in Salem in April 1850. Cady Stanton urged the delegates by letter to amend the state constitution to include woman suffrage.[45] From then on, until the inception of the Civil War, meetings were held throughout New York, Massachusetts, Pennsylvania, Ohio, and Indiana.

For Elizabeth Cady Stanton, the Seneca Falls Convention served to coalesce her thinking and philosophy of feminism. It allowed her to act publicly as a reform speaker and advocate. It legitimized her beliefs, caused her to put them into words, and gave them public attention. Cady Stanton noted:

> The effect of the [Seneca Falls] convention on my own mind was most salutary. The discussions had cleared my ideas as to the primal step to be taken for woman's emancipation, and the opportunity of expressing my self fully and freely on a subject I felt so deeply about was a great relief. I think all women who attended the convention felt better for the statement of their wrongs, believing that the first step had been taken to right them.[46]

The convention thus served as means to clarify the exigency of woman's social handicaps, and Cady Stanton was to continue playing a role in cultivating interest, in gathering followers and in creating momentum for the movement.

As a movement gathers momentum and more people begin expressing their concerns over perceived wrongs, it progresses fully to the stage of social unrest.[47] Leaders begin to organize the far-flung members, meet initial resistance by the establishment, and gain new members. Elizabeth Cady Stanton would find rhetoric moving her from solitary philosopher to agitator as she was thrust more into the public eye.

Following the Seneca Falls Convention, Cady Stanton founded the Seneca Falls Conversation Club, which argued topics of the day from slavery to immigration, territorial rights to women's rights. Amelia Bloomer published a six-page monthly temperance paper called the *Lily*, and Cady Stanton was soon writing articles for it under the pen name "Sunflower."[48] There followed a series of articles refuting man's claim to superiority. Growing bolder, Cady Stanton dropped the pseudonym and signed her initials. Her topics, ranging from woman's vote to free schools to sewing, startled and stimulated her readers. She also began her lifelong campaign against woman's false traditions, including women paying for their share of "dates." The *Lily* also published Cady Stanton's letters to various conventions and provided information about the proceedings. Thus the *Lily* became the earliest principal written medium for spreading among women accurate news of the growing woman's rights movement.

PARTNERSHIP

The shock waves created by the conventions attracted the attention of a young Quaker teacher, Susan Brownwell Anthony (1820-1906), whose reform activities and alliance with Cady Stanton were to have a marked effect on the progress of Cady Stanton's rhetoric and of American feminism.[49] It is Anthony who should be credited with building a national women's coalition, for the early conventions were spontaneously conceived and loosely affiliated. It took Anthony's administrative genius to create the national organization. Just as Lucretia Mott as mentor had been vital to the formation of Cady Stanton's intellectual independence, Susan B. Anthony was essential to her rhetorical independence.

As Stewart notes, during the social unrest phase, a movement's leaders believe that if they can raise society's consciousness, then it will take appropriate actions.[50] Leaders remain convinced that success will come via "petitioning" or by aiming most of its rhetorical energies at the chain-of-command. The emergence of the Cady Stanton-Anthony team at this point in the woman's rights movement's life would place them at the center of attempts to work within the established framework of both reform causes and society. That partnership would, however, move from the mainstream as the movement lost momentum; Cady Stanton's written and spoken rhetoric eventually displayed her frustration and alienated1 her from the cause and its membership.

Both Anthony and Cady Stanton were active in antislavery causes, and in May 1851, the two met at a convention in Seneca Falls. At this time, Anthony was more curious about rather than sympathetic to Cady Stanton's woman's rights ideas, but she was eventually converted. A letter from April 2, 1852, illustrates their life-long collaborative relationship. Suggesting an approach to a temperance address, Cady Stanton cautioned Anthony against conservatism; further, she warned about the dangers of religion. Cady Stanton said:

> The Church is a terrible engine of oppression, especially as concerns woman. [Cady Stanton then volunteered her aid in preparing an address.] I will gladly do all in my power to aid you in getting up such a lecture as you desire . . . if my speech as it stands would serve you as a kind of skeleton for a lecture I will send it to you and you can fill out the heads more fully. Men and angels give me patience! I am at the boiling point! If I do not find some day the use of my tongue on this question, I shall die of an intellectual repression, a woman's rights convulsion! [51]

Their half-century collaboration found the pair complementing each other's abilities. Anthony was the stimulus mobilizing Cady Stanton to work, and together they wrote addresses and essays for causes ranging from temperance to women's rights. Cady Stanton reminisced: "We forged resolutions, protests, appeals, petitions, agricultural reports, and constitutional arguments; for we made it a matter of conscience to accept every invitation to speak on every question, in order to maintain woman's right to do so."[52] She also commented on the relationship, noting:

> It has been said, by those who know me best, that I forged the thunderbolts and she in the early days fired them. In thought and

sympathy we were one, and in the division of labor we exactly complimented each other. I am the better writer, she the better critic. She supplied the facts and statistics, I the philosophy and rhetoric, and together, we have made arguments that have stood unshaken through the storms of long years; arguments that no one has answered.[53]

In 1868 Theodore Tilton described the Cady Stanton-Anthony alliance in the following manner:

Mrs. Stanton is a fine writer, but a poor executant; Miss Anthony is a thorough manager, but a poor writer . . . neither has any selfish ambition for celebrity; but each view with the other in a noble enthusiasm for the cause to which they are devoting their lives. These two women have . . . been diligent forgers of all manners of projectiles, from fireworks to thunderbolts, and have hurled them with unexpected explosion into the midst of all manner of educational, reformatory, religious, and political assemblies. I know of no two more pertinacious incendiaries in the whole country. In fact, this noise-making twain are the two sticks of a drum, keeping up what Daniel Webster called "The rub-a-dub of agitation." [54]

Susan B. Anthony suffered through reproaches to keep silent at the Rochester 1852 Convention convened by the Sons of Temperance. Such treatment aroused her zeal, and she called for a Woman's State Temperance Convention to be held in Rochester several months later. Enlisting Cady Stanton's aid, Anthony attempted to build the strength and importance of women in that cause. Cady Stanton saw temperance as a stepping-stone to woman's rights, and she used the opportunity to broach previously ignored topics. While temperance advocates believed that liquor was the cause of family problems, Cady Stanton dissented, saying that only when women could own their wages, hold property, and be legally recognized guardians of their children would they be able to protect the family. When the first Woman's State Temperance Convention met in Corinthian Hall on April 20, 1852, Elizabeth Cady Stanton served as presiding officer. Her opening address advocated temperance, modification of marriage and divorce laws, and ended with radical remarks aimed at the Church.

PUBLIC ADDRESS

Anthony called for a State Woman's Rights Convention in Albany in February 1854, planning for Cady Stanton to deliver an address on the legal disabilities of women both to the convention and to the Joint Judiciary Committee of the legislature. The 1854 speech greatly enlarged Elizabeth Cady Stanton's reputation as the philosopher and intellect of the women's rights movement. Speaking invitations began to pour in, and Horace Greeley offered to publish her columns in his *New York Tribune.*

The movement had now moved into stage three, "enthusiastic mobilization," where optimism is the key.[55] There were numerous conventions and public lectures on women's rights issues. A national dialogue on topics of suffrage, education, and work ensued in public forums and newspapers. Movement members and leaders began to feel optimistic about the inevitability of their desired change. However, several different factors would force a halt to this momentum.

Cady Stanton's public career created struggles at home, as her father, husband, and friends opposed her activities which removed her from woman's "true sphere." Surprisingly, she surrendered to their appeals for a traditional mother and wife and stayed home, choosing to restrict her public activity. Without the activity of a public life, Cady Stanton channeled her energy into raising her children. She continued contributing to journals and newspapers such as the *Lily* and *Una* (a paper devoted to the "elevation of women"); in addition, she was published regularly in Horace Greeley's *New York Tribune.* The birth of two more children provided an undercurrent of disharmony in her marriage; the delay of her public career and sense of subordination were part of the difficulty she had to face as her domestic responsibilities grew.

The voluntary retirement of Cady Stanton was echoed by the marriages and childbirths in the lives of feminists Lucy Stone (1818-1893) and Antoinette Brown Blackwell (1825-1921); the movement began to suffer from a lack of centralized leadership. In addition, the advent of the Civil War stopped the momentum of the movement, as the abolitionists in the group who had supported the movement funnelled their energies into a single cause. Enthusiastic mobilization ground to a halt.

1859 found Cady Stanton's life changing: a difficult pregnancy, her father's death, and several heroes (including John Brown and Gerrit Smith) facing public disdain due to radical abolitionist activity caused her to reevaluate her life. In 1860, Cady Stanton became active again in speechmaking; Anthony had "volunteered" her services for three major occasions. In March, she testified before the New York Judiciary Committee on married women's property rights; in May, she argued for suffrage for black and white females at the American Anti-Slavery Society; two days later, she advocated divorce at the National Women's Rights Convention.[56] The speeches renewed her opportunities for public debate, and she found herself again actively espousing her feminist philosophy.

WAR AND RECONSTRUCTION

War changed life for the Stanton family, as they moved to New York City in 1862. In addition, Cady Stanton and Anthony argued over the effects of the war effort on the women's movement. Anthony believed that the war focus would interrupt and reverse the progress they had made. Cady Stanton believed that women would be rewarded with suffrage if they aided the war effort. This disagreement was the first major policy conflict between the two, and in the end, Anthony's perception of the war's effects proved correct. For five years, there was no organized group that met to debate woman's legal disabilities, for during the war years, everyone's attentions was elsewhere.

For a movement to regain its momentum and return to enthusiastic mobilization, its leaders must vanquish many crises. Externally, they have to "employ harsh rhetoric and stage symbolic acts designed to pressure institutions into capitulation or compromise."[57] Internally, they must deal with competing ideologies and coalitions. In order to keep the movement fresh, they must attempt to diversify in issues, develop alternative ideologies or strategies, and keep a united front. As the years following the war progressed, Elizabeth Cady Stanton would play a major rhetorical role in damaging those objectives, partly due to her more radical ideology which had initiated much of the movement's progress, and partly due to her advocacy of unpopular causes. Reconstruction proved deleterious to the women's movement, because not only would the abolitionists' ideals be compromised, but the support that they had previously given women would largely be withdrawn. In the five years after the war, feminists found themselves defeated in every encounter with the political authority. Cady Stanton would feel compelled to utilize more radical rhetoric, becoming controversial and often notorious at every turn, and finally causing a split within the membership of the movement.

In 1865, Cady Stanton adopted a more independent private life. Political disagreements with Henry, his instable employment status, and by 1870 eventual separation into two households demonstrated her determination to place the demands of her own life first. Her partnership with Susan B. Anthony also began to change, as Cady Stanton grew less dependent on Anthony's leadership. Prior to this time, Cady Stanton had responded to Anthony's requests for letters and speeches on issues of temperance and education, while her own advocacy for divorce reform and suffrage were left as secondary. As a result, Cady Stanton placed the issue of women's rights as the central argument in every talk. Now Cady Stanton was developing a more active role, and her emphasis on agitation as a control strategy would prove divisive. As Cady Stanton became more visible, she also became more assertive and aggressive. The two women became equal partners.

With the advent of the Fourteenth Amendment, which granted suffrage only to all male citizens, Cady Stanton was outraged and provoked by the treachery of her previous antislavery allies, who insisted that to argue for woman suffrage would cause losses for the Negro.[58] In their effort to rally the women's right advocates, Cady Stanton and Anthony convened the first women's rights convention since the war, but because of their agitation against the Fourteenth Amendment, few reformers came.

The Eleventh National Women's Rights Convention was called for May 1866 and was scheduled to coincide with the first meeting of Theodore Tilton's new organization, the American Equal Rights Association (AERA). The group, with Mott as president, Cady Stanton as vice-president, and Anthony as corresponding secretary, argued for universal suffrage. However, the AERA convened in a session without Cady Stanton or Anthony and complied with Wendell Phillips's desires to argue solely for Negro male citizenship. With the support of AERA, the Fourteenth Amendment was ratified in 1868; it excluded women from citizenship and therefore from voting rights.

As though to reenergize the movement and perhaps reinterpret the Fourteenth Amendment, Elizabeth Cady Stanton announced in 1866 that she would run as an independent for Congress in the Eighth District of New York City; although women could not vote, she reasoned they could hold office if elected. Her platform of universal suffrage, free speech, free press, and free trade stirred up much publicity, and she received twenty-four votes. She was the first woman to run for Congress.

The Kansas campaign was the next event designated to transfuse new life to the cause, since a referendum was being held there on the vote for women and for blacks. Both Anthony and Cady Stanton stumped the state speaking on behalf of woman suffrage, for they believed that if they could win in Kansas, then public sentiment would be further roused. While a strong case for black male suffrage was made by abolitionist reformers and three major newspapers

(Greeley's *New York Tribune*, Tilton's *Independent,* and Phillips's *Anti-Slavery Standard*), none advocated woman suffrage.[59] Although the referendum failed, the partners met the flamboyant George F. Train, who was to play an important role in their next venture, and who would further harm the reuniting of the movement's early leadership.

THE REVOLUTION

Train, Cady Stanton, and Anthony had a shared commitment to women's rights and to educated suffrage; in essence, the idea was to exclude immigrants and blacks from suffrage unless women were granted the same right. What made Train even more appealing was his offer to finance a newspaper they could edit, one which could be devoted to women's rights. *The Revolution* became the first major national newspaper devoted to that cause; it promoted the feminist agenda, but it also enhanced the growing split within the movement. [60] By associating with the Democrat Train, Cady Stanton and Anthony alienated the Republican party as well as the AERA. William Lloyd Garrison warned them against Train, saying, "You will only subject yourselves to merited ridicule and condemnation, and turn the movement which you aim to promote into unnecessary contempt."[61]

The newspaper was first issued on January 8, 1868 with Cady Stanton as senior editor and primary author of most columns; Parker Pillsbury (1809-1898), a Massachusets reformer and former editor of the *Anti-Slavery Standard*, served as co-editor; Anthony was office manager and accountant. The newspaper, with the masthead motto "Principle, not Policy; Justice, not Favors; Men, their rights and nothing more; Women, their rights and nothing less," was indeed devoted more to principle than to policy. It reported on issues such as the status of women tailors, divorce reform, Colorado suffrage, infanticide, prostitution, conditions of prisons and tenements, temperance, and the defeat of the Fifteenth Amendment. It also served as a clearinghouse for information on suffrage lectures, meetings, and conventions, as well as publishing essays, poetry stories and reviews by leading American and international writers. Its title can probably be attributed to Cady Stanton; in a letter defending the name on December 28, 1869, she wrote to Susan B. Anthony:

> The establishing of woman on her rightful
> throne is the greatest revolution the world
> has ever known or will know . . . . A journal
> called the *Rosebud* might answer for those

> who come with kid gloves and perfumes to
> lay immortal wreaths on the monument . . .
> but for us . . . there is no name like *T h e*
> *Revolution.* [62]

The untimely end of *The Revolution* may be attributed to several causes. The paper had barely been published one month when Train departed for England, leaving the financial support on diminished (and finally vanished) grounds. Cady Stanton's strict stand against patent medicines cut advertising and circulation revenues. With few advertisers and subscriptions (it peaked at 3,000 but had few renewals), the paper became more dependent upon Train for nonexistent financial help. Also, the major subscribers were women, who were not major money-makers. Anthony also insisted on high quality paper and female typesetters; she borrowed money from her family, pleaded for contributors, and poured every penny into the enterprise.

Another cause of *The Revolution's* demise was the growing split in the women's movement.[63] The confrontation between conservatives of the AERA and Cady Stanton and Anthony, begun with the Kansas campaign and their alliance with Train, came to a head at the May 1869 convention. Frederick Douglass used that platform to call for a resolution supporting the Fifteenth Amendment, granting suffrage to black males. Anthony and Cady Stanton, who appeared blind to political reality, argued for its defeat; their vehemence against the issue stunned former allies and lessened their support. Anthony and Cady Stanton then broke away, forming the National Woman Suffrage Association (NWSA) to counter the AERA. This split would further undermine the earlier successes of the movement.

The NWSA refused males entry and demanded national suffrage, and as its president, Cady Stanton brought her liberal ideas of unionism and suffrage to the platform. The more militant NWSA was willing to discuss any subject related to women's independence. To a growing number of reformers, Cady Stanton and Anthony were becoming embarrassing troublemakers; their paper, organization, and highly active public oratory advocated discussion of topics such as free love, unwed mothers, and equal wages. As an alternate group, disenchanted reformers founded the American Woman Suffrage Association (AWSA) in November 1869 and dedicated themselves to winning suffrage state by state. The AWSA focused solely on woman suffrage and appealed to the conservative wing of the movement. The AWSA also published its own newspaper, the *Woman's Journal*, which was well financed, respectable, and ultimately successful. The split in means and ends, begun in large part by the positions voiced in *The Revolution,* were to separate the woman's movement until

1890. After two and one-half years of operation, *The Revolution* failed, leaving Anthony with a $10,000 personal debt. In May 1870, it was sold for one dollar to Laura Ballard, who altered the paper to a more literary society journal, losing most of its controversial content. Eighteen months later, it was merged into the *New York Christian Enquirer*.

LYCEUM LECTURES

Lyceum lectures provided a new outlet for Cady Stanton's rhetoric. Because of their popularity such speeches could be on all sorts of topics and paid very well. For twelve years, from 1869 through 1881, Cady Stanton lectured for the New York Lyceum Bureau for eight months each year. A typical tour had her traveling to three dozen cities and small towns in six weeks, usually speaking once daily and twice on Sundays. Her fees of $3,000 to $4,000 per year ($100 to $200 per appearance) gave her enough income to provide higher education for her children. On the platform, Cady Stanton usually wore a matronly black silk dress with lacy white cuffs and collar, an artfully arranged crown of white hair, and displayed a powerful, clear voice. She further legitimized her maternal identification by offering to help with crying infants and giving advice on baby care; on free afternoons, she met alone with women of the community. Her most popular lectures covered topics of children and marriage, where her advice ranged from household management to divorce reform to birth control. In a December 1, 1872 letter to daughter Margaret, she explained her mission: "I feel that I am doing an immense amount of good in rousing women to thought and inspiring them with new hope and self-respect, that I am making the path smoother for you and Hattie and all the other dear girls."[64]

While a movement might achieve victories during the enthusiastic mobilization stage, its early visions of sweeping reform usually remain unfulfilled. Stewart notes that "the social movement may look within and decide that some members are incapable of true understanding or involvement in the cause. These members are purged to purify the movement in time of decision."[65] In addition, those who were once viewed as imaginative visionaries may now be ridiculed by new leaders and members. Stewart argues that "the maturing social movement needs new leadership and a less impassioned and strident rhetoric as it enters the 'maintenance' stage."[66] This describes precisely what occurred to the leadership and participation of Elizabeth Cady Stanton once the movement began to win what she considered minor victories and shifted into a more conservative bent.

During her lyceum days, Cady Stanton was only remotely involved in the organizational concerns and conventions of the NWSA. Isabella Beecher Hooker's ascendency to the leadership of the NWSA was cause for further alienation; Hooker suggested that Cady Stanton not attend the January 1871 meeting, probably due to Cady Stanton's radical ideas and notoriety. Cady Stanton would continue to advocate the position of women in the 1869 Hester Vaughan infanticide trial, the 1870 McFarland-Richardson murder case, and the 1872 Beecher-Tilton trials. Her advocacy combined suffrage causes with scandal in the public eye. In addition, Anthony's assertion of leadership at convention soured Cady Stanton on such meetings, and although she would participate as leader and speaker at later ones, she did so reluctantly.

NEW DIRECTIONS

Upon her retirement from the lyceum circuit in 1879, Cady Stanton turned her energies to the completion of the *History of Woman Suffrage*, the compilation of documents and reminiscences of the movement's progress, which she, Anthony, and Matilda Josyln Gage had begun in 1876. Cady Stanton and Gage were to collect, edit, and write the material; Anthony was charged with its publication details. Although originally, the *History of Woman Suffrage* was to be written in pamphlet form, the volume of collected material made it apparent that several large volumes would be required.

On November 2, 1880, Cady Stanton and Anthony appeared at the polling place ready to vote. Cady Stanton explained that she was three times the legal voting age, had been a Tenafly resident for twelve years, paid real estate and poll taxes and was a property holder, could read and write and therefore, since her legal representative (Henry) was not present, she wished to vote. Although denied, she asserted that acts, not words, were called for in attempting to push woman suffrage to the fore.

Upon completion of volume two of the *History of Woman Suffrage*, Cady Stanton journeyed to Europe with her daughter Harriot Stanton, who had enrolled in a French university to work on her master's degree in mathematics. In London, Cady Stanton was honored as a renowned reform speaker. She gave numerous speeches, met with suffragists, and wrote. Anthony joined her in February 1883, and they made plans for a future international meeting of women to discuss women's rights issues. The two returned to America in November 1883.

In 1885, Cady Stanton presided over the NWSA Washington meeting, where she delivered the principal address, "The Limitations of Sex." Her primary argument was that the concept of separate spheres was outmoded. However, she met opposition by supporting a controversial resolution and later tabled by Anthony which condemned all religious creeds that taught that woman had a subordinate position according to God. Cady Stanton continued an active writing career, completing essays on current events for magazines and newspapers. Topics such as "Religion for Women and Children" (*The Index*, 11 March 1886); and "Our Boys on Sunday" (*Forum*, April 1886) maintained her public presence.

WIDOWHOOD

In October 1886, she returned to England, where she resumed her previous domestic life with Harriot, her granddaughter Nora, and a nanny: she played games, read, wrote regularly, and met with English suffragists and other reformers. Her peaceful sojourn was abruptly ended with news of Henry Stanton's death on January 14, 1887. Although much of their married life had been spent apart, with Henry maintaining his house and law practice in New York City, the two had become closer and often attended parties and family celebrations with each other. Griffith maintains that family history suggests that the two were estranged when he died, with the children split in placing the blame.[67] It is likely that Cady Stanton did love Henry, although no longer in a romantic fashion, for her youthful ideals of marriage as a partnership of equals had long been dashed. Their informal and unofficial separation apparently had satisfied both of them.

She discovered that widowhood gave her legitimacy to her independent nature, for being a widow gave her status as well as a newfound freedom. At a time when many older people become dependent, she became increasingly self-reliant. She supported herself by writing; politically, she remained an eminent philosopher now aloof from organizational clashes; she proclaimed her total independence from all others by synthesizing her feminist ideology in "The Solitude of Self."[68]

Cady Stanton returned to America in March 1888 in time for the first International Council of Women meeting in Washington, largely at Anthony's urging, for this meeting was to honor the fortieth anniversary of the Seneca Falls Convention. Although the two women had conceived the idea of such an international gathering in 1883, it took Anthony's organizational genius to bring it to fruition: she convinced the NWSA, the AWSA, and the Woman's Christian Temperance Union (the latter two being the largest rivals of the National) to participate in the program's financing and structuring. It was the largest gathering of women ever assembled: fifty-three national groups sent delegates, including those from England,

Denmark, France, Norway, Finland, and India. Subjects included education, temperance, professions, social purity, and religious conditions, among others. Anthony presided over the conference, sharing the spotlight with Lucy Stone, Julia Ward Howe, and Frances Willard. Cady Stanton's opening speech emphasized the similarities of the women present, despite national and class differences. The International Council adjourned with the hope that it would prove to be a powerful agitator for the advancement of all women.

The woman's rights movement was now ensconced in the fourth stage of a movement's life: maintenance, where its "persuasion emanates from the legislative or judicial chamber and the conference room or convention hall."[69] Although the movement was splintered into rival groups, in general, their goals of women's rights were being achieved in property, work and education reforms.

Between March 1888 and February 1890, Cady Stanton traveled, visiting children and siblings in an attempt to renew bonds that had grown thin with her celebrity and her busy schedule. Now hailed by newspapers as "the Grand Old Woman of America" (partly due to her maternal, queenly appearance), she exploited the image as she continued her attempts to legitimize her reform strategies. Although she was inactive in the organizational structure of the movement, she answered the call whenever Anthony asked for a speech or an essay. Anthony, in the meantime, was attempting to merge the National and American suffrage associations. The majority of unification details were easy to work out: the name of the united group would be the National American Woman Suffrage Association (NAWSA); a delegate system of representation would be used; and suffrage would be sought both by state and federal means. The most divisive point was who would be the first president; while the American association had always insisted on equal membership for males, the National association admitted only women. In addition, the two sides wanted to place blame on the other for the 1869 schism. Finally, it was agreed not to refer to the split, and Cady Stanton was elected president.

The opening of the first meeting of the NAWSA found President Cady Stanton's inaugural remarks reviewing the history of the movement. Undaunted by the fact that she was addressing many of her critics, she then launched into discussion of several of her favorite liberal, controversial themes: inequality in religion, marriage and divorce reform, and the narrow-mindedness of the new organization's platform. After the presentation's close, Cady Stanton returned to England, leaving Anthony as acting president. Cady Stanton retained misgivings about the union, especially the intolerance of the conservatives. Feeling shut out of new policies and maintaining unpopular attitudes, she absented herself.

The next eighteen months were spent in England, where she continued to visit suffragist friends, made several speeches, and wrote provocative articles for *The Arena*, the *Forum*, and other journals. She sent installments of her Reminiscences back home to be published in the *Woman's Journal.* Mostly, however, she enjoyed the domesticity of family life with Harriot Blatch and her grandchildren. She also continued to send speeches or letters to be read at American suffrage meetings, such as one for the 1891 convention of the NAWSA entitled "The Degradation of Disfranchisement." The deaths of her son Daniel and sister Tryphena Bayard brought her home again in August 1891.

Because she had sold the Tenafly house, she was faced with the decision of where and with whom to live. Anthony encouraged her to live in Rochester, where the two of them could continue their collaboration, but Cady Stanton's children objected, expecting their mother to rest in her old age rather than work. While Cady Stanton acquiesced to their opposition, rather than retiring, she renewed her independence by sharing a penthouse apartment in New York City with her son Robert and widowed daughter Margaret.

SELF-SOVEREIGNTY

Although Cady Stanton and Anthony had not collaborated on any major projects since the completion of the third volume of the *History of Woman Suffrage,* they were still prominent in suffrage work and continued to join forces for various causes, including a petition to urge that the University of Rochester admit women. The NAWSA convention in 1892 found Cady Stanton, now seventy-seven years old, determined to retire as president; it was to be the last convention she attended. She shared the platform with the newly elected president Anthony, outgoing Executive Committee chairman Lucy Stone, and Anna Howard Shaw, who took over as vice-president-at-large. Cady Stanton's relinquishing of the presidential title (even though she had been inactive for several years) freed her to criticize her successors for their decision to move the national convention out of Washington and to close the NAWSA office there. Cady Stanton effectively began to divorce herself totally from her role as leader within the movement. She believed that NAWSA's presence, as maintained by the national office which insured lobbying and access to legislators, was essential to the cause. She perceived the new leaders to be timid, their desires to be too conservative; they shifted their suffrage efforts from congressional federal action to state campaigns. She said: "At present our association has so narrowed its platform for reasons of policy and propriety that our conventions have ceased to point the way." [70]

The speech Cady Stanton delivered as her final public performance was a departure from her typical suffrage rhetoric. "The Solitude of Self" was the culmination of her philosophy, a summary of her principles, crusades, and self-discovery. Her ideology demanded woman's complete self-reliance in physical, social, political, legal, and emotional spheres. She argued that women had to be independent and take responsibility for all aspects of their lives. The speech was delivered three times during a three-day period: once in written form to the House Committee on the Judiciary on January 18; next to the NAWSA convention; finally at a hearing to the Senate Committee on Woman Suffrage.

Retirement from NAWSA in 1892 meant that Cady Stanton finally had achieved total independence from personal and social constrictions. Ironically, a new limitation was placed on her: physical immobility due to her enormous weight. Immobility forced her to limit her outside activities, and after 1897, she was confined to her apartment. However, her mind remained acute, and she continued to write letters, speeches, and resolutions for Anthony. For the 1893 Columbia Exposition she "ghosted" five speeches for Anthony; Anthony once remarked that she couldn't claim credit for her addresses, for they all had been written by Stanton.[71] Cady Stanton wrote on all manner of subjects: on women, bicycles, and religion.[72]

In 1895, in recognition of Cady Stanton's eightieth birthday, she was honored with a public celebration sponsored by the National Council of Women. In New York's Metropolitan Opera House, 6,000 well-wishers gathered to hear tributes. Characteristically, Cady Stanton chose this occasion to emphasize her strong beliefs on woman's sphere; this time, in a speech read by Helen Potter (Cady Stanton saying she was too frail to speak for long), the audience heard potent words about the bondage under which the Church kept women. This attack was to be a precursor of one of her final and more outrageous acts.

The publication of *The Woman's Bible* two weeks later again exposed her to public ridicule and outrage. Cady Stanton had begun work on the *Bible* in England in 1887; its object was to make women aware of derogatory theological doctrines that libeled and subjugated women. She used this platform to attack the accepted interpretations of scripture; she felt that traditional church teachings were hostile to women. In its introduction, she said:

> The canon and civil law, church and state, priests and legislators, all political parties and religious denominations have alike taught that woman was made after man, of man, and for man, an inferior being, subject to man. Creeds, codes, Scriptures, and statutes are all

based on this idea. The fashions, forms, ceremonies and customs of society, church ordinances and discipline all grow out of this idea.[73]

So under the veneer of biblical scholarship, she convened a board of scholarly women to make a thorough revision of the Bible in order to see truthfully what woman's status had been under the original Hebrew and Christian religions. Because all the Bible's revised versions had been written by men, she reasoned that it was likely that males had misinterpreted scripture in their own favor; why not have a more accurate revision by women?

Although the authorship is credited to both Cady Stanton and "The Revising Committee," most of *The Woman's Bible* was written by Cady Stanton. She bought cheap Bibles, cut out negative parts which referred to women, pasted them on blank paper, and wrote her commentaries. Published in two parts, the work served to show discrepancies in interpretations, or areas where she felt women had been slighted. For instance, she demonstrated that while in one passage in Genesis, the "rib" story dominated; in another passage, Adam and Eve came into being at the same time. While *T h e Woman's Bible* is still interesting to read, Cady Stanton's sarcastic tone and obvious animosity toward traditional religion make her seem irreverent. To a society that didn't question the doctrine that the accepted Bible was the direct word of God, this work must have appeared as heresy. In fact, many of the interpretations Cady Stanton made are widely accepted today.

Public reaction to *The Woman's Bible* was marked by dismay and scandal. It rapidly became a best seller, went through seven printings in one year and was translated into many languages. Churches rang with the sermons of clergy condemning the work, calling it a travesty of the Scriptures. Libraries limited its access, keeping it for reference only and denying it circulation. The conservatives in the NAWSA opposed any association with it; in fact a resolution of censure at the convention that year was offered to deny any connection with the work. This is in spite of the fact that Cady Stanton had compiled it as an individual who was no longer an active member and who had not even attended a meeting in five years. Anthony gave an eloquent plea against censure, but the resolution passed. Cady Stanton argued Anthony's to resign in protest, but Anthony didn't want to leave the association. The partnership was once again strained by this difference in strategies and goals. In addition, as if in retaliation against the NAWSA, Cady Stanton's next edition of *The Woman's Bible* had the censure resolution appended to it. Whenever possible, she reminded the public of her roles as founder and president of the organization.

However, to the mainstream attempting to maintain the movement's successes, she had become an embarrassment.

In 1898 Cady Stanton published her reminiscences in *Eighty Years and More*. Under the guise of documenting the private history of a public woman, she used the autobiography to reinforce the calculated, visible image she had created of a woman who was nurturing, smart, respectable, intelligent, and most of all, self-reliant. It is not an intimate account of her life, for there is scant mention of her marriage or her children. The crises and conflicts that dominated much of her career and scandalized the public were whitewashed or ignored.

She continued to fill her life with reading and writing. Failing eyesight caused her to slow down, but she hired a typist and a reader to help her cope. During 1902, Anthony visited her several times. Their relationship had weathered distance, animosity, setbacks, and discord. In October, the *New York American* published her essay discussing divorce. On October 25, she wrote an open letter to President Theodore Roosevelt, requesting his support for the federal woman suffrage amendment. On Sunday, October 26, 1902, Elizabeth Cady Stanton died.

2

The Status of Women and Reform

The many reform movements that arose during the mid-nineteenth century embraced the ideal of perfectionism: reformers believed in progress and that humans had a divine spark within them that could improve society. In order to correct society's ills, it seemed that only necessary to eliminate outdated attitudes and the obstacles of past traditions. With these attempts to eliminate evil in order to raise the general status of society, it is no wonder that some reformers attacked the anachronistic subjugation of women. New calls for equal treatment of men and women, that had been faintly heard in the eighteenth century, now became more strident, and the women's rights reformers would not be denied.

American reformers were marked by pragmatic concerns: they were more concerned with discovering and implementing practical means of social improvement than with dealing with the root causes of the problems. In addition, reform was comprehensive in scope; reformers, confident in their abilities, attacked on all fronts. One could work simultaneously on temperance and on Christianizing Africa; one could advocate prison reform and sensible dress for women with equal fervor. Traditions of mutual aid and philanthropy had roots in Calvinism, Quakerism, frontier democracy, and evangelical zeal. The reformers had a faith in progress and the conviction that humans could be improved by self-determination. In addition, they believed in the individual's ability to direct him or herself to the good, toward right thinking and acting.

Another characteristic of American reform was that it was largely regional, centering in the North and West; the South was relatively untouched. Since one reform usually snowballed into another, Southerners could not risk opening the door to even one, for fear of granting inroads to abolitionism. Further, until the mid-nineteenth century, reform movements were largely apolitical, doing their work from outside partisan political frameworks. There was no single national reform leader or party.

Religious evangelism provided reform causes with their earliest bases of support; from evangelical revivalism came the convictions of perfectionism and practicality. Revivalists believed that people were perfectible and were responsible for themselves. This zeal made social reform into a moral imperative, for if people's sins resulted in social evils, then religious conversion could reform the people and therefore affect society.

The instrument chosen to accomplish this reform was the voluntary association, that consisted of like-minded individuals who organized community groups. These groups, consisting of missionary societies, education associations, and moral societies, published journals, organized speakers' bureaus, held conventions, and grew into powerful governmental lobbies. Often, the leaders of one group held similar positions of power in other groups, therefore making the establishment of a coalition and centralized communication more easy to achieve.

Women figured prominently in many of these organizations, even though their subordinate role denied them the speaker's platform or voting rights. Their status remained much as it had been in the eighteenth century: legally women were minors, with married women existing as their husband's chattels and unmarrieds as wards. Little advancement was made before 1840 to free women from restrictive laws. Sir William Blackstone's *Commentaries on the Laws of England* was the standard text of English common law; this became the foundation of America's legal tradition. Woman's role in society was defined as a private one; they were expected to foster interests only in domestic areas such as childraising, housekeeping, and social graces.

Out of the efforts by women to speak for abolition and temperance came a desire and a means for them to take a more active part in public affairs. As their home lives improved, they had time to read tracts, discuss issues, and attend public meetings. The *Vindication of the Rights of Woman* by Mary Wollstonecraft (1792) had presented the argument for a revolution in female matters and status. It was the first document to assert the full humanity of woman. Wollstonecraft's appeal for more opportunities and recognition for women included criticism of marriage, and she fixed the blame for woman's inferior status on society. Sara Grimke's *Letters on the Equality of the Sexes* (1838) and Margaret Fuller's *Woman in the Nineteenth Century* (1845) also argued against women's subjugation. The National Female Anti-Slavery Society was formed in 1833; it was the first effort by an organized women's society to attack a political question from a public forum. The society aroused intolerance and anger from many quarters, with the most vehement being religious groups. While the first efforts of women to improve society were largely ineffectual, their reform attempts did bring them into public contact with assembled listeners of both sexes. Their opportunities for higher education, coupled with their emergence as platform speakers and organized workers, gave women the opportunity to utilize their talents and to compete equally with men. What was needed was further organization and strong leadership. These would be the result of the first woman's rights convention held at Seneca Falls in July 1848.

WOMAN'S SPHERE

The theory of "woman's sphere" was based exclusively upon the belief that women and men were polar opposites. These separate branches or spheres of humankind supposedly had opposing characteristics. Woman was the repository of life-giving maternity, possessed intuition and refinement, and was morally and spiritually superior to man. Man was confronted daily by hardships and labors; he was bold and possessed courage. Woman's sphere defined her as physically weaker than man, inferior to him intellectually, and unsuited for business or worldly pursuits.

However, as society began to distinguish women's work from men's work according to specialized occupational demands, the sphere concept evolved into something different from opposite natures. Woman's sphere was separate because its domain was the home, where the demands for logical behavior and financial success that men faced were peripheral; thus, the domestic sphere began to be seen as the antithesis of an occupation, and therefore of lesser value. Woman's character and nature, as defined by the limits of this conception, was simultaneously glorified and devalued. Woman's societal role was defined as a private one: a wife could neither make a will, sign a contract, or witness a deed without a male's permission. Her property rights were curtailed. Divorce was next to impossible, and its accompanying scandal effectively made a divorced woman a social outcast. Most professions were closed to women.

Following the Revolutionary War, a new middle class emerged in the Northeast. As men began to work away from their homes in commercial enterprise, home and family evolved into an entity separate from the work world. Once money was earned for labor, a new valuation on work and roles began to emerge, and middle-class women were isolated from commerce. This new separation affected women in several significant ways. While they continued to perform traditional domestic work, those endeavors were no longer considered real work because they earned no money. Cut off from a monetary-oriented economy, a woman might labor all day cooking, cleaning, making clothing and essential household goods, and caring for her children, but she would still be subjugated by society. No longer was woman a partner of man; she was now defined as a supported dependent. Factories began producing many essential family goods, which further shifted the value placed upon the woman's domain of family. But while woman's household work and worth were devalued, ideals about home, children, and wife took on new levels of emotional significance. Here were beings to be cherished and protected form the cruelties of the outside world. A wife was legitimized as her husband's "better half." While he was struggling in the demanding, unsympathetic business environment, she could embody all of the purity and goodness he had to stifle. The home and family became the emotional altar for all the sentiment and feelings men felt incapable of expressing in the business world that dominated their lives.

Sexual double standards were acclaimed as divinely ordained. Reform opponents trumpeted biblical injunctions against women speaking in public as their justification for limiting woman's role to the private sector. Most often quoted was the apostle Paul, who, in his letter to the Corinthians, directed women how to act and speak:

> Let your women keep silence in the churches;
> for it is not permitted unto them to speak; but
> they are commanded to be under obedience,
> as also saith the law. And if they will learn
> anything, let them ask their husbands at
> home; for it is a shame for women to speak in
> the church.[1]

The Congregational Church of Massachusetts brought the proper role of women in society to national attention in their famous Brookfield Bull, that said:

> We invite your attention to the dangers which
> at present threaten the female character with
> widespread and permanent injury.
>
> The appropriate duties and influence of
> women are clearly stated in the New
> Testament. Those duties and that influence
> are unobtrusive and private, but the source of
> mighty power . . . .
>
> But when she assumes the place and
> tone of a man as a public reformer our care
> and protection of her seem unnecessary; she
> yields the power which God has given for her

protection and her character becomes
unnatural.[2]

Women were expected to foster interests only in the home; they
were taught domestic arts, sewing, and social graces. Theatrical
productions were viewed as immoral, so women were limited in the
social events that they could attend with propriety.

Although the romantic ideals of happy marriage and contented
family life were widely publicized, many women found that reality
did not match such claims. Not only did their prenuptial property
become the legal possessions of her husband, so did their earnings.
Mothers had no control over their children's destinies; if a father
died when the children were small, the mother was considered an
unfit guardian and a male was appointed by the courts as custodian.
Under the law, the husband was responsible for his wife's conduct
and deportment. These and similar laws negated the existence of a
married women, submerging her life below that of her husband and
legitimizing her total dependence on him.

For women who chose to remain single, once they overcame the
social stigma of failing to secure a mate and bear his children, life
was a bit less restrictive. The single woman could own and control
her property and earnings. However, she was restricted by custom
to a few fields of low-paying employment, such as sewing, teaching,
and domestic service. Women worked thirteen to fourteen hours per
day and were paid one-seventh to one-fourth of men's salaries for
the same work.[3]

By the mid-nineteenth century, social conditions had shifted
and the home was no longer the economic nucleus of family life. The
separation into distinct spheres that emphasized the opposite natures
and duties of the sexes altered the relationships between them, as
well as changing the values attached to their manner and activity.
De Tocqueville remarked: "In no country has such constant care been
taken as in America to trace two clearly distinct lines of action for
the two sexes, in two pathways which are always different."[4] Along
with the shift in economic conditions, society placed new values upon
sexual roles. The home was no longer the economic nucleus of family
life, and as the economic need for woman declined, her own value
changed, as did the respect accorded her. On one hand, tradition and
contemporary literature encouraged the idea of a perfect woman
with requisite virtues.[5] On the other hand, social forces were at
work that impelled woman to change, to play a more active and
creative role in society. Reform movements, westward migration, and
industrialization demanded responses that differed from those
woman had been told were naturally or divinely decreed. As
working hours at home shortened because of technological
advancements, women had time to read tracts, discuss issues, and

conduct public meetings.[6] Out of the efforts of women to speak for abolition and temperance grew the most compelling motive for them to take an active part in public affairs. In this public role, new, dissimilar virtues were imperative. Unfortunately, the values that predominated as part of the "woman's sphere" concept would prove to be major obstacles to reform efforts, especially in the arguments for women's rights.

THE WOMEN'S RIGHTS MOVEMENT

The pioneering effect that Cady Stanton had on the women's rights movement began with her instrumental activity in calling for the first Woman's Rights Convention in Seneca Falls, New York, in 1848. She was not brought to reform because of any discontent with her social status; while she liked elegance and came from a privileged background, she was in sympathy with the needs of the less fortunate. Rather, she came to reform because of her intellectual curiosity and rhetorical skills, her association since childhood with social and legal reform issues, and a personality that compelled her toward activism.

The course of events that propelled Cady Stanton into an early position of leadership within the movement has been charted in the previous chapter. The 1848 Seneca Falls Convention endorsed the first public declaration of the list of women's grievances and demands. Cady Stanton chose the 1776 Declaration of Independence as the agenda's guiding prototype, to describe the compelling list of grievances. These included women's rights to own property, to achieve higher education, and the right to vote. The appropriation of the Declaration of Independence turned out to be a brilliant rhetorical technique; by connecting her cause to the foundation of American liberty, Cady Stanton placed the women's movement in the mainstream of American traditions.

However, by advocating her suffrage demands, Cady Stanton also demonstrated the style that would distinguish her from other feminists. Her emphasis on the basic necessity of enfranchisement was radical, possibly calculated to provoke reformers and opposition alike into confronting social traditions. This militant style became a hallmark: Elizabeth Cady Stanton would constantly battle between the opposite tactics of political and partisan maneuvering and direct confrontation on high moral ground. She was independent and impatient, and the slow progress of politics, coupled with its realistic demands for compromise, were frustrating to her.

In the years after the Seneca Falls convention, when Cady Stanton emphasized her domestic role over the public one, she remained active in the many women's rights organizations that were springing up. She wrote articles and letters to be read at the meetings; she opened her home to reformers on their way to speak. Her public letters were designed to rouse the delegates to act, but her physical absence restricted her influence on policy matters. Her efforts for dress reform kept her in the public eye; however, after much public and private criticism, she abandoned the "Bloomer Costume" in 1853. Although the highly publicized outfit had been comfortable to wear, Cady Stanton found that the derision it received deflected attention from what she felt were more important concerns.

Cady Stanton's fortuitous meeting and eventual partnership with Susan B. Anthony created a blend of complements: Cady Stanton was a brilliant conversationalist and intellect; Anthony was controlled and organized. While Cady Stanton possessed the qualities of an outstanding orator, Anthony was a tireless researcher. As chronicled in the previous chapter, the two women played a central role in the establishment, maintenance, division, and reestablishment of an organized women's rights coalition.

Cady Stanton's presidency of the newly formed New York Woman's Temperance Society in 1852 found her trying to appeal to the more conservative reform advocates. Her speech stressed ending the subjugation of women and the need for divorce for chronic drunkenness as paramount concerns. Still, the speech was severely criticized, and in 1853, she was denied reelection as president. Rather than continuing her "radicalizing" attempts with the group, she and Anthony abandoned the organization they had helped found. This painful lesson granted Cady Stanton new wisdom: while it might be important to attempt to win the conservatives to her position, it was unimportant and perhaps counterproductive to center her activities around them. This made her much more open to the radical groups that called for more revolutionary action, and she would begin to abandon caution in her public demands.

The 1854 address to the Joint Judiciary Committee of the New York legislature marked the growing recognition Cady Stanton was receiving as a woman's rights leader. It was the first address by a woman to such a legislative body, so again, Cady Stanton was at the vanguard of public demands and brought favorable press to the movement's concerns. But in 1860, she shocked members of the Tenth National Woman's Rights Convention by demanding resolutions advocating divorce. Perhaps Cady Stanton felt the time was right to introduce a new woman's rights issue, for property rights for women were gradually being achieved in the various states. Cady Stanton met with strong opposition to her demands; the meeting was widely publicized, and the resultant damaging news stories about divisiveness in the movement also hindered her credibility with many former supporters.

Between 1863 and 1869, Cady Stanton and Anthony attempted to maintain the gains women had made. During the war years, feminist organizations folded or foundered, and many gains were lost. The partners created a far-ranging group of organizations to keep women's issues alive: the Loyal National Woman's League (1863); the American Equal Rights Association (1864); the Workingwoman's Association and Woman's Suffrage Association of America (1868); and the National Woman Suffrage Association (1869). But there were several problems with the feminist situation: there was indecision among leaders, the war was turning attention to other issues, and new reformers were emerging during the Reconstruction. Most importantly, the strong base of abolitionist support women possessed before the war began to desert them in favor of negro male suffrage. This abandonment by allies was a source of animosity and resentment, and it would result in Cady Stanton assuming a more radical position within the movement. Eventually, she would become so disenchanted with the movement's direction that she would disassociate herself from many of its activities.

The campaign for suffrage in Kansas provided Cady Stanton with another means to attempt a renewed leadership role in the women's movement. But her acceptance of George Train's financial backing was in essence a burning of bridges, for conservatives in the movement were adamant in their disapproval of him. She and Anthony formed the National Woman Suffrage Association, that argued liberal positions on a broad range of issues. The publication of *The Revolution* trumpeted a new independent position and allowed Cady Stanton, as editor and primary scribe, to promote all types of radical ideas. These two intertwined events created a schism in the movement that would last for two decades, imperiling the cause of women's rights.

After the disputes of the 1869 Equal Rights Association Convention and the split to form the NWSA, Cady Stanton abandoned her leadership role in woman suffrage conventions. Her concern over the conservatism of the new feminists in the organizations gave her the impetus to seek further autonomy and independence, away from the close partnership with Anthony and from the central cause. Cady Stanton's increasing and enthusiastic involvement in many causes brought her new notoriety. Her crusades for worker's rights, abortion, prostitution, and financial policies broadened her constituency but maintained animosity from many feminists. The lyceum tours gave her increasing fame and visibility among individuals, but they did nothing for her leadership within the movement. However, the highly popular and publicized lyceum speeches did provide her with a new public image, that she carefully fostered. She became the "grand old woman" of the woman's movement, and this matronly, queenly, and brilliant orator image would keep Cady Stanton in the public eye.

Cady Stanton's "return" to suffrage began with the 1876 Centennial celebration and her resumption of the presidency of the NWSA; it was in this role that she conferred with California Senator Aaron Sargeant, who reintroduced the woman suffrage amendment to Congress. She actively lobbied Congress between 1877 and 1890 for the amendment, and here her public image, which was turning her into a living legend, played an important role for the aims of the movement. This lobbying also marked a change in the way Cady Stanton perceived how goals could be accomplished: it seemed she was now resigned to the political maneuverings that were necessary for change to occur.

During the same period, Cady Stanton's impact on the women's rights movement was felt in other ways. The *History of Woman Suffrage* chronicled the first forty years of the movement; it revealed the strengths and weaknesses of the nineteenth century movement. Her founding (with Anthony) of the International Council of Women was an effort to create a broad coalition of women's organizations that could attack feminist issues on a world wide scale.

As a public figure, reformer, movement leader and philosopher, Elizabeth Cady Stanton maintained an essential feminist ideology. Although she argued for issues and causes that others in the movement ignored, her central commitment was legitimizing the demands for woman's rights and independence. More importantly, she wanted to alter the social, religious, and political attitudes people held about women; she wanted self-sovereignty for each person to be a goal and a possibility . This desire often led her in directions away from the mainstream of thought, for hers was a vision of ideals rather than of practical acts. While a movement might need and thus tolerate a visionary such as Cady Stanton in its genesis stages, as it grows, it requires a manager, a statesman, and a compromiser. Elizabeth Cady Stanton was unable to fulfill those roles successfully for any sustained period, and her leadership of and participation in the movement gradually waned.

3

The Struggle for Suffrage

The demand for suffrage was the cohesive force that united various women's associations into a powerful movement. Elizabeth Cady Stanton insisted on the inclusion of a suffrage resolution at the 1848 Seneca Falls convention: "Resolved, that it is the duty of the women of this country to secure to themselves their sacred right to the elective franchise."[1] Such a right seemed basic, fundamental to the achievement of all other rights. She felt that through the ballot, women could gain power, that would help them readily win their freedom. This was the first public demand for woman suffrage, and it was made only through the vision of Cady Stanton. It is Cady Stanton's suffrage arguments that are the most well documented, for the demand for the elective franchise was a constant call in most of her public address.[2]

The calls for woman suffrage mark the start of the movement's social unrest phase, in which leaders feel that by raising society's consciousness, the establishment will feel compelled to take remedial action. In addition, movement leaders are content to petition the establishment, to aim their rhetorical energies at those in power. They assume that society has only recently been made aware of any exigencies, and that they must strip the establishment of the false notions that are responsible for maintaining the exigent situations. Indeed, during the social unrest phase, rhetoric is primarily aimed at educating those in power of the true condition and nature of those agitating for change. Thus, Elizabeth Cady Stanton faced dual rhetorical objectives as a key leader within the movement. First, she had to transform the audience's perceptions of history in order to make them questione their false conceptualization of the essence of womanhood. Second, she had to strip the opposition of its presumed legitimacy, forcing the audience to see that the opposition had violated the basic values upon which America was founded. Cady Stanton chose a very specific strategy to meet these objectives: she asserted a specific policy change, the right to vote, which would alleviate the faulty conditions and conceptualizations under which women were forced to live.

The two texts analyzed here demonstrate Cady Stanton's extensive use of logical argument and extensive proof, which were trademarks of most of her addresses. The first speech, her 1854 Address before the New York State Legislature's Joint Judiciary Committee,3 displayed a masterful use of definition and clarification in its attempt to create a revised image of the true nature of woman and her position in society. Her legitimating tactic of contrasting opinion with reality, of tradition with present conditions, is a hallmark of her organizational method. The 1860 address before the New York State Legislature4 demonstrated Cady Stanton's use of extended metaphors, and her attempts to dissociate falsely held notions from the truth in an attempt to change society's values.

1854 ADDRESS

One of the most important addresses given in the early years of the women's movement was the 1854 address before the New York State Legislature, the first given by a woman to such a body. In it, Cady Stanton described the legal position of woman as woman, wife, widow, and mother in order to establish presence for women's legal disabilities. Her demands for political equality gave feminism a clear strategy and goal to pursue. Cady Stanton understood that the law played a major role in setting men over women; this speech explored four areas of injustice and promoted a new conception of woman's position in society. Although the speech was also presented to the 1854 New York State Woman's Rights Convention, it was the less sympathetic public audience for whom the speech was designed.

Anthony had asked Cady Stanton to prepare and deliver an address to both the State Woman's Rights Convention in Albany and to the Joint Judiciary Committee of the legislature. Enthusiastic allies to the address's development were Rochester Unitarian pastor William Henry Channing and Judge William Hay of Saratoga Springs. Hay prepared notes on points of unjust law and wrote to Anthony: "The person who arranges and condenses our suggestions into an address should, from every consideration, be Mrs. Stanton, because her style is admirably suited to such a subject."5 Channing wrote to Elizabeth Cady Stanton: "On all accounts you are the person to do it. There is not one of us who could tell the story of woman's wrongs as strongly, clearly, tersely, eloquently as yourself."6

Cady Stanton was thus encouraged to develop an address that would meet her supporter's expectations. Laboring under domestic difficulties (including an arrow shot through her daughter's eye by an older son), she nevertheless completed the speech. Channing was its first critic, offering only several more legal references. Henry Stanton also critiqued her, pronouncing her address excellent. Her most potent critic was next: Judge Cady, hoping to dissuade his daughter, urged her to read the speech to him. It appeared, to his chagrin, that Judge Cady's admonitions to his youthful daughter about speaking to the legislators to change the law were about to come true.[7]

When the New York State Woman's Rights Convention met in Albany's Association Hall on February 14, 1854, president Elizabeth Cady Stanton delivered the address that was destined for the legislature. Her appeal to the New York State Legislature came a few days later before a packed Senate chamber; it was the first address by a woman before them. In addition to the entire Joint Judiciary Committee of both houses, the galleries contained many prominent Albany citizens. As Cady Stanton recited case after case of woman's humiliating legal status as wife, widow, and mother, her voice and demeanor became impassioned. She demanded a new, just code of laws, saying: "we ask for all that you have asked for yourselves in the progress of your development, since the Mayflower cast anchor beside Plymouth Rock; and simply on the ground that the rights of every human being are the same and identical."[8]

She began the speech by stating her demands for a revisions of the New York State constitution to include new laws and provisions treating women equally with men. The primary justification for such changes lay in the fact that as "daughters of the revolutionary heroes of '76," women demanded redress of their grievances. Cady Stanton thus defined women in a new light: women were not fragile creatures needing protection; instead, they were equal beings who shared the same revolutionary legacy of American men. This rhetorical strategy hinted at the thrust of the speech: society's values had become corrupted with time, and Cady Stanton, in the role of educator, hoped to reaffirm the basic American value system by examining the true state of the oppressed.

The role of women as perceived in their "proper sphere" was first to be attacked. Cady Stanton asserted that society treated women inconsistently, for

> We are persons; native, free-born citizens;
> property-holders, tax-payers; yet we are
> denied the exercise of our right to the elective
> franchise. We are moral, virtuous, and
> intelligent, and in all respects quite equal to
> the proud white man himself, and yet by your
> laws we are classed with idiots, lunatics, and
> negroes . . . in fact, our legal position is lower

> than that of either . . . we who have guided
> great movements of charity, established
> missions, edited journals, published works on
> history, economy and statistics; who have
> governed nations, led armies, filled the
> professor's chair, taught philosophy and
> mathematics to the savant of our age,
> discovered planets, piloted ships across the
> sea, are denied the most sacred rights of
> citizens, because, forsooth, we came not into
> this republic crowned with the dignity of
> manhood!

Thus, Cady Stanton asserted that man was inconsistent: if woman were the moral and virtuous creature he says her to be, then she should not be treated in the same fashion as those who do not share those qualities. This argument demonstrated the loss of the American value of treating equal beings equally, which is the basis of the Golden Rule.

Other contradictions involved the enactment of laws when women had no say in their development; the violation of basic tenets of English law, from which our law sprang; the fact that women were subject to taxation on all property and still could not vote. Cady Stanton's first objective, to couch the contradictions in familiar political images (no taxation without representation, essential rights under the law), was successful in creating an atmosphere of tolerance within the audience. But tolerance was not her goal: it was not enough to cause the audience to question some of their values. Instead, she wanted action. She knew that her audience of male legislators thought more in concrete, actual terms than in values, so she had to demonstrate not only that social conditions harming women existed, but that the audience had the power to alleviate those harms. In answering potential objections that women didn't need to vote because they were represented by their male family members, Cady Stanton countered with an objection to the lack of trial by peers (since no woman could sit on a jury). She pictured for the audience a degrading situation in which their own women would be faced with a trial, thus making the image of lack of justice in law complete.

Cady Stanton's second argument, the position of woman as wife, began again with the inconsistent application of English common law. Here was Cady Stanton's first clear enunciation of the "contract" argument, which she would develop and hone in her later speeches:

> But if you regard marriage as a civil contract,
> then let it be subject to the same laws which

control all other contracts. Do not make it a
kind of half-human, half-divine institution,
which you may build up, but can not regulate.
Do not, by your special legislation for this one
kind of special contract, involve yourselves in
the grossest absurdities and contradictions. So
long as by your laws no man can make a
contract for a horse or piece of land until he is
twenty-one years of age . . . upon what
principle of civil jurisprudence do you permit
the boy of fourteen and the girl of twelve, in
violation of every natural law, to make a
contract more momentous in importance than
any other, and then hold them to it, come
what may.

Here Cady Stanton also foreshadowed her later arguments for
divorce, because she suggested that the signing of the marriage
contract is "instant civil death" to woman. She detailed the list of
losses woman must bear upon marriage: the loss of property rights
and wages, the ability to testify against her husband, the power to
sue, and of control of children. Thus, the law violated woman's true
spirit and God-given rights, because man now controlled woman's
destiny. This contradiction in values could not be tolerated.

The speech's third area, covering woman's position as widow,
began with an attempt to dissociate the currently held beliefs about
widows' privileges and powers with the reality of their condition.
While man in theory appeared to treat the widow fairly, in practice
he restricted her and reaped benefits from her loss. Cady Stanton
developed several powerful images of the true state of the woman as
"cared for" by society:

But, alas for human hopes! The husband dies,
and without a will, and the stricken widow, at
one fell blow, loses the companion of her
youth, her house and home, and half the little
sum she had in the bank. For the law, which
takes no cognizance of widows left with
twelve children and not one cent, instantly
spies out this widow, takes account of her
effects, and announces to her the startling
intelligence that but one-third of the house
and lot, and one-half the personal property
are hers . . . . This is the much-talked-of
widow's dower. Behold the magnanimity of
the law in allowing the widow to retain a life

> interest in one-third and one-half, and taking
> the lion's share to itself! Had she died first,
> the house and land would all have been the
> husband's still . . . . How, I ask you, can that
> be called justice, which makes such a
> distinction as this between man and woman?

The contradictions in the widow's position were further carried out as Cady Stanton described the taxation without self-representation widows had to endure. Again, she pointed out corrupted values, and though Cady Stanton had yet to articulate her policy proposal, she was laying the groundwork for change.

The address's final area of concern was the position of woman as mother. Here, Cady Stanton pointed out the inconsistencies that gave men the power over a child: fathers were given full legal right over unmarried children under age twenty-one; they were allowed to apprentice children out, to will away guardianship, and to degrade them through vice. Such a litany of man's mistreatment stripped the audience of its presumed legitimacy in actions as well as values.

By reviewing these four positions of woman, Cady Stanton demonstrated the severe contradictions inherent in man's law; she showed how ridiculously mistaken current beliefs about women were. Her task now shifted to help the audience conceive of a new reality and a means by which to right the wrongs it had perpetuated through its ignorance. She began the structuring of this new reality with a pragmatic argument: woman's moral power could best speak through the ballot box. She believed that men are deluded in their thinking and that they were unable to see the indignation women felt at legal injustices perpetuated upon them. She advocated Christ's Golden Rule: "Do unto others as you would have others do unto you." Justice suggested that all women want is the same protection the laws grant men. This "sacred right" was found securely within the mainstream of the audience's values, and Cady Stanton placed the audience in the position of adhering to that call or being in violation of a basic tenet that they professed guided their lives. In her impassioned conclusion, Cady Stanton touched upon a psychic kind of injustice: the demeaning of the spirit of women. Women were not asking for special favors; they only wanted what American men had possessed since the Mayflower landed, the right to be treated as equal beings.

The address before the New York State Legislature in 1860 was Cady Stanton's argument for passage of a woman's suffrage bill currently in the Senate.[9] In this second appearance before the legislature, Cady Stanton focused upon the contradictions within the concept of "woman's sphere," utilizing an extended analogy between the position of slaves and that of women. She wanted to reform the audience's mistaken beliefs about the true nature of women. By causing them to question their basic conceptualization, she hoped to energize them into changing the laws that maintained this false notion.

The address began with an assertion that rights were God-given, not legally conferred; in fact, "every individual comes into this world with rights that are not transferable." Thus, those in power (men) should have no voice in appropriating the rights of others, no matter the reason. In comparing woman's position with that of the negro slaves, Cady Stanton attempted to create an understanding of the degradation the "chains" of laws create. A slave had no name, had no right to his earnings, could call nothing his own. He had no right to his children and no legal existence. So, too, with woman:

> The prejudice against color, of which we hear
> so much, is no stronger than that against sex.
> It is produced by the same cause, and
> manifested very much in the same way. The
> negro's skin and the woman's sex are both
> *prima facie* evidence that they were intended
> to be in subjection to the white Saxon man.
> The few social privileges which the man gives
> the woman, he makes up to the negro in civil
> rights . . . . As citizens of a republic, which
> should we most highly prize, social privileges
> or civil rights? The latter, most certainly.

Cady Stanton suggested that an alien who would read the law books would wonder at the condition of women and negroes that they must be so "fenced in, so guarded against."

To those who would object that women must be protected from the ugliness of life by shielding her from the polls, Cady Stanton reminded the audience of the true condition of most women: consorts to vulgar, debased drunkards. Not all women were delicate and refined, and even those who were had to face brutal situations daily. By confronting the reality of life, Cady Stanton hoped to convince her audience of the need for change.

Another likely objection from the audience was that the majority of women did not want legal changes, and that when they wanted the ballot, as a class they would demand it. Cady Stanton associated the wise statesmen who legislated for the best interests of the nation, and the Christian who attempted to convert the world, with the women who argue for suffrage. She said: "Because they [the silly butterflies of fashion] know nothing of governments, or rights, and therefore ask nothing, shall my petitions be unheard? I stand before you the rightful representative of woman, claiming a share."

All she wanted, Cady Stanton claimed, was the ability to take care of herself, her property, her children, and her home. She requested the striking down of all special legislation and the erasing of the words "white male" from all laws; then, she said, all humans would sink or swim together. This rhetorical ploy was effective in several ways. It asserted the demands of the abolitionists, who often also supported woman's rights causes. It echoed the American notion that at times in history, leaders have to emerge who will fight for the rights of those who do not necessarily know that they are oppressed. It also reminded the audience of the equal nature and interdependence of all beings.

Cady Stanton's final extended analogy ridiculed the image of woman as created by the sculptor man: "He has made a woman . . . from his low standpoint . . . fair and beautiful, a being without rights, or hopes, or fears . . . neither noble, virtuous, nor independent." Men could not understand how their notion of "woman's superiority" was so false and unwanted a vision. Cady Stanton pictured true womanhood as the "crowning glory of the model republic among the nations of earth," and suggested that men and women together could build a future. Her metaphor of a lifeless sculpture versus a living, breathing being attempted to dissociate false images from reality, because as she saw it, the essence of true woman outdistanced society's false, dead conceptualization.

Her goal, that of restructuring society's illegitimate views of women, was achieved. The response to this speech was highly supportive. The Married Women's Property Act was passed on March 20, 1860. Lydia Mott, in a letter to a friend, described the speech by saying "The press is very complimentary . . . the House was packed, but so still that not one word was lost. It was worth as much to our cause as our whole convention, though we could not have spared either." [10]

These two suffrage addresses demonstrate some of Cady Stanton's most effective rhetorical strategies as a movement leader speaking out during its social unrest stage. She was able to place her values in the mainstream of public attitudes. In the 1854 speech, she showed that the natural, God-given rights women deserved were part of the traditional American system of values. She was also able to make her opponents' position vulnerable by pointing out inconsistencies in their treatment of women: if, for instance, widows were to be revered, why were they treated so shabbily? In 1860, she reasoned that a mistake must have been made to grant slaves rights before women. Her underscoring of this contradictory behavior was designed to make listeners question their beliefs.

The two addresses also demonstrated Cady Stanton's extensive use of legal precedent, extended examples, statutes, and historical images to illustrate her basic argumentative structure. She appeared intelligent and conversant with the facts; this enhanced her stature with the key audience, the powerful legislators. After all, the primary duty of a movement leader during this early phase is to educate the audience, to reshape their way of looking at the world. Cady Stanton also displayed a ready wit and satire; the irony of society's false beliefs about woman's true condition did not escape her listeners. In demonstrating society's misconceptions, she was able perhaps to create an attitude that would allow society to reconsider (or at least to question) its positions. Her speech's use of recognized authority, its extended and skillfully designed analogies, and its logical structure were all rhetorical strategies upon which Cady Stanton built her reputation as a leading orator within the movement.

Thus, Elizabeth Cady Stanton's suffrage addresses were marks of oratorical success in many ways. She was able to transform the audience's perceptions of their own history, reminding them of the values upon which the nation had been founded, creating in them the willingness to return to a more ideal state. She was able partially to strip the opposition of its assumed legitimacy by forcing it to question its policies that maintained false values and images. Cady Stanton chose a very specific means by which she asserted change would come. The right to vote, she claimed, would alleviate the faulty conditions and conceptualizations under which women were forced to live.

Cady Stanton's calls for suffrage remained constant through her public career. Although she altered her demands from universal suffrage to educated suffrage, it is safe to say that her suffrage addresses were highly regarded and well received. She was among a handful of women orators who were noted for fidelity and true belief in this cause, and she was called upon throughout her life to speak articulately and fervently for the movement on the suffrage issue before federal and state legislatures as well as the public.

4

Discontent and Reform

Elizabeth Cady Stanton's challenges to many of society's mores and customs startled and provoked her allies and enemies alike. Her disquieting calls for change caused society to review its established values and beliefs, and she persisted in demanding reform in divorce and marriage, religion, education, and labor. As a movement leader, Cady Stanton was a study in success and failure: while she altered society's conception of the essence of woman, her demands for alterations in accepted laws and roles often caused her to be ridiculed and lambasted. She was often censured for her outspoken views, but she continued to assert that woman could only achieve self-sovereignty when society based its ideas about woman on the true nature of female autonomy.

Many of Cady Stanton's addresses contained demands for reform in the laws and traditions that maintained woman's degrading role in society, such as religious tenets, the marriage contract, and the denial of equal educational opportunities. She argued that woman's basic nature guaranteed her the right to self-determination, and that society's restrictions were significantly damaging to that right. The rhetorical goals that Cady Stanton set for herself were challenging. She wanted to transform the audience's perceptions of history; she had to make them believe that the problems women faced were caused by a false conceptualization of the essence of womanhood that had mistakenly evolved over time. These false beliefs resulted in the audience's denial that women felt wronged. She wanted to strip the opposition of its presumed legitimacy, forcing the audience to see that they were responsible for allowing intolerable conditions to exist. She also wanted to prescribe courses of action, pressing a list of demands and solutions which would allow women to achieve self-sovereignty.

Because Cady Stanton proposed radical alterations in social perceptions and actions, her rhetorical goals were not always met. In some cases, she achieved a measure of success: progress in the coeducation of the sexes, and some loosening of divorce laws, did occur during her lifetime, and she had been a most vocal advocate of both of those causes. Cady Stanton desired immediate change, but when a rhetor challenges accepted standards and philosophies, alterations are slow in coming. Her rhetorical failures were often due to her inability to move the audience far enough from their initial conceptual and perceptual positions so that actual social and legal changes could occur.

There is a wealth of speeches that reflect the nature of Cady Stanton's reform oratory, many of which may be found in the Elizabeth Cady Stanton papers.[1] These discontent and reform addresses establish her rhetorical purposes of affirming propositions of fact and value, and they demonstrate Cady Stanton's range of success and failure in oratory.

RELIGION

Unfortunately, the historical record of Cady Stanton's oratory on religion is severely limited; in fact, in several instances in the *History of Woman Suffrage*, it is noted that due to length, her remarks about the Bible were omitted. The researcher can get a flavor of Cady Stanton's antireligious stance by her presentation and support of several resolutions denouncing religions whose dogma suggested that women were divinely ordained to a subordinate position. In her presidential address to the Seventeenth National Woman Suffrage Association 1885 meeting, Cady Stanton presented a speech entitled "The Limitations of Sex."[2] Although the main theme was the denial of the separate spheres argument, the speech also sounded her religious doubts. She said, for example, that the "most fatal dogma of the Christian religion" was that it commanded man to withdraw from all companionship with women in order to attain the "Divine ideal." Shortly after her speech, she supported a resolution condemning all religious creeds that taught that women were subordinate creatures, doomed to misfortune because of their sex. In her advocacy for resolution at the 1885 convention, she said:

> You may go over the world and you will find that every form of religion which has breathed upon this earth has degraded woman. There is not one which has not made her subject to man . . . . So long as ministers stand up and tell us that as Christ is the head of the church, so is man the head of the

woman, how are we to break the chains which
have held women down through the ages?

Now I ask you if our religion teaches the
dignity of woman? Can we ever cultivate any
proper sense of self-respect as long as women
take such sentiments (that motherhood is a
curse and woman is the author of sin) from
the mouths of the priesthood? We must
demand that our religion shall teach a higher
idea in regard to woman. We want to help roll
off from the soul of woman the terrible
superstitions that have so long repressed and
crushed her.[3]

Her outspoken approval of the resolution created a public dispute
with Susan B. Anthony, who had the resolution tabled.

One can get more of a sense of Cady Stanton's anticlerical
stance from her written rhetoric, especially in articles contained in
The Revolution and in *The Woman's Bible.* Yet a religious theme runs
through many of her addresses, and her impious position would
prove to be very damaging in her attempts at creating a climate of
legitimacy for some of her more revolutionary proposals.

MARRIAGE AND DIVORCE

To discuss divorce in the nineteenth century was to invite
ridicule and derision, for popular opinion held that only adulterers
and other sinners would want divorce, and further, that in granting
such a right, society would condone *free love.* Elizabeth Cady Stanton
first broached the subject in 1852, when she asserted to the
Women's State Temperance Society that habitual drunkenness should
be grounds for divorce action. In 1856, she wrote a letter to the
National Women's Rights Convention that concluded that marriage
"stripped womankind of true virtue, dignity and nobility."

At the Tenth National Women's Rights Convention, on May 10,
1860, Cady Stanton produced ten resolutions which favored divorce,
including the following:

Resolved, That any constitution, compact, or
covenant between human beings, that failed
to produce or promote human happiness,
could not, in the nature of things, be of any
force or authority; and it would not only be a
right, but a duty, to abolish it . . . .

> Resolved, That an unfortunate or ill-assorted
> marriage is ever a calamity, but not ever,
> perhaps never, a crime--and when society or
> government, by its laws or customs, compels
> its continuance, always to the grief of one of
> the parties, and the actual loss and damage of
> both, it usurps an authority never delegated
> to man, nor exercised by God himself.[4]

Her speech then spoke in favor of divorce, because marriage
was inherently unjust to women, it being a man-made convention.
Because marriage and divorce are private matters not subject to the
mistakes of civil law, they should be treated as such. She asserted:

> If marriage is a human institution, about
> which man may legislate, it seems but just
> that he should treat this branch of his
> legislation with the same common-sense that
> he applies to all others. If it is a mere legal
> contract, then should it be subject to the
> restraints and privileges of all other
> contracts . . . . The least concealment, fraud,
> or deception, if proved, annuls the contract.[5]

Cady Stanton demanded authorization for divorce in situations
involving insanity, desertion, adultery, drunkenness, and
incompatibility; such divorce would allow for escape from "one
unfortunate step." The address also depicted bad marriages as being
harmful to society, because "one unhappy, discordant man or woman
in a neighborhood, may mar the happiness of all the rest."[6]

The discussion following Cady Stanton's address was strident;
indeed, there was a raging debate. Wendell Phillips sought to have
the discussion removed from the record on the grounds that such a
subject was out of order at a women's rights convention. Susan B.
Anthony finally prevailed, and the resolutions were tabled. Elizabeth
Cady Stanton's promotion of the resolutions and her radical remarks
were portents of her increasingly unpopular positions on issues that
would distance her from the mainstream of movement thought.

This analysis examines two of her major addresses on the
theme of marriage and divorce. The first speech text is entitled
"Speech on Marriage and Divorce" (1869);[7] there is no description of
audience or setting, but it may have been one of her lyceum lectures.
Its thrust is to clarify the definition and true meaning of marriage as
part of Cady Stanton's attempt to transform society's perceptions of
history and of itself. In a similar vein, the second address was
delivered October 20, 1870 at the Decade Meeting on Marriage and

Divorce in New York's Apollo Hall. These two speeches on marriage and divorce display some of the hallmarks of Elizabeth Cady Stanton's rhetorical style as a movement leader during the stage of "enthusiastic mobilization." During this time, the movement enjoys a surge of optimism about the inevitability of change. Externally, leaders must stage symbolic acts which will force the opposition to examine itself, its values, and its positions. In addition, divisive and attacking rhetoric may be employed to cause further pressure and capitulation. Internally, leaders must deal with competing ideologies and coalitions. In order to keep the movement fresh, they must attempt to diversify their issues, and to develop alternative ideologies or strategies, yet keep a united front.

Elizabeth Cady Stanton was faced with the task of altering society's perceptions of truth by changing their conceptions of the past and present. Her basic thesis was that marriage and divorce were private matters, which civil and religious law had no right to regulate. In addition, she asserted that most of society already believed in the basic value of marriage, which was the freedom to choose a good life for oneself, not the false slavery that statutes had created.

Since one of the primary duties of a leader is to transform perceptions of the past and the present, Cady Stanton began by confronting the audience's conception of the marriage contract. By shifting their perceptions, she hoped to move them to view her message as reasonable. At the same time, she did not want to deny the essential values the audience placed in marriage: the sharing, love, and respect that two individuals pledge to each other for life. Instead, Cady Stanton's rhetorical task was to demonstrate that divorce was the means to allow unfortunate people a way out of false marriages, which were damaging to society. Her task was to move the audience away from its two-sided orientation: marriage was good, divorce was its antithesis. Instead, Cady Stanton wanted to develop within the audience a new orientation, that true marriage (as she defined it) was good, and that the freedom of divorce might sometimes be necessary to attain that valued state.

The 1869 address began by calling the contemporary definition of marriage ill-conceived, for it was "a compulsory bond enforced by the law and rendered perpetual by that means." This destructive bond, Cady Stanton asserted, subverted the true nature of marriage by making the partners into master and slave. She presented a definition of *true marriage* as the union of soul and intellect that allowed partners jointly to attain paradise. Such unions were possible only if both partners were free.

Cady Stanton also tried to answer audience suspicions that she was advocating the unlimited freedom of divorce, which would create a society doomed to free love. Her ethos was at stake, for while the audience might acknowledge her attempts at women's rights reform, primarily suffrage, as laudatory, divorce was too scandalous an issue. She effectively countered dissent with her assertions that the best constitutional lawyers had already supported her position, thus legitimating the notion of divorce. Of great effect were her historical reviews of the development of marriage as a religious and legal institution, for these reviews indicated not only that the concept of *marriage* had become perverted over time, but that progress in recognizing the disabilities caused by false marriages was already underway. To contradict further the audience's traditional definition of marriage, Cady Stanton cited the vacillating laws from state to state, which created three kinds of polygamy:

> First. There is the Mohammedan or Mormon form of polygamy, many wives known to each, living in daily contact.
>
> Second. There is the form known to our laws as bigamy, where one man has two or more wives living in different places, each supposing herself the legal wife.
>
> Third. There is the form well known to society, where a man lives with one wife but has many mistresses.

The effectiveness of this position lay in Cady Stanton's allegation that the meaning of marriage had been subverted over time, and that their idealized image of the marriage contract no longer held true. Cady Stanton attempted to create a new definition of *true marriage* based on common ground with her audience. True marriage, she proclaimed, was that state where two equal partners shared and grew together, raised children, and were an integral part of society. She successfully identified with the audience, allowing them to see her as a defender of the marriage institution, and she created a clearer sense of what she was defending.

Cady Stanton had to provide the audience with value-based criteria so they could assess the marriage contract: did contemporary marriage law support the audience's newly conceived ideal of *true marriage*? She utilized the criteria that the audience had already expressed in its objections to divorce: that divorce would break up family relations; that divorce would promote free love; that children's best interests were served in marriage, and that divine revelation condemned divorce. By identifying her own criteria as those established by the audience, Cady Stanton effectively created a shared ethos. She argued that it was untrue that divorce would break up the family, because the person who seeks and attains a divorce does not exist in a true marriage. In addition, divorce would not mean that men would take a new wife every Christmas, because the law would strengthen women by making them less likely to be the prey of such libertines. Furthermore, she provided examples that education, which was now becoming more common for women, was creating a new sense of inner strength that would be further liberated by less reliance on the false marriage contract. Free love would not be condoned, because true love was pure and not fickle or trifling; thus, social mores would not be abandoned. Cady Stanton argued there was a "demoralizing influence on children trained in an atmosphere of discord and dissatisfaction, such as a false marriage relation." Divorce would allow a wise mother to remove children from corrupting influences. Finally, religious objections to divorce, she asserted, derived from mistaken interpretations of Scripture rather than from Divine decree. She recognized potential objections from the audience and attempted to answer them, utilizing the audience's own higher values of freedom of choice and salvation. In particular, this 1870 address utilized extensive testimony, historical examples, and narratives in illustrating its points.

Both addresses placed themselves firmly in the mainstream of American values: freedom, equality, and justice for all. Cady Stanton articulated a sense of the inevitability and goodness of change, rather than uprooting the soul, rather than being a negative, destructive force, change would result in greatness By recognizing that their conception of marriage had become subverted through time and mistaken law, the audience now would want to stop maintaining an evil institution. According to Cady Stanton, the audience had the means to correct their error.

Both addresses employed common rhetorical themes common to most of Cady Stanton's addresses: the need for education; a demand for recognition of the true nature of women; claims of the perversion of original intents into something man-made and wrong; and a scope of historical fact that placed her arguments into the rational mainstream.

The difficulties these addresses faced were nearly insurmountable, because the concept of *true marriage* as Cady Stanton conceived of it was considered redundant by her listeners. Even though she was trying to create a new definition of the concept *marriage*, the audience was unable to break from its traditional perspective. The misplaced public attachment of the negative concept of *free love*, even with the new definitional parameters that Cady Stanton attempted to assert, did not aid her argument. Although marriage might be a contract, in the public's mind it was somehow different from other civil contracts, for the marriage contract had divine backing as well as innumerable consequences attached. It could not be broken, for in allowing divorce, society would crumble around the disintegrating family. The same could not be said for breaking a civil contract, despite Cady Stanton's numerous analogies between the two.

A second problem that her divorce and marriage positions faced was that her audience already knew what marriage was, and it was defined by both God's law and man's. Despite her many illustrations to the contrary, Cady Stanton was perceived as denying the basic precepts of God's divine plan. Marriage was a divinely ordained and sanctioned condition, with its boundaries and rights clearly prescribed. To question the sanctity of the marriage vows meant to doubt all religion. Cady Stanton's childhood problems with restrictive religious tenets had led to a new personal theology that emphasized independence in interpreting Scripture, self-reliance in constructing a moral code, and autonomy over the religious dogma as proscribed by the clergy. She despaired of the sycophantic believers who accepted religious proclamations without question. In her attack on marriage and defense of divorce, she argued against the underpinnings of religious belief. Thus, her arguments for divorce, although not based on the antireligious values that others ascribed to her, caused Cady Stanton's divorce messages to be misrepresented.

Cady Stanton's progressive arguments in favor of marriage reform were unpopular with many in the women's movement, since they called for a radical alteration of the traditional family. Opponents saw her calls as a demand for total permissiveness, immorality, and selfishness; in contrast, she felt that true marriage would join two equal partners, and that her pleas to all were for choice, freedom, and autonomy. For Cady Stanton, marriage reform was only one aspect of wider social change; legitimization of divorce would grant women the independence they needed. In order to be free to choose to marry or remain single, women had to have equal rights, which would allow them to vote on the educational and economic issues that affected their lives. Thus, divorce was only one means to an ultimate end. Her ultimate message was the significance of the self-sovereignty that freedom of choice would allow. But her audiences were largely unable to see the larger picture, for they believed that by removing one essential social element, the marriage laws, all of society would crash. This clash of values was insurmountable, and her notorious stance on divorce caused the alienation of many former allies. Indeed, Cady Stanton was widely censured for her remarks on marriage and divorce, and her unpopular position caused her ridicule from friends and enemies. Her ethos within and without the movement was significantly damaged by her position on these controversial issues.

CO-EDUCATION

Elizabeth Cady Stanton's addresses on education were more successful attempts at persuading society to place a new definition on the value and role of women and to grant them the power of self-determination. Her goal in these speeches was to demonstrate that educational problems threatened the welfare of society, and that the barriers to coeducation had to be removed. Thus, she had to help her audience to understand the nature and importance of the problems facing women who were denied education. Whereas speeches that advocate a value are designed to develop standards and judgments, speeches that attempt to create beliefs or concern for problems are designed as a prelude to advocating a specific solution. Cady Stanton's calls for educational reform were primarily designed to show that specific social conditions had to be defined as problems, and more important, that the value of equal education was essential to society's welfare. She wanted to undermine the audience's sense of superiority, forcing them to see that they were responsible for allowing unequal educational conditions to exist. In creating this dichotomy she could then promote specific courses of action that would allow women to achieve educational independence and equality.

Cady Stanton had an unusual educational upbringing, for until she was fifteen, she attended classes with boys. Her dedication to equal rights in education for the sexes had a long history. In 1856, she helped draft a speech for Susan B. Anthony to present to the New York State Teachers' Association calling for all colleges and universities to open their doors to women. The address entitled "Co-Education" presented in this volume, however, was probably one of Cady Stanton's lyceum lectures.[8]

The address demonstrated the hallmarks of the Cady Stanton style: strong organization marked by the debate tactics of enumerating arguments, countering objections, and supplying conclusive evidence from credible sources. She also succeeded in depicting coeducation as a fact already in existence that should no longer be debated; the concern should instead be shifted to the means for attaining coeducation.

By beginning with a historical review of the gains made in education, Cady Stanton set a tone of progress in the making. The speech began with an analogy: the seasons and planets change, often without our awareness. So too, she insisted, were the facts about coeducation of the sexes changing, and this change had been occurring for most of the century. Coeducation was no longer a theory, and it was time to wake up society to the facts. Cady Stanton then presented testimony from a variety of academicians involved in higher education in order to demonstrate that the real argument should no longer lie in "would the experiment work," but instead with the point, "shall we build similar colleges for girls when there already exist well endowed ones for boys."

Once she had identified for her audience the reality of the present condition of education, Cady Stanton proceeded to counter societal objections to coeducation. She had already demonstrated that leading educators believed in coeducation, and that coeducation was in fact occurring successfully in various parts of the country. She had to demonstrate that popular objections to coeducation were in violation of society's own standards. She called the unequal conditions that marked educational opportunities in America the result of misinformation and mistaken belief. If Cady Stanton achieved success in dissociating reality from perception, then her coeducation arguments would lead to educational equality for the sexes.

Cady Stanton's first point was the disparity of funds made available to women and men for higher education. Justice would say that what is good for one half of the state must be also good for the other half. She demonstrated unfair treatment by reviewing the endowments and educational advantages of the various colleges and universities in New York; the disparity in funding displayed the prejudice that society held against the higher education of women. She then turned attention to the reasons for this prejudice. One objection to the higher education of women lay in the sphere concept, which she dispelled by a series of analogies:

> Behold! Man eats, drinks, sleeps, and so does woman. He loves, is religious, penitent, prayerful, reverent; and so is woman. He is noble, courageous, self-reliant, generous, magnanimous; and so is woman . . . . Are not our hopes and fears for time and eternity the same?

Men had unjustly labeled women inferior, and this label had prevented women from obtaining that which was rightly theirs.

A second popular objection was that attending school with boys would demoralize both sexes. Cady Stanton asked how it could be that young girls and boys could associate at theaters and operas in safety; why not so under the watchful eyes of teachers? She also wondered if the moral atmosphere of our colleges is so evil that women cannot be safe, should then we be sending our future statesmen there?

A third popular objection was that scholarship standards would be lowered if women were admitted. This objection was overruled by her recitations of testimony from universities that already admitted women, where it had been found that not only did women often best the men in scholarly achievement, but they also influenced a stimulating challenge to their peers. In presenting such evidence, Cady Stanton affirmed her ethos; she was not alone in her assertions of the social benefits of coeducation. Her expert witnesses were all powerful males of high educational and professional repute.

A fourth public objection was that girls did not have the stamina for college study. Cady Stanton asserted that where coeducation already existed, girls were healthy and free of misery, in contrast with "the aimless, hopeless, pleasure seekers, for whom good fathers think they have done their utmost, when they have supplied every meal and have left heads and hearts and minds alike unfulfilled." She again backed up her comments with expert agreement.

The final objection was that instead of studying, boys and girls would spend their time flirting, or conversely, that women would be turned from marriage. Here, Cady Stanton reasserted her ideas about marriage, saying that marriage would continue, and that a well-educated girl would demand a higher type of young men and would "not be governed in marriage by the law of attraction and not by sordid motives of policy." This argument would appear to be bringing in a side issue, but it should be remembered that an audience might hear two or three of Cady Stanton's lyceum addresses during her stay. Thus, it seems logical that the marriage argument might be linked to the coeducation one, because her rhetorical success in one area would be linked with the other in the minds of her audience.

The speech's tone was optimistic and challenging; it demonstrated Cady Stanton's keen wit. The extensive use of testimony from a variety of credible witnesses added to the weight of her arguments, providing the address with a debate-like foundation. When describing the supposed differences between men and women, she aptly demonstrated through analogy and example how in all ways they were identical. There could be no objection to coeducation, she claimed, for it already was a successful fact of life. Indeed, if the audience consisted of rational men and women, they would realize that Cady Stanton was simply reviewing the facts for them, and they would see that their notions of reality were based upon false assumptions.

The emphasis on self-reliance in education in this speech echoed Cady Stanton's belief that the rights and responsibilities of individuals held superiority over those of society; thus, education was a right, and to say that a woman didn't need it because she would always be taken care of was a moot point. Girls deserved the chance at equal education, had proven their ability to compete and excel in coeducational situations, and were being held back by mistaken beliefs and misappropriation of funds. Cady Stanton argued that education was the vehicle by which society could create a new race of moral citizens; instead of causing distractions and flirtations, coeducation would improve the moral climate of classrooms. Coeducation was a positive moral force, not a disintegrating one. The only demoralizing factor, she posited, was in the treatment of women's higher education; although she didn't use the term "separate but equal," her speech was, in essence, asserting that it existed. If education was good, if it could be shown to work, and if we had schools already funded and equipped, then, she concluded, it made good sense to utilize the resources and get ahead with meeting the rights due equally to all citizens.

This speech is quite similar to her suffrage addresses in its use of well-regarded expert testimony. In this case, rather than asserting that change needed to come, Cady Stanton used historical precedent to demonstrate that change was already here, and it had worked. It is this explanation of reality that distinguished the speech; Cady Stanton quite ably met every potential objection to the "dangerous possibilities of co-education" with credible and undeniable testimony that helped to define the truth. The address was able to show the audience that their false beliefs about coeducation could not meet the test of reality, and that therefore they had to alter those beliefs. It was a masterfully designed piece of argumentation.

The coeducation speech was probably delivered at the height of Elizabeth Cady Stanton's lyceum career. She was enormously popular, bringing both entertainment and information to small communities across the nation. She found the lyceum lectures an opportunity to bring her messages of radical reform into the home rather than the convention hall. With a low and appealing voice and a gracious, feminine stature, she was perceived as maternal and eminently respectable. This speech, like her other lyceum addresses (including the one on "Marriage and Divorce"), kept her ideas at the center of public view, despite the distance she was apparently feeling from the movement's directions on many issues. In fact, while her feminist ideology was not the center of her lectures, it is easy to see her primary thesis: women have the right to self-determination, whether it be through education, marriage, or both.

The success of Elizabeth Cady Stanton's reform oratory must be judged by two measures. First, did she cause alterations in the audience's perceptions of the true nature of women, and second, did she attain the courses of action that she believed would create an equal world for women? The answer to the first question is a guarded yes. Cady Stanton's arguments demonstrated that in many ways, the audience's conception of social institutions was not in line with reality. The standard views of *marriage*, *divorce*, and *free love* were all shown to lack clarity and appropriateness, given the legal and moral entanglements of the times. It may be that her new conceptualizations failed to gain much acceptance because the audience was too deeply entrenched in values that discounted such new definitions. For example, the audience might concur with her argument that modern *marriage* did not allow women to be treated in the idealized manner that its definition expected, but other overriding concerns (family structure, religious decrees) took precedence over any abuse of the ideal. Another rhetorical success was Cady Stanton's demonstration of the progress that had occurred: indeed, she showed through many examples that reforms in marriage laws and educational practices had been successfully integrated into society with no alarming repercussions.

Was she successful in attaining the course of action that she called for, those proposals that would grant women equal status in the world? The immediate answer is no, because changes in marriage laws were the concern of states rather than the federal government, and such changes were slow in coming. So, too, were alterations in educational matters, because each institution was allowed to set its own standards. Cady Stanton's success lay more in pointing out the discrepancies between reality and impression, between mistaken perception and fact, than in obtaining any particular law or program. While she may have felt that success was being measured in too small steps, in retrospect, perhaps she met the larger goal of any movement's leader during its enthusiastic mobilization stage. She was able to force the opposition to reexamine its traditional values and beliefs, thus creating the potential for the legitimation of a new way of thinking about women, as well as diversifying the issues that the movement would deal with. At the same time, her "harsh rhetoric" developed into an internal struggle over ideologies that divided the movement.

5

Woman's Self-Image

The final speeches discussed in this survey exhibit the evolution of
Cady Stanton's feminist ethic of female independence. Indeed, one of
the bases of all of her oratory was the persistent identification of the
essence of womanhood while dissociating false beliefs about the
nature and desires of woman and arguing the need for woman to
recognize her God-given right to self-sovereignty. Although most of
Cady Stanton's addresses on the topic of woman reiterated her
central theme of female autonomy in some way, the two speeches
discussed in this chapter were arguably her more memorable and
well renowned in emphasizing her conviction that women could not
achieve anything close to a full life without first achieving total
autonomy. Cady Stanton insisted that women must stand on their
own before they could choose whether or not they wished to be
allied with men. She challenged her female audience to rethink their
limits, to abandon false restrictions, and to find solace in
themselves.[1]

Thus, these speeches, unlike many of the others, seemed
directed at a very specific audience: women who were allowing
themselves to be held back. This makes these addresses unique in
Cady Stanton's repertoire. As demonstrated in previous chapters,
her suffrage and reform speeches were most often directed at those
in power who could create change: in other words, at audiences
consisting primarily of men. The addresses also found willing
listeners in women, but these women were in power positions
because of status, wealth, or reform advocacy rather than political
strength. Women were incapable of writing the legal statutes that
would transform their lesser political and legal status. These two
speeches focused more attention on social and psychological barriers
which women could overcome in order to achieve autonomy. The
speeches are distinctive in their central concern with female
independence.

"OUR GIRLS"

For the lyceum tours, Cady Stanton developed a broad repertoire of topics: her titles included "The Subjection of Women," "Home Life, "Our Girls," "Our Boys," "Prison Life," "The True Republic," "Co-Education," (discussed above) "Marriage and Divorce," "Marriage and Maternity," "Thurlow Weed, William Seward and Horace Greeley," "Famous Women in the Bible," and "The Bible and Women's Rights." The most popular of Cady Stanton's lyceum lectures was "Our Girls."[2] In it, she urged the upcoming female generation to prepare themselves for self-sovereignty, and she urged males to acknowledge the need for female independence.

"Our Girls" displayed Cady Stanton's expressiveness in language and images, which audiences had come to expect in her addresses. She urged the women in the audience to prepare themselves for self-sovereignty. She reminded them that while they may never play the role of wife or mother, they would always be women. The speech began with a description of young, free girls frolicking at equal play with boys, but who evolved into passive and unsatisfied subjugated females:

> And why? They have awakened to the fact that they belong to a subject, degraded, ostracized class; that to fill their man-appointed sphere, they can have no individual character, no life purpose, personal freedom, aim or ambition. They are simply to revolve around some man, to live only for him, in him, with him; to be fed, clothed, housed, guarded and controlled by him . . . never to know the freedom and dignity that are secured in self-dependence and self-support.

Her vivid descriptions of the degradations felt by young women depicted the humiliation they must endure. Society confronted young women, telling them in not-so-subtle ways that they were inferior to men. Custom perpetuated this myth, teaching it to boys and girls alike. The resultant condition was that their ambitions were thwarted and unnecessary obstacles were placed in girls' way.

Cady Stanton attempted to dispel the mistaken ideas many held about woman's sphere. The speech explored the desires of women to paint, to act, to control their own fortunes. She proposed a plan for reforms that would allow the full development of women in all facets of their lives.

First, educational reform was needed for the physiological requirements of woman. This educational change began with creation of a new, healthy girl who was unfettered by the trivial demands of fashion and custom. Cady Stanton decried the unnatural restraints placed on girls by fashion, which denied Nature's intentions:

> Woman, as she is today, is men's handiwork. With iron shoes, steel-ribbed corsets, hoops, trains, high heels, chignons, paniers, limping gait, feeble muscles, with her cultivated fears of everything seen and unseen . . . women die ten thousand deaths, when if educated to be brave and self-dependent, they would die but one.

A sound body, according to Cady Stanton, was like the foundation to a house. She lamented the misplaced attention paid in the search for youthful beauty, which prompted women to utilize all types of harmful nostrums. The search for true beauty should begin from within.

Cady Stanton's use of irony played upon the ridiculous ideas fostered by popular patent products. For example, she decried Hagan's Magnolia Balm, which boasted that it would make a lady of thirty look like a girl of sixteen. She scoffed at such a claim, asking: "What sensible woman of thirty with all the marks of intelligence and cultivation that well-spent years must give would desire to look like an inexperienced girl of sixteen?" She progressed into a vivid exhibition of the harmful effects of the chalk, alcohol, and white lead that many of the products contained. She declared that these potions could not provide the beauty that comes from inside the person:

> Remember that beauty works from within, it cannot be put on and off like a garment, and it depends far more on the culture of the intellect, the tastes, sentiment, and affections of the soul than the color of the hair, eyes or complexion . . . . Be kind, noble, generous, well mannered, be true to yourselves and your friends . . . we cannot be one thing and look another . . . . There are indelible marks in every face showing the real life within.

It should be noted that Cady Stanton was quite willing to use her own physique and demeanor as prime examples of a healthy, active live. During her lyceum period, she was widely recognized as a model speaker, and she played upon her matronly image for the audience's recognition. In speaking against the false search for beauty, she offered herself as one whose "well-spent years" still provided her with a pleasing countenance.[3]

As a scholar in Emma Willard's school, Elizabeth Cady Stanton had studied physiology, which was an advanced (and shocking) topic for the times. She used this address to expose the physiological problems created by needless concern for fashion. Cady Stanton asserted that the question of health mandated the reform of dress. She described the damage done to woman by restrictive clothing:

> But look at the forms of all our young girls to appreciate the violence done Nature in the small waists and constrained gait and manners of all we meet. Ordinarily a girl of fourteen is a healthy, happy being in short hair, short dress, in clothes hung loosely on her shoulders. But as soon as her skirts trail and her dressmakers lace and tighten her clothes "to form the waist" as they say, a change takes place at once in her whole manner and appearance. She is moody, listless, weary, strolls when she should run, cries when she should laugh, and this at the very age when she should manifest newfound vigor and enthusiasm. Much of this may be attributed to the many unnatural restraints placed on all girls . . . the tight waist prevents a free circulation of the blood and action of the heart and lungs, contracts the ribs and paralyzes a belt of the nerves and muscles at least six inches in width round that part of the body. The long dress prevents all freedom of motion. When we remember that deep breathing has much to do with deep thinking, we see the relation between scholarship and clothes.

The address described the refreshment gained from walking, which girls were unable to do because of interference from their dress and uncomfortable shoes. Cady Stanton even reflected upon her own childhood habits of walking five miles before breakfast or ten miles on horseback and how her father refused to have her ribs taped. She avowed that these early habits resulted in her continuing health today. Cady Stanton did not place blame on men for the results of this fashion-slavery; instead, she asserted that women should claim responsibility for their physical condition. She regarded the artificial restraints caused by fashion and tradition as grievously harmful. Woman's independence from this slavery to fashion was the first type of educational reform to be achieved.

A second educational reform that would create autonomy would be to impress the truth that women were "independent, creative wildflowers made primarily for her own happiness." If women were misleadingly told that during all of their lives they would be taken care of and that they could always count on some male to tend to their needs, then they would be unprepared to deal with the facts of life when thrown on their own resources. Thus, Cady Stanton argued, women needed to be educated to some profitable career to eliminate the possibility of being left helpless without skills. She asserted that marriages, even good ones, were not without financial danger, for "good husbands sometimes die bankrupt, leaving a young wife . . . helpless, friendless, alone, with no trade or profession by which she can gain a livelihood."

Cady Stanton introduced statistics about the number of women in New York who had to work in low paying but decent employment for a living. She then turned her listeners' eyes to the depths to which many women would fall in search of money. Her exposure of the world of vice as a logical outlet for such women was calculated to shock her audience, who probably had not considered that they or their daughters could be reduced to such a condition. But Cady Stanton backed her conjecture with compelling narratives:

> Go to the departments of Washington and what do you find there, a large majority of the female clerks from the first families in the land. Go to the mercantile establishments, the garrets and cellars of our metropolis, the sinks of iniquity and vice, the busy marts of trade in your own city, and there are the daughters and sisters of Supreme Court judges, presidents, senators, congressmen, priests and bishops. Remember, vice recruits its ranks not from the children of lust but from the gay, the fashionable, the helpless, those who know not how to work, but yet must eat. The stern question presses itself on our consideration: what can these soft white hands and listless brains do for an honorable support?

Cady Stanton described women who were thrown on the mercy of the streets and told of the vice and disease that lurked there. She contrasted that seedy narrative with the benefits gained by women who had skills and earned wages for living. She suggested professions such as the ministry, commerce, and law as particularly suited to women. For those who still did not believe, Cady Stanton provided a list of potential jobs and salaries, such as a teacher who could earn thirty dollars per week, paying six dollars per week for room and board, or a waitress or chambermaid able to earn twelve dollars per month. She argued that it would be better to educate women in freedom, so that they could look forward to some life work and the means of self-support that a trade or profession would offer. Again, she provided a litany of such jobs and salaries: a minister in San Francisco at $2000 per year, a telegraph operator at twenty dollars per week, and so on.

This employment argument might appear to be contradictory. Cady Stanton could be accused of using the sphere concept when convenient and railing against its strictures when it suited her. Cady Stanton did not use the concept in the same way as her detractors, for rather than suggesting that there were separate, distinct natures for the sexes, she asserted that certain qualities were inherent in men and women's beings. While those qualities might exist in different degrees, both sexes could function in the professional arena. Woman could do well in the ministry, she claimed, for its duties were chiefly research, teaching, and sympathy. As the argument unfolded, Cady Stanton provided cases of women (Elizabeth Fry and John Wesley's mother) who were excellent ministers of the faith. She pointed out that the Methodist Church had recognized that when dispensing God's spirit, no sexual boundaries existed. Thus, rather than suggesting that woman was better suited than man for the ministry, she simply suggested that woman was at least his equal in promoting religious belief.

She continued her indictment of the lack of professional training for women by reviewing the position of women in the mercantile arena and how female physicians were already affecting society. In an extended analogy, Cady Stanton referred to Shakespeare, a literary allusion that was probably familiar to the audience because plays were acceptable forms of public entertainment. She reminded her listeners that during Shakespeare's day, female characters were performed by men, yet today no one wondered at women treading the boards. Cady Stanton successfully argued that change is not necessarily bad. Progress was underway without negative social consequences. Thus, she concluded, alterations in professional development should be explored.

Cady Stanton recognized that some in the audience might be alarmed at women taking such a public role in the professions. She inquired,

Is a lawyer's office with a dozen clients, all
sober men engaged in the practical business
of life, where your daughters must sit plainly
and comfortable dressed, pen and book in
hand, as public as a ball room where
assembled hundreds may look at her as she
minces about, immodestly draped now in the
dance taking anybody by the hand, and now
in the giddy waltz, whirling about in the arms
of some licentious debaucher.

In exploring this new argument, that woman's employment affected
public morals, Cady Stanton concluded that not only would a working
woman enjoy greater independence, but society would be rid of
licentiousness and excess.

Cady Stanton then opposed another commonly held belief that
educating women for professions would turn them away from
marriage and motherhood. In a brief passage, she returned to her
familiar conception of the true state of marriage, wherein partners
were equals. Cady Stanton advised that no girl should marry until
she is at least twenty-five, when she had gained physical maturity
and had devoted the preceding years to reading, thought, and study
in order to become a greater life companion. She said, "If husbands
found this companionship in their wives in science, philosophy, and
government, our whole social life would be refined and educated and
marriage would be a far more happy and permanent relation than it
is today." She also used this argument to focus attention on her
anticlerical position, for in her way of thinking, religion had been the
devil that kept women subjugated. Cady Stanton complimented the
Methodist church for dropping the word "obey" from the marriage
ceremony, but she lambasted the Episcopal church for its uncivilized
rules. She detailed a lengthy example of one woman's humiliation
because of the church's insistence on the ritual of giving the bride
away. She concluded by rebuking those who insisted upon such
degradation, proposing that they should be impeached for violating
the Thirteenth Amendment, which outlawed involuntary servitude.
Because marriage was based on the superiority of the husband, it
degraded women and thus supported slavery. This was a recurrent
theme in Cady Stanton's public advocacy.

The speech concluded with an old German proverb, that "every
girl is born into the world with a stone upon her head." In an
apparent attack on society, particularly men, Cady Stanton alleged
that society's laws and customs were such stones, but today's well-
educated and independent young girls would soon rise despite the
burdens placed upon their heads. She provided a litany of famous
women in the professions, a sort of triumphant march of champions

in order to prove that women were overcoming their burdens. This exultation of Nature over man's law served as a challenge and a reminder: change was occurring, and a transformation of woman was attainable, despite the obstacles society placed in her way.

"Our Girls" was typical of Cady Stanton's speeches in several ways. It relied upon analogy and contrast to demonstrate the falsehood of beliefs currently held by the audience. This dissociation with truth and reality was designed to let the audience recognize how their ideas of the truth had become perverted through time and false custom. Cady Stanton perfected elaborate graphic accounts of social conditions; she painted word pictures that expanded the senses; and her language was highly picturesque and evocative of strong emotions. For example, she spoke of the "artificial barriers of custom" and "puny legislation," and called out: "Strike off these chains!" When discussing one young girl whose longing to be educated for the stage was denied, she avowed that "the weary hours of such a blasted life cannot be cheated with the dull sound of ordinary duties, with the puerile pleasures said to be legitimate to woman's sphere." In fact, when speaking of young girls, Cady Stanton selected words that symbolized the ideal girl as being strong, shining, ambitious, healthy, cunning, spirited, and skillful, while the unfortunate victims of society's customs were contrasted as dull, weak, gloomy, diseased, lazy, malicious, idle, frivolous, ill tempered, and impatient. The audience was left with no doubt as to the more desired condition.

However, the speech lacked a coherent unity in its progression. Although Cady Stanton suggested that she would present several ways in which educational reforms could reverse the negative burdens placed upon women, she abandoned that arrangement halfway through the speech. First, she talked about educating for health. She meant that woman had to be taught that Nature intended her to be active, healthy, and unfettered, and that social custom had created artificial boundaries of dress and activity that made woman weak. The next argument, educating for careers, was was barely underway when Cady Stanton returned to the good health issue for several more pages. Her reviews of beauty practices, a comparison between the health and character of American and of foreign women, and other arguments extended the first type of educational reform rather than the second. Although the accounts were vivid and eye-opening, they were misplaced, and it is likely that the audience suffered some confusion as to where the address was progressing. When Cady Stanton returned to the theme of career education, she presented a compelling distinction between professional women who were self-supporting, and the poor, weak creatures who were life long dependents on some male. The effectiveness of these passages lay in the statistical evidence presented concerning the salaries that women could earn.

Her final thrust against religion seemed out of place with the generally positive feelings about woman's possibilities that the address had thus far generated.   The audience had come to understand a new truth of how custom greatly harmed women and therefore society.   But then Cady Stanton digressed into her anticlerical views, focusing on the unfairness of the marriage vows. Her comments on the "degradation of the marriage ceremony" probably caused members of the audience some discomfort, and the address ended with a negative, accusatory tone that was not prevalent in the rest of the text. Cady Stanton had addressed both men and women throughout the speech, showing how both were responsible for woman's devaluation. However, she professed hope that progress had occurred due to changes in woman's self-perception. That progress was reflected in society's gradual acceptance of a more active female role in education and the professions. The speech was an attempt to encourage those measured steps of progress.

The memorable aspects of this speech were its picturesque language, its compelling juxtaposition between truth and reality, and its narrative zest. The germ of Cady Stanton's feminist ideology was found throughout the speech: woman must be able to achieve self-dependence. Without independence, woman would be unable to face life's crises and demands. In addition, dependence on others and false beliefs hurt not only woman's growth but society's future. Without full partnership of all humans, the nation would decay from lack of morals and a usurpation of the true nature of the individual. Each individual must find within him or herself the self-love, composure, peace, and virtue with which Nature has endowed all people. As a movement leader maintaining progress during the movement's maintenance phase, Cady Stanton was faced with the challenge of reminding the audience of truths that had been achieved, with keeping the faithful from backsliding, and with moving the ideals forward. By focusing attention on the autonomous nature of woman, this speech was able to attain her purposes. This theme of self-sovereignty was echoed throughout many of Cady Stanton's speeches and would come to be the central motif in her final address, "The Solitude of Self."

"THE SOLITUDE OF SELF"

This address was considered by many, including Cady Stanton, to be her best. In it, she reiterated her commitment to human rights and her personal philosophy of independence. The address was to be the definitive statement of her feminist ideology. It reviewed her arguments for woman's absolute intellectual, physical, emotional, social, religious, and legal self-dependence at the end of Cady Stanton's public oratorical career.

"The Solitude of Self" was delivered three times over a three-day period. The first presentation, in written form, was sent to the House Committee on the Judiciary on January 18, 1892, in Washington, D.C. That afternoon, she personally delivered it before the NAWSA convention; it was to be her final appearance before that group, and the speech was the final public address she made, although later her speeches were read for her. On January 20, she again delivered the speech personally to the Senate Committee on Woman Suffrage at a Washington hearing; it was her last appearance before Congress. The speech was reprinted both in the *Woman's Journal* and the *Congressional Record*. Admirers felt it was her finest effort. Susan B. Anthony said, "This is pronounced the strongest and most unanswerable argument and appeal made by the moral pen or tongue for the full freedom and franchise of women."[4]

The address was a call for rights based upon tradition and nature. Instead of displaying optimism, Cady Stanton reflected in somber and tragic tones on the essential isolation of each person. No one could represent any one else, because no two people shared the same experiences. No matter what laws or reforms existed, individuals were unique and ultimately alone, which meant they were responsible for themselves. No one could depend on legal remedies to improve their condition, as they would have to confront their trials alone. Women were more vulnerable than men because they were not expected or prepared to fend for themselves. Women had to cope with the "awful solitude" existing in childhood, marriage, childbirth, widowhood, old age, and death.

Cady Stanton began the address by reflecting that all people were like an "imaginary Robinson Crusoe with her woman Friday on a solitary island." This natural isolation and the requirements for self-dependence necessitated that woman be educated, be allowed to develop her faculties, and be given complete emancipation from fear, false bonds, and custom. Early in the address, she asserted:

> The strongest reason for giving woman all the opportunities for higher education, for the full development of her faculties, her forces of mind and body; for giving her the most enlarged freedom of thought and action; a complete emancipation from all forms of bondage, of custom, dependence, superstition; from all the crippling influences of fear; is the

solitude and personal responsibility of her
own individual life.

Rather than using the speech to repeat her well-known
arguments for women's rights, Cady Stanton chose to argue that such
rights were due because of one unfailing cause: all people have
responsibilities for themselves. She said:

> The strongest reason for giving woman all the
> opportunities for higher education, for the full
> development of her faculties, her forces of
> mind and body; for giving her the most
> enlarged freedom of thought and action; a
> complete emancipation from all forms of
> bondage, of custom, dependence, superstition;
> from all the crippling influences of fear; is the
> solitude and personal responsibility of her
> own individual life . . . . No matter how
> much women prefer to lean, to be protected
> and supported, nor how much men desire to
> have them do so, they must make the voyage
> of life alone.

She said that each soul must be prepared for independent action,
simply because no two persons or circumstances are identical. We
each must bear our own burdens: "We come into the world alone,
unlike all who have gone before us; we leave it alone under
circumstances peculiar to ourselves." We live our tragedies alone,
unable to share the inner agonies with others. For instance, she
described how

> In youth our most bitter disappointments, our
> brightest hopes and ambitions are known
> only to ourselves; even our friendship and
> love we never fully share with another; there
> is something of every passion in every
> situation we conceal. Even so in our triumphs
> and defeats.

Cady Stanton pictured woman as handicapped by law and
custom, forced to fight her own battles unprepared. She affirmed this
state by describing a series of compelling metaphors:

> To throw obstacles in the way of a complete
> education, is like putting out the eyes; to deny
> the rights of property, like cutting off the

> hands. To deny political equality is to rob the
> ostracized of all self-respect; of credit in the
> market place; of recompense in the world of
> work; of a voice among those who make and
> administer the law, a choice in the jury before
> whom they are tried, and in the judge who
> decides their punishment.

Young wives and mothers, shielded by kind husbands, had safety;
nevertheless, they had to stand alone in fighting the battles of
running a home, raising moral children, training servants, and so on.
Uneducated women who were trained only for dependence failed.
Without full development of the faculties, people grow feeble and
passive. She lamented:

> If they cannot find companionship in books, if
> they have no interest in the vital questions of
> the hour, no interest in watching the
> consummation of reforms, with which they
> might have been identified, they soon pass
> into their dotage . . . . Nothing strengthens
> the judgement and quickens the conscience
> like individual responsibility. Nothing adds
> such dignity to character as the recognition of
> one's self-sovereignty; the right to an equal
> place, everywhere conceded; a place earned
> by personal merit, not an artificial attainment.

Cady Stanton described various life crises in which men and women
found themselves. Because one could never predict the situation,
limited training that stultified the full development of all the
faculties of mind and body had to be wrong.

The address showed that man could not protect woman from
the pains of childbirth, in which she suffers perhaps the ultimate
moment of solitude:

> Whatever the theories may be of a woman's
> dependence on man, in the supreme moments
> of her life he can not bear her burdens. Alone
> she goes to the gates of death to give life to
> every man that is born into the world. No one
> can share her fears, no one can mitigate her
> pangs; and if her sorrow is greater than she
> can bear, alone she passes beyond the gates
> into the vast unknown.

If woman must meet eternity alone, how could it be appropriate that she was denied the opportunity to prepare herself fully? Cady Stanton used the religious allusion of Christ at Gethsemane and on the cross to further this sense of loneliness that each person must bear. Even Christ felt the "awful solitude of self" as He was deserted by His friends. She mourned:

> And so it ever must be in the conflicting scenes of life, in the long weary march, each one walks alone. We may have many friends, love, kindness, sympathy and charity to smooth our pathway in everyday life, but in the tragedies and triumphs of human experience each moral stands alone.

Rather than reasserting her arguments about coeducation, Cady Stanton expressed deep concern about training the self toward autonomy. No longer did she feel compelled to argue that women be granted admission into schools and permitted specific fields of study. The issue now was a broader conception of education, the training of an individual's mind toward liberty and development. Women were already man's equals in art, music, science, literature, and government. Such triumphs raised women over the false theories of the past. Women now needed the training to allow them to be guided by their own conscience and judgement, "trained to self-protection by a healthy development of the muscular system" as well as stimulated to be self-supporting. Women's ambitions and hopes had changed with the invention of the spinning wheel and loom, with the ingress of woman to the platform and bars of justice. Thus,

> We see reason sufficient in the outer conditions of human beings for individual liberty and development, but when we consider the self-dependence of every human soul we see the need of courage, judgment, and the exercise of every faculty of mind and body, strengthened and developed by use, in woman as well as man.

Rather than advocating specific curriculums, Cady Stanton now petitioned for the right of woman to develop all of her senses. Woman's outer conditions may have appeared to be nearing fulfillment through society's gradual acknowledgement of her intellectual capabilities in music, art, and some professions; however, woman's inner conditions were poorly exercised. All humans faced crises alone, and man's sympathy and love could not ease the way for woman. The inner being yearned for self-dependence. Cady Stanton closed with the thought that "In that solemn solitude of self, that links us with the immeasurable and the eternal, each soul lives alone forever." No one had the right to take responsibility for another soul.

The address culminated Elizabeth Cady Stanton's decades-old argument that woman had to be free to assume responsibility for her life, because in the end, all people were ultimately alone. Without the education, experience, and the desire to deal effectively and independently with life's exigencies, woman was helpless and thus suffered greatly. The address asserted Cady Stanton's own standards of independence and self-reliance. In that sense, the speech charted and affirmed her own evolution to self-sovereignty.

"The Solitude of Self" displayed marked differences from other Cady Stanton speeches. Unlike most of her previous addresses, Cady Stanton here employed little logical argumentation, cited few narrative examples detailing conditions and situations, and failed to develop specific instances of wrongs or even contradictions within society's values and actions. She referred briefly to the position of woman as mother, as widow, and ultimately as an individual through a string of general allusions rather than pointed, specific references, as in her earlier addresses before the New York State Legislature.[5] And in "The Solitude of Self," she mentioned suffrage, divorce, and other favorite issues only in passing. In addition, the address lacked structural unity. There was no true introduction, and it had no ending, because the abrupt, pleading final question failed to consummate the message.

Rather than employing familiar rhetorical strategies and cliched examples, Cady Stanton chose a different route and developed a singular theme: the essential solitude of the self in all its daily encounters. The speech focused on the nature of human individuality and the need for women to achieve their birthright as unique human beings. Karlyn Kohrs Campbell has asserted that what made this address extraordinary was its philosophical statement and defense of humanistic individualism as well as its unusual lyric tone.[6] Cady Stanton painted a picture of a universal woman and contrasted her position to that of the rest of humanity. The images she created demonstrated that because of the ultimate aloneness each individual must endure, society had no right to limit women.

"The Solitude of Self" is unique in Cady Stanton's repertoire of addresses. Rather than inspiring or challenging her audience, she spoke mournfully about the essential isolation of each person. This existential argument belied the claim that politics alone could remedy woman's condition. Nor could people reform society enough to change their fates. Instead, Cady Stanton's tragically powerful case asserted that people had to be prepared to live with themselves, to fight for themselves, and to suffer for themselves. Women, she claimed, were poorly prepared to do so because of mistaken notions about the ability of others to share the burdens that life presented.

Cady Stanton's tone was somber, in contrast with other speeches where she displayed linguistic wit, aggression, and optimism. Instead, "The Solitude of Self" emphasized the tragic nature of human self-dependence. It focused upon the isolation all people feel when faced with tragedy and triumph. In a sense, Cady Stanton downplayed the legal gains that the movement had achieved, because she wanted to stress that all life ends in desolate personal solitude. Woman was largely unprepared to deal with that autonomy. The only thing that mattered is the preparation for the here and now, for the future was sealed. Thus, Cady Stanton avowed the need for changes in the inner lives of women in the present so that they could better face their destiny alone. Self-sovereignty was an ethic that had ruled her own life. This was Cady Stanton's valedictory address; in it, she presented the basic principle that guided her leadership during the first fifty years of the women's movement.

Conclusion

Elizabeth Cady Stanton was one of the founding mothers of the woman's rights movement. She was its earliest major philosopher and advocate, one of its organizational mainstays, and eventually became one of its leading critics. She invented the movement's agenda, articulated its ideals, developed its issues in public forums, and led the movement through birth, establishment, and rebirth. At times, she was its outspoken advocate, and she garnered national recognition for her public stands. Because of Cady Stanton's advocacy on a breadth of issues, including suffrage, divorce, abortion, work laws, and education, detractors accused her of lacking direction. Others charged her with a radicalism that destroyed any hopes women had of gaining significant political or social change. More than most other female reform advocates of her time, Elizabeth Cady Stanton was an impatient visionary. She charged ahead, fearlessly confronting society's perceptions of woman's duties and roles wherever she encountered them: in the church, the court, the workplace, the immigration station, the schools, and the home.

Cady Stanton believed that effective social change could come only through total autonomy and self-reliance. Once people were freed from encumbering social, moral, legal, and religious traditions, she felt they could then achieve their true potential. Her native curiosity, audacious thinking, and bold advocacy of diverse issues, combined with her galvanized spirit of reform, had a major impact on the women's movement and on society.

Cady Stanton's role in the women's movement was that of philosopher, agitator, key speaker, and torchbearer. Because of her visionary ability, she was the first to argue that the power of the ballot was essential to gain all rights, whether they were social or religious, economic or educational, individual or group. Elizabeth Cady Stanton forged the early threads of the women's rights movement into a national organization that grew in power and demands. She argued that the basis of all rights was an individual's right to self-determination. Her leadership style idealized this self-sovereignty ethic. As the movement began to flourish, Cady Stanton's early visionary role evolved into a more public one. She achieved the national spotlight because of her utter convictions in the truth, her oratorical prowess, and her determination to be heard in every available forum. She was among a handful of women who spoke eloquently to legislatures and conventions detailing the social and legal wrongs that were perpetuated on women. Gradually, as progress in changing statutes occurred, Cady Stanton grew impatient with the movement's slowness to demand broader societal changes. She derided and criticized the conservative direction that the movement's leaders were charting, and she became an object of embarrassment and ridicule. All the while, she remained firmly convinced that her vision of the inherent self-sovereignty of the individual was correct; in her rhetoric, she espoused this philosophy for all causes.

Hers was a life moved by varying intellectual and emotional currents. Sometimes dominated by controversy, she steeped her rhetoric in aggressive attacks on falsely held attitudes, in the creation of new definitions of traditional ideas such as freedom and marriage, and in a powerful grasp of rhetorical strategies developed from debate traditions. She seemed to relish the role of agitator within the movement as she attempted to wrestle it from a too conservative path. On other occasions, she served as the movement's key public advocate, and the national attention paid to her addresses gave the movement form and impetus.

Cady Stanton's speeches attacked fundamental social objections to the rightful enlargement of woman's sphere, even as they argued for the creation of a self-sovereign sphere where each individual could reign supreme over him or herself. She demanded that people be treated as individuals without regard for the incidental relations of life such as mother or father, wife or husband. In order to be free, she felt, people had to be released from all forms of superstition, custom, and bondage. According to Judith Nies, Cady Stanton once told an inquisitive reporter to put this down in capital letters: "SELF-DEVELOPMENT IS A HIGHER DUTY THAN SELF-SACRIFICE. The thing which most retards and militates against woman's self-development is self-sacrifice."[1] This is not to say that Cady Stanton only believed in the individual. She viewed society as interconnected, an organic whole that was bettered when the rights of one were improved. But unless the individual was permitted to achieve all due freedoms and self-sovereignty, the good of society was diminished.

Cady Stanton addressed her attacks to both men and women, although males were the more frequent targets because they held more power. She despaired over the dependency of women, especially on their husbands, for this sycophantic behavior made them incapable of achieving true womanhood. Instead, such reliance made women passive, listless, slave-like creatures who stood in the shadows.

Because the "woman's sphere" concept was so widely believed, many of Cady Stanton's arguments met with adamant denials from her tradition-bound audiences. Yet she was a more successful advocate than others of the day, such as Victoria "Free Love" Woodhull, because Cady Stanton recognized that values must be addressed and agreed upon before change could come. Generally, she professed common ground with her listeners, suggesting that her ideas were theirs. She wanted the audience to recognize that misplaced values and mistaken conceptions had shifted their thoughts. As a speaker, she tried to refocus attention on the original rights that all Americans had once shared. As the speeches examined in this text demonstrate, Cady Stanton grasped the necessity of meeting the audience on its own ground, showing how that ground was ill-conceived, and then leading the listeners to a new consciousness and reality.

Her addresses and essays displayed a wide range of rhetorical strategies. Cady Stanton was especially adept in using extensive testimony and precedent, vivid imagery, extended metaphor and analogy, humor and irony. She structured her speeches with precision and utilized the logical argumentation skills she learned in her father's law office. She gently, but sometimes sarcastically, juxtaposed truth and reality with false beliefs by citing examples of the conditions woman was forced to endure. Cady Stanton displayed a unique ability to draw from wide-ranging sources in legal, religious, political, and literary arenas. She developed compelling narratives replete with imagery that evoked emotions ranging from despair to elation. According to contemporary sources, she was reported to be a confident and serene speaker, self-assured and motherly on the platform. In fact, she was one of the more popular female orators of her day.

However, Cady Stanton's speeches, like her wide-ranging intellect, occasionally took off on contradictory paths. One time she would assert that men and women were equal; the next she would articulate woman's inherent superiority over man. Although she was a staunch supporter of education for all, she later turned to educated suffrage as a right, portraying the uneducated as undeserving of the elective franchise.

Elizabeth Cady Stanton was not always successful. Indeed, some of her arguments angered, embarrassed, and alienated even her allies. Her behavior sometimes outraged the conservative members of society. In a life centered around controversial issues, Elizabeth

Cady Stanton regularly found herself to be the notorious cause of more conflict. She advocated dress reform with her adoption of the Bloomer costume, which freed women from encumbering skirts by dressing them in pants. She called for marriage reform, saying that religious and social hypocrisy were more evil than divorce. She wanted sweeping reforms in education. Cady Stanton was impatient with slow-moving progress and often proceeded into new territory without thought about the consequences. Elizabeth Cady Stanton was sometimes contradictory, always outspoken on many issues, and rarely admitted mistakes. She was a larger-than-life figure.

The major thrust of Cady Stanton's argumentative positions revolved around four essential societal assumptions:

1. The sphere argument, which insisted that anatomy is destiny;

2. The theological argument, which asserted God's divine limitations on woman and her subservience to man;

3. The domestic argument, which said that woman's role as mother and wife was paramount and that her sole duty was to the family;

4. The legal argument, which claimed that woman needed special judicial protection.

In attacking each of these fundamental assumptions, Cady Stanton was faced with the challenge of altering society's mistaken ideas into a newly conceptualized belief. She had to convince the listeners that their dominant beliefs were based on inconsistencies, false notions, and outmoded customs. In order to create such arguments, Cady Stanton grounded them in principles that formed the basis of American democracy: freedom, no taxation without representation, and the desire to achieve autonomy. She espoused the natural rights philosophy of the American Enlightenment. According to Cady Stanton, whatever differences existed between women and men were culturally rather than physically based. She believed that these false notions could be changed through society's political, religious, legal, and cultural realignment. There was no justification for denying women the freedoms that Nature promised, because woman possessed the same natural abilities as man. All restrictions or presumed disabilities were artificial or misguided. In her earliest public document, the "Declaration of Sentiments," she reminded the audience of this natural right: "We hold these truths to be self-evident: that all men and women were created equal."

The degradation of women, she posited, came from an aristocracy of sex that man had dictatorially created. Her rhetoric emphasized the detrimental effects on woman's physical, legal, religious, moral, economic, and intellectual development that male-dominated society had created and maintained. This aristocracy of sex was harmful to all of society, because it promoted rape, prostitution, discrimination, and oppression as well as the moral disintegration of society. Such a patriarchical dictatorship, she claimed, would eventually cause the downfall of society. It directly opposed the shining ideals upon which the nation had been founded.

Elizabeth Cady Stanton's social vision was to liberate society from false perceptions, outmoded customs, illogical laws, and false religious doctrine. In order to alter the attitudes and values of society, Cady Stanton utilized oratory and journalism in a campaign that lasted over fifty years of her adult life. She learned from her experiences and filtered the lessons through her gradually developing ethic of autonomy and self-development. She fearlessly attacked false beliefs about whatever issue or topic she encountered.

What was the effect of Cady Stanton's rhetoric? Her spoken oratory has been largely ignored by rhetorical historians and critics, due partly to ignorance and partly because of the traditional male dominance of the study of American public address. Her multitudinous contributions to the foundation, formation, and generation of the broad women's rights movement has been overshadowed by those of the less controversial Susan B. Anthony, although Anthony herself admitted that most of her public addresses came from Cady Stanton's pen. Even feminists have ignored many of her contributions, perhaps due to the controversial or radical nature of some of her arguments, or to unfamiliarity with the wide range of historical documents that await further exploration.

Elizabeth Cady Stanton, advocate, philosopher, and critic, addressed the exigencies of her era. She witnessed many reforms in female property laws, wage and work rules, schools and prisons, and even partial suffrage. Federal suffrage came within two decades after her death, when the Nineteenth Amendment was added to the Constitution in August 1920. Elizabeth Cady Stanton was a dominant rhetorical figure in American society for over fifty years. As a leader, her visionary foresight set the course for the women's movement. As a woman, she triumphantly attained her ultimate goal of self-sovereignty.

II

COLLECTED SPEECHES

Address to the Joint Judiciary Committee, New York Legislature, 1854

"The thinking minds of all nations call for change. There is a deep dying struggle in the whole fabric of society; a boundless, grinding collision of the New with the Old."

The tyrant, Custom, has been summoned before the bar of Common-Sense. His majesty no longer awes the multitude--his sceptre is broken--his crown is trampled in the dust--the sentence of death is pronounced upon him. All nations, ranks, and classes have, in turn, questioned and repudiated his authority; and now, that the monster is chained and caged, timid woman, on tiptoe, comes to look him in the face, and to demand of her brave sires and sons, who have struck stout blows for liberty, if, in this change of dynasty, she, too, shall find relief. Yes, gentlemen, in republican America, in the nineteenth century, we, the daughters of the revolutionary heroes of '76, demand at your hands the redress of our grievances--a revision of your State Constitution--a new code of laws. Permit us then, as briefly as possible, to call you attention to the legal disabilities under which we labor.

1st. Look at the position of woman as woman. It is not enough for us that by your laws we are permitted to live and breathe, to claim the necessaries of life from our legal protectors-to pay the penalty of our crimes; we demand the full recognition of all our rights as citizens of the Empire State. We are persons; native, free-born citizens; property-holders, tax-payers; yet are we denied the exercise of our right to the elective franchise. We support ourselves, and, in part, your schools, colleges, churches, your poor-houses, jails, prisons, the army, the navy, the whole machinery of government, and yet we have no voice in your councils. We have every qualification required by the Constitution, necessary to the legal voter, but the one of sex. We are moral, virtuous, and intelligent, and in all respects quite equal to the proud white man himself, and yet by your laws we are classed with idiots, lunatics, and negroes; and though we do not feel honored by the place assigned us, yet, in fact, our legal position is lower than that of either; for the negro can be raised to the dignity of a voter if he possess himself of $250; the lunatic can vote in his moments of sanity, and the idiot, too, if he be a male one, and not more than nine-tenths a fool; but we, who have guided great movements of charity, established missions, edited journals, published works on history, economy and statistics; who have governed nations, led armies, filled the professor's chair, taught philosophy and mathematics to the savants of our age, discovered planets, piloted ships across the sea, are denied the most sacred rights of citizens, because, forsooth, we came not into this republic crowned with the dignity of manhood! Woman is theoretically absolved from all allegiance to the laws of the State. Section #1, Bill of Rights, 2 R.S. 301 says that no authority can, on any pretense whatever, be exercised over the citizens of this State but such as is or shall be derived from, and granted by the people of this State.

Now, gentlemen, we would fain know by what authority you have disfranchised one-half the people of the State? You who have so boldly taken possession of the bulwarks of this republic, show us your credentials, and thus prove your exclusive right to govern, not only yourselves, but us. Judge Hurlburt, who has long occupied a high place at the bar in this State, and who recently retired with honor from the bench of the Supreme Court, in his profound work on Human Rights, has pronounced your present positions rank usurpation. Can it be that here, where we acknowledge no royal blood, no apostolic descent, that you, who have declared that all men were created equal-that governments derive their just powers from the consent of the governed, would willingly build up an aristocracy that places the ignorant and vulgar about the educated and refined-the alien and the ditch digger above the authors and poets of the day-an aristocracy that would raise the sons above the mothers that bore them? Would that the men who can sanction a Constitution so opposed to the genius of this government, who can enact and execute laws so degrading to womankind, had sprung, Minerva-like, from the brains of their fathers, that the matrons of this republic need not blush to own their sons!

Woman's position, under our free institutions, is much lower than under the monarchy of England. In England the idea of woman holding official station is not so strange as in the United States. The countess of Pembroke, Dorset, and Montgomery held the office of hereditary sheriff of Westmoreland, and exercised it in person. At the assizes at Appleby, she sat with the judges on the bench. In a reported case, it is stated by counsel and substantially assented to by the court, that a woman is capable of serving in almost all the offices of the kingdom, such as those of queen, marshal, great chamberlain and constable of England, the champion of England, commissioner of sewers, governor of work-house, sexton, keeper of the prison, of the gate-house of the dean and chapter of Westminster, returning officer for members of Parliament, and constable, the latter of which is in some respects judicial. The office of jailor is frequently exercised by a woman.

In the United States a woman may administer on the effects of her deceased husband, and she has occasionally held a subordinate place in the post-office department. She has therefore a sort of post-mortem, post-mistress notoriety; but with the exception of handling letters of administration and letters mailed, she is the submissive creature of the old common law. True, the unmarried woman has a right to the property she inherits and the money she earns, but she is taxed without representation. And here again you place the negro, so unjustly degraded by you, in a superior position to your own wives and mothers; for colored males, if possessed of a certain amount of property and certain other qualifications, can vote, but if they do not have these qualifications they are not subject to direct taxation; wherein they have the advantage of woman, she being subject to taxation for whatever amount she may possess.[1]

But, say you, are not all women sufficiently represented by their fathers, husbands, and brothers? Let your statute books answer the question.

Again, we demand in criminal cases that most sacred of all rights, trial by a jury of our own peers. The establishment of trial by jury is of so early a date that its beginning is lost in antiquity; but the right of trial by a jury of one's own peers is a great progressive step of advanced civilization. No rank of men have ever been satisfied with being tried by jurors higher or lower in the civil or political scale than themselves; for jealousy on the one hand, and contempt on the other, has ever effectually blinded the eyes of justice. Hence, all along the pages of history, we find the king, the noble, the peasant, the cardinal, the priest, the layman, each in turn protesting against the authority of the tribunal before which they were summoned to appear. Charles the First refused to recognize the competency of the tribunal which condemned him; for how, said he, can subjects judge a king? The stern descendants of our Pilgrim Fathers refused to answer for their crimes before an English Parliament. For how, said they, can a king judge rebels? And shall woman here consent to be tried by her liege lord, who has dubbed himself law-maker, judge, juror, and sheriff too?-whose power, though sanctioned by Church and State, has no foundation in justice and equity, and is a bold assumption of our inalienable rights. In England a Parliament-lord could challenge a jury where a knight was not impaneled; an alien could demand a jury composed half of his own countrymen; or in some special cases, juries were even constituted entirely of women. Having seen that man fails to do justice to woman in her best estate, to the virtuous, the noble, the true of our sex, should we trust to his tender mercies the weak, the ignorant, the morally insane? It is not to be denied that the interests of man and woman in the present undeveloped state must be antagonistic. The nobleman can not make just laws for the peasant; the slaveholder for the slave; neither can man make and execute just laws for woman, because in each case, the one in power fails to apply the immutable principles of right to any grade but his own.

Shall an erring woman be dragged before a bar of grim-visaged judges, lawyers, and jurors, there to be grossly questioned in public on subjects which women scarce breathe in secret to one another? Shall the most sacred relations of life be called up and rudely scanned by men who, by their own admission, are so coarse that women could not meet them even at the polls without contamination? And yet shall she find there no woman's face or voice to pity and defend? Shall the frenzied mother, who, to save herself and child from exposure and disgrace, ended the life that had but just begun, be dragged before such a tribunal to answer for her crime? How can man enter into the feelings of that mother? How can he judge of the agonies of soul that impelled her to such an outrage of maternal instinct? How can he weigh the mountain of sorrow that crushed that mother's heart when she wildly tossed her helpless babe into the cold waters of the midnight sea? Where is he who by false vows thus blasted this trusting woman? Ah, he is freely abroad in the dignity of manhood, in the pulpit, on the bench, in the professor's chair. The imprisonment of his victim and the death of his child, detract not a tithe from his standing and complacency. His peers made the law, and shall law-makers lay nets for those of their own rank? Shall laws which come from the logical brain of man take cognizance of violence done to the moral and affectional nature which predominates, as is said, in woman?

Statesmen of New York, whose daughters, guarded by your affection, and lapped amidst luxuries which your indulgence spreads, care more for their nodding plumes and velvet trains than for the statute laws by which their persons and properties are held-who, blinded by custom and prejudice to the degraded position which they and their sisters occupy in the civil scale, haughtily claim that they already have all the rights they want, how, think ye, you would feel to see a daughter summoned for such a crime-and remember these daughters are but human-before such a tribunal? Would it not, in that hour, be some consolation to see that she was surrounded by the wise and virtuous of her own sex; by those who had known the depth of a mother's love and the misery of a lover's falsehood; to know that to these she could make her confession, and from them receive her sentence? If so, then listen to our just demands and make such a change in your laws as will secure to every woman tried in your courts, an impartial jury. At this moment among the hundreds of women who are shut up in prisons in this State, not one has enjoyed that most sacred of all rights-that right which you would die to defend for yourselves-trial by a jury of one's peers.

2nd. Look at the position of woman as wife. Your laws relating to marriage-founded as they are on the old common law of England, a compound of barbarous usages, but partially modified by progressive civilization-are in open violation of our enlightened ideas of justice, and of the holiest feelings of our nature. If you take the highest view of marriage, as a Divine relation, which love alone can constitute and sanctify, then of course human legislation can only recognize it. Men can neither bind nor loose its ties, for that prerogative belongs to God alone, who makes man and woman, and the laws of attraction by which they are united. But if you regard marriage as a civil contract, then let it be subject to the same laws which control all other contracts. Do not make it a kind of half-human, half-divine institution, which you may build up, but can not regulate. Do not, by your special legislation for this one kind of contract, involve yourselves in the grossest absurdities and contradictions.

So long as by your laws no man can make a contract for a horse or piece of land until he is twenty-one years of age, and by which contract he is not bound if any deception has been practiced, or if the party contracting has not fulfilled his part of the agreement-so long as the parties in all mere civil contracts retain their identity and all the power and independence they had before contracting, with the full right to dissolve all partnerships and contracts for any reason, at the will and option of the parties themselves, upon what principle of civil jurisprudence do you permit the boy of fourteen and the girl of twelve, in violation of every natural law, to make a contract more momentous in importance than any other, and then hold them to it, come what may, the whole of their natural lives, in spite of disappointment, deception, and misery? Then, too, the signing of this contract is instant civil death to one of the parties. The woman who but yesterday was sued on bended knee, who stood so high in the scale of being as to make an agreement on equal terms with a proud Saxon man, today has no civil existence, no social freedom. The wife who inherits no property holds about the same legal position that does the slave on the Southern plantation. She can own nothing, sell nothing. She has no right even to the wages she earns; her person, her time, her services are the property of another. She can not testify in many cases, against her husband. She can get no redress for wrongs in her own name in any court of justice. She can neither sue nor be sued. She is not held morally responsible for any crime committed in the presence of her husband, so completely is her very existence supposed by the law to be merged in that of another. Think of it; your wives may be thieves, libelers, burglars, incendiaries, and for crimes like these they are not held amenable to the laws of the land, if they but commit them in your dread presence. For them, alas! there is no higher law than the will of man.[2]

How could man ever look thus on woman? She, at whose feet Socrates learned wisdom--she, who gave to the world a Savior, and witnessed alike the adoration of the Magi and the agonies on the cross. How could such a blessing, so blessed and honored, ever become the ignoble, servile cringing slave, with whom the fear of man could be paramount to the sacred dictates of conscience and the hold love of Heaven? By the common law of England, the spirit of which has been but too faithfully incorporated into our statute law, a husband has a right to whip his wife with a rod not larger than his thumb, to shut her up in a room, and administer whatever moderate chastisement he may deem necessary to insure obedience to his wishes, and for her healthful moral development! He can forbid all persons harboring or trusting her on his account. He can deprive her of all social intercourse with her nearest and dearest friends. If by great economy she accumulates a small sum, which for future need she deposit, little by little, in a savings bank, the husband has a right to draw it out, at his option, to use it as he may see fit.[3]

There is nothing than an unruly wife might do against which the husband has not sufficient protection in the law. but not so with the wife. If she have a worthless husband, a confirmed drunkard, a villain, or a vagrant, he has still all the rights of a man, a husband, and a father. Though the whole support of the family be thrown upon the wife, if the wages she earns be paid to her by her employer, the husband can receive them again. If, by unwearied industry and perseverance, she can earn for herself and children a patch of ground and a shed to cover them, the husband can strip her of all her hard earnings, turn her and her little ones out in the cold northern blast, take the clothes from their backs, the bread from their mouths; all this by your laws may he do, and he has done, oft and again, to satisfy the rapacity of that monster in human form, the rum-seller.

But the wife who is so fortunate as to have inherited property, has, by the new law in this State, been redeemed from her lost condition. She is no longer a legal nonentity. This property law, if fairly construed, will overturn the whole code relating to woman and property. The right to property implies the right to buy and sell, to will and bequeath, and herein is the dawning of a civil existence for woman, for now the *femme covert* must have their right to make contracts. So, get ready, gentlemen; the "little justice" will be coming to you one day, deed in hand, for your acknowledgment. When he asks you "if you sign without fear or compulsion," say yes, boldly, as we do. Then, too, the right to will is ours. Now what becomes of the "tenant for life"? Shall he, the happy husband of a millionaire, who has lived in yonder princely mansion in the midst of plenty and elegance, be cut down in a day to the use of one-third of this estate and a few hundred a year, as long as he remains her widower? And should he, in spite of this bounty on celibacy, impelled by his affections, marry again, choosing for a wife a woman as poor as himself, shall he be thrown penniless on the cold world, though, in the sympathies of many women who have passed through just such an ordeal. But what is property without the right to protect that property by law? It is mercy to say a certain estate is mine, if, without my consent, you have the right to tax me when and how you please, while I have no voice in making the tax-gatherer, the legislator, or the law. The right to property will, of necessity, compel us in due time to the exercise of our right to the elective franchise, and then naturally follows the right to hold office.

3d. Look at the position of woman as widow. Whenever we attempt to point out the wrongs of the wife, those who would have us believe that the laws can not be improved, point us to the privileges, powers, and claims of the widow. Let us look into these a little. Behold in yonder humble house a married pair, who, for long years, have lived together, childless and alone. Those few acres of well-tilled land, with the small, white house that looks so cheerful through its vines and flowers, attest to the honest thrift and simple taste of its owners. This man and woman, by their hard days' labor, have made this home their own. Here they live in peace and plenty, happy in the hope that they may dwell together securely under their own vine and fig-tree for the few years that remain to them, and that under the shadow of these trees, planted by their own hands, and in the midst of their household gods, so loved and familiar, they may take their last farewell of earth. But, alas for human hopes! The husband dies, and without a will, and the stricken widow, at one fell blow, loses the companion of her youth, her house and home, and half the little sum she had in the bank. For the law, which takes no cognizance of widows left with twelve children and not one cent, instantly spies out this widow, takes account of her effects, and announces to her the startling intelligence that but one-third of the house and lot, and one-half the personal property, are hers. The law has other favorites with whom she must share the hard-earned savings of years. In this dark hour of grief, the coarse minions of the law gather round the widow's hearth-stone, and, in the name of justice, outrage all natural sense of right; mock at the sacredness of human love, and with cold familiarity proceed to place a moneyed value on the old arm-chair, in which, but a few brief hours since, she closed the eyes that had ever beamed on her with kindness and affection; on the solemn clock in the corner, that told the hour he passed away; on every garment with which his form and presence were associated, and on every article of comfort and convenience that the house contained, even down to the knives and forks and spoons--and the widow saw it all--and when the work was done, she gathered up what the law allowed her and went forth to seek another home! This is the much-talked-of widow's dower. Behold the magnanimity of the law in allowing the widow to retain a life interest in one-third the landed estate, and one-half the personal property of her husband, and taking the lion's share to itself! Had she died first, the house and land would all have been the husband's still. No one would have dared to intrude upon the privacy of his home, or to molest him in his sacred retreat of sorrow. How, I ask you, can that be called justice, which makes such a distinction as this between man and woman?

By management, economy, and industry, our widow is able, in a few years, to redeem her house and home. But the law never loses sight of the purse, no matter how low in the scale of being its owner may be. It sends its officers round every year to gather in the harvest for the public crib, and no widow who owns a piece of land two feet square ever escapes this reckoning. Our widow, too, who has now twice earned her home, has her annual tax to pay also--a tribute of gratitude that she is permitted to breathe the free air of this republic, where "taxation without representation," by such worthies as John Hancock and Samuel Adams, has been declared "intolerable tyranny." Having glanced at the magnanimity of the law in its dealings with the widow, let us see how the individual man, under the influence of such laws, doles out justice to his helpmate. The husband has the absolute right to will away his property as he may see fit. If he has children, he can divide his property among them, leaving his wife her third only of the landed estate, thus making her a dependent on the bounty of her own children. A man with thirty thousand dollars in personal property, may leave his wife but a few hundred a year, as long as she remains his widow.

The cases are without number where women, who have lived in ease and elegance, at the death of their husbands have, by will, been reduced to the bare necessaries of life. The man who leaves his wife the sole guardian of his property and children is an exception to the general rule. Man has ever manifested a wish that the world should indeed be a blank to the companion whom he leaves behind him. The Hindoo makes that wish a law, and burns the widow on the funeral pyre of her husband; but the civilized man, impressed with a different view of the sacredness of life, takes a less summary mode of drawing his beloved partner after him; he does it by the deprivation and starvation of the flesh, and the humiliation and mortification of the spirit. In bequeathing to the wife just enough to keep soul and body together, man seems to lose sight of the fact that women, like himself, takes great pleasure in acts of benevolence and charity. It is but just, therefore, that she should have it in her power to give during her life, and to will away at her death, as her benevolence or obligations might prompt her to do.

4th. Look at the position of woman as mother. There is no human love so strong and steadfast as that of the mother for her child; yet behold how ruthless are your laws touching this most sacred relation. Nature has clearly made the mother the guardian of the child; but man, in his inordinate love of power, does continually set nature and nature's laws at open defiance. The father may apprentice his child, bind him out to a trade, without the mother's consent--yea, in direct opposition to her most earnest entreaties, prayers and tears.

He may apprentice his son to a gamester or rum-seller, and thus cancel his debts of honor. By the abuse of this absolute power, he may bind his daughter to the owner of a brothel, and, by the degradation of his child, supply his daily wants; and such things, gentlemen, have been done in our very midst. Moreover, the father, about to die, may bind out all his children wherever and to whomsoever he may see fit, and thus, in fact, will away the guardianship of all his children from the mother.[4]

Thus, by your laws, the child is the absolute property of the father, wholly at his disposal in life or at death.

In case of separation, the law gives the children to the father; no matter what his character of condition. At this very time we can point you to noble, virtuous, well-educated mothers in this State, who have abandoned their husbands for their profligacy and confirmed drunkenness. All these have been robbed of their children, who are in the custody of the husband, under the care of his relatives, whilst the mothers are permitted to see them but at stated intervals. But, said one of these mothers, with a grandeur of attitude and manner worthy the noble Roman matron in the palmiest days of that republic, I would rather never see my child again, than be the medium to hand down the low animal nature of its father, to stamp degradation on the brow of another innocent being. It is enough that one child of his shall call me mother.

If you are far-sighted statesmen, and do wisely judge of the interests of this commonwealth, you will so shape your future laws as to encourage woman to take the high moral ground that the father of her children must be great and good. Instead of your present laws, which make the mother and her children the victims of vice and license, you might rather pass laws prohibiting to all drunkards, libertines, and fools the rights of husbands and fathers. Do not the hundreds of laughing idiots that are crowding into our asylums, appeal to the wisdom of our statesmen for some new laws on marriage-to the mothers of this day for a higher, purer morality?

Again, as the condition of the child always follows that of the mother, and as by the sanction of your laws the father may beat the mother, so may he the child. What mother can not bear me witness to untold sufferings which cruel, vindictive fathers have visited upon their helpless children? Who ever saw a human being that would not abuse unlimited power ? Base and ignoble must that man be who, let the provocation be what it may, would strike a woman: but he who would lacerate a trembling child is unworthy the name of man. A mother's love can be no protection to a child; she cannot appeal to you to save it from a father's cruelty, for the laws take no cognizance of the mother's most grievous wrongs. Neither at home nor abroad can a mother protect her son. Look at the temptations that surround the paths of our youth at every step; look at the gambling and drinking saloons, the club rooms, the dens of infamy and abomination that infest all our villages and cities-slowly but surely sapping the very foundations of all virtue and strength.

By your laws, all these abominable resorts are permitted. It is folly to talk of a mother moulding the character of her son, when all mankind, backed up by law and public sentiment, conspire to destroy her influence. But when woman's moral power shall speak through the ballot-box, then shall her influence be seen and felt; then, in our legislative debates, such questions as the canal tolls on salt, the improvement of rivers and harbors, and the claims of Mr. Smith for damages against the State, would be secondary to the consideration of the legal existence of all these public resorts, which lure our youth on to excessive indulgence and destruction.

Many times and oft it has been asked us, with unaffected seriousness, "What do you women want? What are you aiming at?" Many have manifested a laudable curiosity to know what the wives and daughters could complain of in republican America, where their sires and sons have so bravely fought for freedom and gloriously secured their independence, trampling all tyranny, bigotry, and caste in the dust, and declaring to a waiting world the divine truth that all men are created equal. What can woman want under such a government? Admit a radical difference in sex, and you demand different spheres--water for fish, and air for birds.

It is impossible to make the Southern planter believe that his slave feels and reasons just as he does-that injustice and subjection are as galling as to him-that the degradation of living by the will of another, the mere dependent on his caprice, at the mercy of his passions, is a keenly felt by him as his master. If you can force on his unwilling vision a vivid picture of the negro's wrongs, and for a moment touch his soul, his logic brings him instant consolation. He says, the slave does not feel this as I would. Here gentlemen, is our difficulty: when we plead our cause before the law-makers and savants of the republic, they can not take in the idea that men and women are alike; and so long as the mass rest in this delusion, the public mind will not be so much startled by the revelations made of the injustice and degradation of woman's position as by the fact that she should at length wake up to a sense of it.

If you, too, are thus deluded, what avails it that we show by your statute books that your laws are unjust-that woman is the victim of avarice and power? What avails it that we point out the wrongs of woman in social life; the victim of passion and lust? You scorn the thought that she has any natural love of freedom burning in her breast, any clear perception of justice urging her on to demand her rights.

Would to God you could know the burning indignation that fills woman's soul when she turns over the pages of your statute books, and sees there how like feudal barons you freemen hold your women. Would that you could know the humiliation, she feels for her sex, when she thinks of all the beardless boys in your law offices, learning these ideas of one-sided justice--taking their first lessons in contempt for all womankind--being indoctrinated into the incapacities of their mothers, and the lordly, absolute rights of man over all women, children, and property, and to know that these are to be our future presidents, judges, husbands, and fathers; in sorrow we exclaim, alas! for that nation whose sons bow not in loyalty to woman. The mother is the first object of the child's veneration and love, and they who root out this holy sentiment, dream not of the blighting effect it has on the boy and the man. The impression left on law students, fresh from your statute books, is most unfavorable to woman's influence; hence you see but few layers chivalrous and high-toned in their sentiments toward woman. They can not escape the legal view which, by constant reading, has become familiarized to their minds: "*Femme covert*," "dower," "Widow's claims," "protection," "incapacities," "encumbrance," is written on the brow of every woman they meet.

But if, gentlemen, you take the ground that the sexes are alike, and, therefore, you are our faithful representatives--then why all these special laws for woman? Would not one code answer for all of like needs and wants? Christ's Golden Rule is better than all the special legislation that the ingenuity of man can devise: "Do unto others as you would have others do unto you." This, men and brethren, is all we ask at your hands. We ask no better laws than those you have made for yourselves. We need no other protection than that which your present laws secure to you.

In conclusion, then, let us say, in behalf of the women of this State, we ask for all that you have asked for yourselves in the progress of your development, since the Mayflower cast anchor beside Plymouth Rock; and simply on the ground that their rights of every human being are the same and identical. You may say that the mass of women of this State do not ask the demand; it comes from a few sour, disappointed old maids and childless women.

You are mistaken; the mass speak through us. A very large majority of the women of this State support themselves and their children, and many their husbands too. Go into any village you please, of three or four thousand inhabitants, and you will find as many as fifty men or more, whose only business is to discuss religion and politics, as they watch the trains come and go at the depot, or the passage of a canal boat through a lock; to laugh at the vagaries of some drunken brother, or the capers of a monkey dancing to the music of his master's organ. All these are supported by their mothers, wives, or sisters.

Now, do you candidly think these wives do not wish to control the wages they earn--to own the land they buy--the houses they build? to have at their disposal their own children, without being subject to the constant interference and tyranny of an idle, worthless profligate? Do you suppose that any woman is such a pattern of devotion and submission that she willingly stitches all day for the small sum of fifty cents, that she may enjoy the unspeakable privilege, in obedience to your laws, of paying for her husband's tobacco and rum? Think you the wife of the confirmed, beastly drunkard would consent to share with him her home and bed, if law and public sentiment would release her from such gross companionship? Verily, no! Think you the wife with whom endurance has ceased to be a virtue, who, through much suffering, has lost all faith in the justice of both heaven and earth, takes the law in her own hand, severs the unholy bond, and turns her back forever upon him whom she once called husband, consents to the the law that in such an hour tears her child from her--all that she has left on earth to love and cherish? The drunkards' wives speak through us, and they number 50,000. Think you that the woman who has worked hard all her days in helping her husband to accumulate a large property, consents to the law that places this wholly at his disposal? Would not the mother whose only child is bound out for a term of years against her expressed wish, deprive the father of this absolute power if she could?

For all these, then, we speak. If to this long list you add the laboring women who are loudly demanding remuneration for their unending toil; those women who teach in our seminaries, academies, and public schools for a miserable pittance; the widows who are taxed without mercy; the unfortunate ones in our work-houses, poor-houses, and prisons; who are they that we do not now represent? But a small class of the fashionable butterflies, who, through the short summer days, seek the sunshine and the flowers; but the cool breezes of autumn and the hoary frosts of winter will soon chase all these away; then they, too, will need and seek protection, and through other lips demand in their turn justice and equity at our hands.

Address to the New York State Legislature, 1860

GENTLEMEN OF THE JUDICIARY:

There are certain natural rights as inalienable to civilization as are the rights of air and motion to the savage in the wilderness. The natural rights of the civilized man and woman are government, property, the harmonious development of all their powers, and the gratification of their desires. There are a few people we now and then meet who, like Jeremy Bentham, scout the idea of natural rights in civilization, and pronounce them mere metaphors, declaring that there are no rights aside from those the law confers. If the law made man too, that might do, for then he could be made to order to fit the particular niche he was designed to fill. But inasmuch as God made man in His own image, with capacities and powers as boundless as the universe, whose exigencies no mere human law can meet, it is evident that the man must ever stand first; the law but the creature of his wants; the law-giver but the mouthpiece of humanity. If, then, the nature of a being decides its rights, every individual comes into this world with rights that are not transferable. He does not bring them like a pack on his back, that may be stolen from him, but they are a component part of himself, the laws which insure his growth and development. The individual may be put in the stocks, body and soul, he may be dwarfed, crippled, killed, but his rights no man can get; they live and die with him.

Though the atmosphere is forty miles deep all round the globe, no man can do more than fill his own lungs. No man can see, hear, or smell but just so far; and though hundreds are deprived of these senses, his are not the more acute. Though rights have been abundantly supplied by the good Father, no man can appropriate to himself those that belong to another. A citizen can have but one vote, fill but one office, though thousands are not permitted to do either. These axioms prove that woman's poverty does not add to man's wealth, and if, in the plenitude of his power, he should secure to her the exercise of all her God-given rights, her wealth could not bring poverty to him. There is a kind of nervous unrest always manifested by those in power, whenever new claims are started by those out of their own immediate class. The philosophy of this is very plain. They imagine that if the rights of this new class be granted, they must, of necessity, sacrifice something of that they already possess. They can not divest themselves of the idea that rights are very much like lands, stocks, bonds, and mortgages, and that if every new claimant be satisfied, the supply of human rights must in time run low. You might as well carp at the birth of every child, lest there should not be enough air left to inflate your lungs; at the success of every scholar, for fear that your draughts at the fountain of knowledge could not be so long and deep; at the glory of every hero, lest there be no glory left for you . . . .

If the object of government is to protect the weak against the strong, how unwise to place the power wholly in the hands of the strong. Yet that is the history of all governments, even the model republic of these United States. You who have read the history of nations, from Moses down to our last election, where have you ever seen one class looking after the interests of another? Any of you can readily see the defects in other governments, and pronounce sentence against those who have sacrificed the masses to themselves; but when we come to our own case, we are blinded by custom and self-interest. Some of you who have no capital can see the injustice which the laborer suffers; some of you who have no slaves, can see the cruelty of his oppression; but who of you appreciate the galling humiliation, the refinements of degradation, to which women (the mothers, wives, sisters, and daughters of freemen) are subject, in this the last half of the nineteenth century? How many of you have ever read even the laws concerning them that now disgrace your statute-books? In cruelty and tyranny, they are not surpassed by any slaveholding code in the Southern States; in fact, they are worse, by just so far as woman, from her social position, refinement, and education, is on a more equal ground with the oppressor.

Allow me just here to call the attention of that party now so much interested in the slave of the Carolinas, to the similarity in his condition and that of the mothers, wives, and daughters of the Empire State. The negro has no name. He is Cuffy Douglas or Cuffy Brooks, just whose Cuffy he may chance to be. The woman has no name. She is Mrs. Richard Roe or Mrs. John Doe, just whose Mrs. she may chance to be. Cuffy has no right to his earnings; he can not buy or sell, or lay up anything that he can call his own. Mrs. Roe has no right to her earnings; she can neither buy nor sell, make contracts, nor lay up anything that she can call her own. Cuffy has no right to his children; they can be sold from him at any time. Mrs. Roe has no right to her children; they may be bound out to cancel a father's debts of honor. The unborn child, even by the last will of the father, may be placed under the guardianship of a stranger and a foreigner. Cuffy has no legal existence; he is subject to restraint and moderate chastisement. Mrs. Roe has no legal existence; she has not the best right to her own person. The husband has the power to restrain, and administer moderate chastisement.

Blackstone declares that the husband and wife are one, and learned commentators have decided that that one is the husband. In all civil codes, you will find them classified as one. Certain rights and immunities, such and such privileges are to be secured to white male citizens. What have women and negroes to do with rights? What know they of government, war, or glory?

The prejudice against color, of which we hear so much, is no stronger than that against sex. It is produced by the same cause, and manifested very much in the same way. The negro's skin and the woman's sex are both *prima facie* evidence that they were intended to be in subjection to the white Saxon man. The few social privileges which the man gives the woman, he makes up to the negro in civil rights. The woman may sit at the same table and eat with the white man; the free negro may hold property and vote. The woman may sit in the same pew with the white man in church; the free negro may enter the pulpit and preach. Now, with the black man's right to suffrage, the right unquestioned, even by Paul, to minister at the altar, it is evident that the prejudice against sex is more deeply rooted and more unreasonably maintained than that against color. As citizens of a republic, which should we most highly prize, social privileges or civil rights? The latter, most certainly.

To those who do not feel the injustice and degradation of the condition, there is something inexpressively comical in man's "citizen woman." It reminds me of these monsters I used to see in the old world, head and shoulders woman, and the rest of the body sometimes fish and sometimes beast. I used to think, What a strange conceit! but now I see how perfectly it represents man's idea! Look over all his laws concerning us, and you will see just enough of woman to tell of her existence; all the rest is submerged, or made to crawl upon the earth. Just imagine an inhabitant of another planet entertaining himself some pleasant evening in searching over our great national compact, our Declaration of Independence, our Constitutions, or some of our statute-books; what would he think of those "women and negroes" that must be so fenced in, so guarded against? Why, he would certainly suppose we were monsters, like those fabulous giants or Brobdingnagians of olden times, so dangerous to civilized man, from our size, ferocity, and power. Then let him take up our poets, from Pope down to Dana; let him listen to our Fourth of July toast, and some of the sentimental adulations of social life, and no logic could convince him that this creature of the law, and this angel of the family altar, could be one and the same being. Man is in such a labyrinth of contradictions with his marital and property rights; he is so befogged on the whole question of maidens, wives, and mothers, that from pure benevolence we should relieve him from this troublesome branch of legislation. We should vote, and make laws for ourselves. Do not be alarmed, dear ladies! You need spend no time reading Grotius, Coke, Puffendorf, Blackstone, Bentham, Kent, and Story to find out what you need. We may safely trust the shrewd selfishness of the white man, and consent to live under the same broad code where he has so comfortably ensconced himself. Any legislation that will do for man, we may abide by most cheerfully . . . .

But, say you, we would not have woman exposed to the grossness and vulgarity of public life, or encounter what she must at the polls. When you talk, gentlemen, of sheltering woman from the rough winds and revolting scenes of real life, you must be either talking for effect, or wholly ignorant of what the facts of life are. The man, whatever he is, is known to the woman. She is the companion, not only of the accomplished statesman, the orator, and the scholar; but the vile, vulgar, brutal man has his mother, his wife, his sister, his daughter. Yes, delicate, refined, educated women are in daily life with the drunkard, the gambler, the licentious man, the rogue, and the villain; and if man shows out what he is anywhere, it is at his own hearthstone. There are over forty thousand drunkards in this State. All these are bound by the ties of family to some woman. Allow but a mother and a wife to each, and you have over eighty thousand women. All these have seen their fathers, brothers, husbands, sons, in the lowest and most debased stages of obscenity and degradation. In your own circle of friends, do you not know refined women whose whole lives are darkened and saddened by gross and brutal associations? Now, gentlemen, do you talk to woman of a rude jest or jostle at the polls, where noble, virtuous men stand ready to protect her persona and her rights, when alone in the darkness and solitude and gloom of night, she has trembled on her own threshold, awaiting the return of a husband from his midnight revels?--when, stepping from her chamber, she has beheld her royal monarch, her lord and master--her legal representative--the protector of her property, her home, her children, and her person, down on his hands and knees slowly crawling up the stairs. Behold him in her chamber-in her bed! The fairy tale of "Beauty and the Beast" is far too often realized in life. Gentlemen, such scenes as woman has witnessed at her own fireside, where no eye save Omnipotence could pity, no strong arm could help, can never be realized at the polls, never equaled elsewhere, this side the bottomless pit. No, woman has not hitherto lived in the clouds, surrounded by an atmosphere of purity and peace--but she has been the companion of man in health, in sickness, and in death, in his highest and in his lowest moments. She has worshipped him as a saint and an orator, and pitied him as madman or a fool. In Paradise, man and woman were placed together, and so they must ever be. They must sink or rise together. If man is low and wretched and vile, woman can not escape the contagion, and any atmosphere that is unfit for woman to breathe is not fit for man. Verily, the sins of the fathers shall be visited upon the children to the third and fourth generation. You, by your unwise legislation, have crippled and dwarfed womanhood, by closing to her all honorable and lucrative means of employment, have driven her into the garrets and dens of our cities, where she now revenges herself on your innocent sons, sapping the very foundations of national virtue and strength. Alas! for the young men just coming on the stage of action, who soon shall fill your vacant places--our future Senators, our Presidents, the expounders of our constitutional law! Terrible are the penalties we are now suffering for the ages of injustice done to woman.

Again, it is said that the majority of women do not ask for any change in the laws; that it is time enough to give them the elective franchise when they, as a class, demand it.

Wise statesmen legislate for the best interests of the nation; the State, for the highest good of its citizens; the Christian, for the conversion of the world. Where would have been our railroads, our telegraphs, our ocean steamers, our canals and harbors, our arts and sciences, if government had withheld the means from the far-seeing minority? This State established our present system of common schools, fully believing that educated men and women would make better citizens than ignorant ones. In making this provision for the education of its children, had they waited for a majority of the urchins of this State to petition for schools, how many, think you, would have asked to be transplanted from the street to the school-house? Does the State wait for the criminal to ask for his prison-house? the insane, the idiot, the deaf and dumb for his asylum? Does the Christian, in his love to all mankind, wait for the majority of the benighted heathen to ask him for the gospel? No; unasked and unwelcomed, he crosses the trackless ocean, rolls off the mountain of superstition that oppresses the human mind, proclaims the immortality of the soul, the dignity of manhood, the right of all to be free and happy.

No, gentlemen, if there is but one woman in this State who feels the injustice of her position, she should not be denied her inalienable rights, because the common household drudge and the silly butterfly of fashion are ignorant of all laws, both human and Divine. Because they know nothing of governments, or rights, and therefore ask nothing, shall my petitions be unheard? I stand before you the rightful representative of woman, claiming a share in the halo of glory that has gathered round her in the ages, and by the wisdom of her past words and works, her peerless heroism and self-sacrifice, I challenge your admiration; and, moreover, claiming, as I do, a share in all her outrages and sufferings, in the cruel injustice, contempt, and ridicule now heaped upon her, in her deep degradation, hopeless wretchedness, by all that is helpless in her present condition, that is false in law and public sentiment, I urge your generous consideration; for as my heart swells with pride to behold woman in the highest walks of literature and art, it grows big enough to take in those who are bleeding in the dust.

Now do not think, gentlemen, we wish you to do a great many troublesome things for us. We do not ask our legislators to spend a whole session in fixing up a code of laws to satisfy a class of most unreasonable women. We ask no more than the poor devils in the Scripture asked, "Let us alone." In mercy, let us take care of ourselves, our property, our children, and our homes. True, we are not so strong, so wise, so crafty as you are, but if any kind friend leaves us a little money, or we can by great industry earn fifty cents a day, we should rather buy bread and clothes for our children than cigars and champagne for our legal protectors. There has been a great deal written and said about protection. We, as a class, are tired of one kind of protection, that which leaves us everything to do, to dare, and to suffer, and strips us of all means for its accomplishment. We would not tax man to take care of us. No, the Great Father has endowed all his creatures with the necessary powers for self-support, self-defense, and protection. We do not ask man to represent us; it is hard enough in times like these for man to carry backbone enough to represent himself. So long as the mass of men spend most of their time on the fence, not knowing which way to jump, they are surely in no condition to tell us where we had better stand. In pity for man, we would no longer hang like a millstone round his neck. Undo what man did for us in the dark ages, and strike down all special legislation for us; strike the words "white male" from all your constitutions, and then, with fair sailing, let us sink or swim, live or die, survive or perish together.

At Athens, an ancient apologue tells us, on the completion of the temple of Minerva, a statue of the goddess was wanted to occupy the crowning point of the edifice. Two of the greatest artists produced what each deemed his masterpiece. One of these figures was the size of life, admirably designed, exquisitely finished, softly rounded, and beautifully refined. The other was of Amazonian stature, and so boldly chiselled that it looked more like masonry than sculpture. The eyes of all were attracted by the first, and turned away in contempt from the second. That, therefore, was adopted, and the other rejected, almost with resentment, as though an insult had been offered to a discerning public. The favored statue was accordingly borne in triumph to the place for which it was designed, in the presence of applauding thousands, but as it receded from their upturned eyes, all, all at once gazed upon it, the thunders of applause unaccountably died away--a general misgiving ran through every bosom--the mob themselves stood like statues, as silent and as petrified, for as it slowly went up, and up, the soft expression of those chiselled features, the delicate curves and outlines of the limbs and figure, became gradually fainter and fainter, and when at last it reached the place for which it was intended, it was a shapeless ball, enveloped in mist. Of course, the idol of the hour was now clamored down as rationally as it had been cried up, and its dishonored rival, with no good will and no good looks on the part of the chagrined populace, was reared in its stead. As it ascended, the sharp angles faded away, the rough points became smooth, the features full of expression, the whole figure radiant with majesty and beauty. The rude hewn mass, that before had scarcely appeared to bear even the human form, assumed at once the divinity which it represented, being so perfectly proportioned to the dimensions of the building, and to the elevation on which it stood, that it seemed as though Pallas herself had alighted upon the pinnacle of the temple in person, to receive the homage of her worshippers.

The woman of the nineteenth century is the shapeless ball in the lofty position which she was designed fully and nobly to fill. The place is not too high, too large, too sacred for woman, but the type that you have chosen is far too small for it. The woman we declare unto you is the rude, misshapen, unpolished object of the successful artist. From your stand-point, you are absorbed with the defects alone. The true artist sees the harmony between the object and its destination. Man, the sculptor, has carved out his ideal, and applauding thousands welcome his success. He has made a woman that from his low stand-point looks fair and beautiful, a being without rights, or hopes, or fears but in him--neither noble, virtuous, nor independent. Where do we, in Church or State, in school-house or at the fireside, see the much talked-of moral power of woman? Like those Athenians, we have bowed down and worshiped in woman, beauty, grace, the exquisite proportions, the soft and beautifully rounded outline, her delicacy, refinement, and silent helplessness--all well when she is viewed simply as an object of sight, never to rise one foot above the dust from which she sprung. But if she is to be raised up to adorn a temple, or represent a divinity--if she is to fill the niche of wife and counsellor to true and noble men, if she is to be the mother, the educator of a race of heroes or martyrs, of a Napoleon, or a Jesus--then must the type of womanhood be on a larger scale than that yet carved by man.

In vain would the rejected artist have reasoned with the Athenians as to the superiority of his production; nothing short of the experiment they made could have satisfied them. And what of your experiment, what of your wives, your homes? Alas! for the folly and vacancy that meet you there! But for your club-houses and newspapers, what would social life be to you? Where are your beautiful women? your frail ones, taught to lean lovingly and confidingly on man? Where are the crowds of educated dependents-- where the long line of pensioners on man's bounty? Where all the young girls, taught to believe that marriage is the only legitimate object of a woman's pursuit--they who stand listlessly on life's shores, waiting, year after year, like the sick man at the pool of Bethesda, for some one to come and put them in? These are they who by their ignorance and folly curse almost every fireside with some human specimen of deformity or imbecility. These are they who fill the gloomy abodes of poverty and vice in our vast metropolis. These are they who patrol the streets of our cities, to give our sons their first lessons in infamy. These are they who fill our asylums, and make night hideous with their cries and moans.

The women who are called masculine, who are brave, courageous, self-reliant and independent, are they who in the face of adverse winds have kept one steady course upward and onward in the paths of virtue and peace--they who have taken their gauge of womanhood from their own native strength and dignity--they who have learned for themselves the will of God concerning them. This is our type of womanhood. Will you help us raise it up, that you too may see its beautiful proportions--that you may behold the outline of the goddess who is yet to adorn your Temple of Freedom? We are building a model republic; our edifice will one day need a crowning glory. Let the artists be wisely chosen. Let them begin their work. Here is a temple to Liberty, to human rights, on whose portals behold the glorious declaration, "All men are created equal." The sun has never yet shone upon any of man's creations that can compare with this. The artist who can mold a statue worthy to crown magnificence like this, must be godlike in his conceptions, grand in his comprehensions, sublimely beautiful in his power of execution. The woman--the crowning glory of the model republic among the nations of the earth--what must she not be?

"The Limitations of Sex," 1885

. . . Those people who declaim on the inequalities of sex, the
disabilities and limitations of one as against the other, show
themselves as ignorant of the first principles of life as would that
philosopher who should undertake to show the comparative power of
the positive as against the negative electricity, of the centrifugal as
against the centripetal force, the attraction of the north has against
the south end of the magnet. These great natural forces must be
perfectly balanced or the whole material world would relapse into
chaos. Just so the masculine and feminine elements in humanity
must be exactly balanced to redeem the moral and social world from
the chaos which surrounds it. One might as well talk of separate
spheres for the two ends of the magnet as for man and woman; they
may have separate duties in the same sphere, but their true place is
together everywhere. Having different duties in the same sphere
neither can succeed without the presence and influence of the other.
To restore the equilibrium of sex is the first step in social, religious,
and political progress. It is by the constant repression of the best
elements in humanity, by our false customs, creeds and codes, that
we have thus far retarded
civilization . . . .

There would be more sense in insisting on man's limitations
because he can not be a mother, than on woman's because she can
be. Surely maternity is an added power and development of some of
the most tender sentiments of the human heart and not a
"limitation." "Yes," says another pertinacious reasoner, "but it unfits
woman for much of the world's work." Yes, and it fits her for much of
the world's work; a large share of human legislation would be better
done by her because of this deep experience.

If one-half the effort had been expended to exalt the feminine
element that has been made to degrade it, we should have reached
the natural equilibrium long ago. Either sex, in isolation, is robbed of

one-half its power for the accomplishment of any given work. This was the most fatal dogma of the Christian religion-that in proportion as men withdrew from all companionship with women, they could get nearer to God, grow more like the Divine Ideal . . . .

Speech on Marriage and Divorce, 1869

Ladies and Gentlemen:

I have been asked in your hearing my comments on marriage and divorce, such as I gave in the legislature of New York years ago, such as I have recently delivered in many places, such as I shall permit to stand the test of future consideration. But the law of all things is progress, and I profess at this hour to take a step forward. We progressed in our (?)[2] theories in the past by the growth of ideas in our own minds, in part by the growth of ideas in the social medium which surrounds us, in part by the growth in us of that boldness which dare lay openly and wholly what we do think. I have said in the proceeding lecture that what I claimed would not destroy but would simply influence and perfect marriage. But stop! I will not be guilty of fake pretense, I will not skulk under the pretentious ambiguity in the meaning of the term marriage; in some sense all will be disturbed, will be abrogated in time by the progress of reform, in the only sense indeed in which it is defined in the dictionary, in the law book, in what it is understood by 99% of the whole people. Marriage, I mean, as a compulsory bond enforced by the law and rendered perpetual by that means. This element of legal compulsion is all that distinguishes marriage from the natural and free adjustments which the sentiment of love would spontaneously organize for itself and I do not know that I, as you, have the right to say what these adjustments should be. I have (?) in behalf of the equality of the sexes because it has seemed to me that the recognition of that equality was, as I still think it is, the first requisite, the first step in the search to social emancipation, social happiness. But I have perceived all along somewhat dimly, and I perceive more and more clearly every day, that the recognition of the equality of woman with man in all the senses in which it is justifiable that they should be equal is not enough, that it is only a first step and nothing more. It is just as justifiable, though understandably somewhat less usual and likely, that equals should oppress and endure each other, as it is for their to hold a relation of superior and subordinate is for the superior to suppress the subordinate. Two nations each acknowledging the unlimited sovereignty of the other acting therefore perfectly in the capacity of equals may enter into entangling alliances which will destroy the independence and freedom of each as may bind each other by impolitic and oppressive treaties and even by conditions impossible of execution without ruin to each other, so may two individuals thoroughly ensnare each other with the (?) founded in particularly in their mutual differences and needs. I know parties, man and wife, who have worked hard and honestly almost for a lifetime and together in behalf of what has been known as women's rights . . . working in the equality of the sexes, neither of whom dares say their souls were their own, making each other mutually and equally the abject slaves, simply because each has classified and established the right of ownership over the other and because each had in ignorant good faith--conceded the right, had in a word abdicated their own individual sovereignty--sinking it in the cortex of marriage. Luck in fact--I think is the social condition of the great man not if married conflicts at large merely but even of the prominent advocates of women's rights, to say nothing of the more timid and conservative claimants of female merely. They live the lives through married conflicts generally of mutual spies and tyrants over each other, and it is the most (?) form of slavery ever instituted, because it is seemingly so fair, bounded as if in mutual agreement and not insurmountable with all the full compassion of the equality of the parties to this mutant treaty of self-stultification. What is wanted therefore, is not mere suffrage and civic rights and not merely in the second place, the social recognition of the equal ranks of the sexes, though both of these must be had, but freedom, freedom from all unnecessary entanglements of concessions, freedom from binding obligations involving impossibilities, freedom to repair mistakes; to express the manifestations of our own nature, and to progress is to advance to higher planes of development.

But at this point probably your suspicions are aroused, freedoms in this subject, why that is something short of unlimited freedom of divorce, freedom to initiate at the option of the parties new awaking relationships, that put above marriage and in a (?) the obnoxious doctrine of free love. Well, yes, that is what I mean. We are all free lovers at heart, although we may not have thought so. We all believe in a good time coming either in this world or in another, when men and women will be good and nice, when they will not be (?) themselves and when therefore the external laws of compulsion will no longer be needed. Nobody thinks of the legislature at Albany or the police court as permanent necessities to interfere in the regulation of the most current relation of human hearts . . . . Now whenever confusion and restraint, whether of the law or of a dogmatic and oppressive public opinion are removed, whatever results will be free love. If every man selects one woman and every woman one man, if they live together as they [wish] . . . that is just as much free love as the (?) in promiscuity. It is indeed of the essence of freedom that it does not attempt to proscribe what the result shall be, trusting to the laws of nature and to the enlightenment, good conscience and culture, as good taste of the parties to be affected by it. And if I mistake not this, just this is what meant and all that is meant by the intelligent advocates of free love. When a bad sense is thrust upon the souls, that is I apprehend, the fault of us who hear them and interpret them in a bad sense in accordance with the (?) of our own natures. If I mistake not, the true free lovers are among the most progressive, the most virtuous of women and of men. The true nobility and virtue of Mary Wollstonecraft compelled her admission with the most aristocratic and most moral circles in England, despite of her sins (?) and while she rejected all intelligence to the marriage institution and lived in her land openly as the mistress of the man of her choice. Freedom is demanded at this day, by the most enlightened and most virtuous, not by the victims . . . .

It is the refined natures of delicate sensibilities and tender consciences who loathe the compulsory adulteries of the marriage bed, and it is the men of vigorous logic and love of justice who insist on the same freedoms for others as for themselves, even when the freedom may be used to do what they think wrong. We blunder habitually. I have done so myself perhaps sometimes, and I see others doing so every day in compromising freedoms with the uses good or bad which may be made of freedom. The freedom of the press is one thing, but whether I should be engaged in the exercise of that freedom in writing and publishing ribald stories and silly trash, or in pursuing the sublimest truths of the intellect, is wholly another question. Freedom is demanded to do good; if some use their freedoms to do evil, that is the function of the machinery. The bad investment which goes to profit and loss is the business of progress, but freedom nevertheless is the watchword of truth, the *sine qua non* of development of the badge of the enlightened confidence of God, or the force of powers of nature to accomplish her own ends.

Well, then, it is agreed, we are all free lovers in some time or stage or development. It is only a question of time. We ought then, friends, to question whether the freedom of affections is or would be safe and profitable for the world here and now or whether it must be postponed till the world has learned (?) this freedom to be nice and good. This is the same issue as that of immediate or gradual emancipation in the slavery question. Freedom is one of indivisible (?), whether we say freedom of political action, freedom of conscience, free thinking freedom, freedom of intellectual speculation, freedom from the slavery of servitude, freedom of the press, freedom of locomotion, or whatnot. The law of the subject is the same. Evil, great evil, comes in every case, apparent evil at any rate from the confusions of freedom. Some people will and do make a bad use of their freedoms, but, whether freedom is therefore is a bad thing, as whether with all its attendant evils, it will not be an invaluable boon, an indefensible condition of true living, and in a word the fundamental idea of human rights, is the other more rudimentary question. It is a question too, with which all we Americans have had a good deal to do in answering, in other respects and with which now we are going to have a good deal to do in answering with respect to marriage and love. Andrew Jackson Davis tells an excellent story of an old gentleman who had the (?) badly, and who, being asked to try bran bread declined perpetually and said that he would rather die than do it, for he had always noticed that if anybody began with bran bread, he was sure to end with infidelity. There was a profound instinct of a great truth hid away in this old man's brain. He felt what is true that all reforms, innovations, logically affiliated with each other, and that whosoever says A will sooner or later say B.

The men and women who are dabbling with the suffrage amendment for women should be at once therefore, emphatically warned, that they mean logically, if not consciously in all they say, is that the next logical equality and next freedom is in a word "free love." And if they wish to get out of the bout, they should for surely get out now for delayed are dangerous. Indeed the two first questions have already been argued and already settled. It is the freedom question which is now open. But again freedom is not enough, it is only the stepping stone to something higher and better. The next better thing is wisdom, to know how rightly to use and enjoy freedom, in other words, the whole science of the subject. License must be called on to investigate radically every part of the subject, the sole nature and legitimate demands of men and of women the truth of the one, of the many relations between them and in a word to discover the divine social case. But equality and freedom and science--all of these are not enough. The next good and necessary and indisputable thing is virtue, which seems the love of truth and goodness, of beauty. Men and women must fall in love, not so much with each other as contributors to their own selfish wants as with each others' highest held being . . . . And in time one other result, a new religion, a religion that shall be to all their (?) of human nature, what the string which binds the stem of flowers is to the bouquet. The day was when religion was allied with all that was progressive in human affairs. Today it has somehow got in the wrong side and has been retarding and obstructive.

The best word is then a new catholicity which shall not merely tolerate but which shall adorate and enforce by its influence all that reform shall aspire after and all that science shall discover and divine--in a word, the new Catholic Church in this radical and progressive signification of the term.

"Co-Education," 1872

The planetary world with its changing seasons, days and nights, evolved for centuries in order and harmony before Newton discovered the law of gravitation.

This western continent slumbered peacefully amid the tidal waves of the Atlantic and Pacific long before Columbus prophesized of this far-off land.

And so, in social life, great facts maintain themselves before we take cognizance of their existence, in spite of theories that would block every step in progress, as abundant as the sands of the sea, and as easily washed away. Ofttimes, we have heard conceit in ignorance declare this or that cannot be, and lo! it is.

The co-education of the sexes, as a practical experiment, has been going on in this country for the greater part of a century. Although "the Nation," president Eliot of Harvard College, Dr. Edward Clarke of Boston, and others just aroused to the consideration of this question, declare such an experiment "dangerous," "impracticable," "contrary to nature," "at variance with the ordinance of God," "destructive of the health, morals, and manners of our girls"; in fact, "would tend to undermine the whole foundation of our social edifice."

Such solemn warnings from the pulpit, the forum, and the professor's chair are given in face of the facts, that in district schools, high schools, academies, boys and girls, "young men and women of marriageable age," coming from distant homes have been and are being educated together, in all the northern states. In almost every Western college and university, we find boys and girls studying all branches, side by side, mathematics, languages, law, medicine, theology. The girls, maintaining good morals, manners, and health, and also equal rank in scholarship. The presidents, professors, regents, and principals at the head of these institutions have given strong unqualified testimony in favor of the co-education of the sexes in colleges and universities, as well as academics in district schools. It is over thirty years since Western colleges began the experiment and now, the great state of New York, in opening Cornell University to girls, has set her seal of approbation in the system.

Hence, this is no longer a matter of theory in America, but an established fact. It is a loss of time, of effort to rest this question a single hour on the judgement of men bound by custom and prejudice who have never fairly considered the ethics of the subject nor the facts that exist around them.

President White of Cornell University, in his able majority support of admitting girls to that institution, says the committee in search of facts corresponded with numbers of persons in various parts of the country where experience in the education of the sexes together made their statements of value, but they did not consult the authorities of colleges that have never tried the system. That would have been as if the Japanese authorities, roused to the necessity of railroads and telegraphs, had corresponded with eminent Chinese philosophers regarding the ethics of this subject instead of sending persons to observe the workings of railroads and telegraphs where they are already in use.

Following this plan, I have collected abundant testimony as to the wisdom of the experiment that we have so long tried in this country; to give it all would make my paper too voluminous; moreover, the real question today is not the safety or wisdom of co-education, for that is already proven. But rather shall the wealthy, endowed colleges of the east, with all their advantages, be thrown open to girls or shall the people of the several states be taxed to build similar ones for them?

When we consider the thought, effort, time, and energy required to do the latter, it is evident that the present generation of girls would pass away before that could be accomplished. Moreover, the same arguments that would rouse popular sentiment to do this work would open Harvard, Yale and Columbia. In a financial kind of (?)[2] it would be far easier to open the colleges we have to girls than to open others. And this is a point, that common sense, men and legislators, are wanted to consider. When they are told that there are sixteen colleges and universities for boys in the state of New York, with 200 professors and 15 million dollars and grants of land in addition, some with empty halls, they would say rather than repeat the labor and expense to build separate colleges let our daughters enter existing institutions, use our means, all educational funds and appropriations to influence and make them what they should be. Buildings, libraries, scientific apparatus, all the appliances for complete education, cannot be spoken into existence; they are the results of oft-repeated acts of state, of individuals' munificence, they grow, like systems of government, religion and education. Other

Harvards, Yales, and Columbias for girls are impossible for generations, and we should be satisfied with nothing less.

Women of wealth have contributed to these institutions for boys, all over the land; directly, by munificent bequests, and indirectly by the taxes they have paid for their commitments; therefore, they have a right to an equal share in their benefits.

It is important for the girls knocking at the doors of these venerable institutions to know that they have a right inside. There is no law, human or divine, nothing in their churches that forbids. Nothing but the crochets of a few conservative minds, to combat and conquer.

In a recent discussion on co-education before the Social Science Association in Boston, Wendell Phillips declared the right of every girl born in Massachusetts to walk up and down Harvard's halls. He says,

> Harvard College belongs to the Commonwealth of Massachusetts; and if he had a daughter and her health was such and her disposition was such that she wanted to go, he would carry it to the Supreme Court--if he supposed there were an honest one--and claim it as a right. If Harvard College wants to draw back within the line of certain theories and her own conceptions, let her disgorge the contributions of the state, and then, when she relies upon her own funds, when she is a private way, she may put up a sign, "this is a private way; dangerous passing here." But while it is opened by the State, accepted by the commissioners, graded and hardened by the commonwealth, must it be opened to all.

President Pierce, in an address to the graduating class of Rutgers College, maintains the same right. He says,

> If then, the law of the land creates privileged class, such for instance as orders of nobility on whom it bestows powers not given to others, it makes distinctions that are repugnant alike to the teachings of Christianity and of experience. The utter rejection of this sort of feudalism from the Constitution of the United States was a great step in the progress of Christian civilization and is soon to be followed throughout the

world. But if the state fulfills its duty to a part of the people in the bestowment of that which is a benefit for them to receive and a duty for the state to give, and does not do the same for the whole, or if it does this for such other part in a less degree, its neglect of these or its less complete fulfillment of its duty to them against whom it discriminates, this is in the nature of a wrong, and tends to create an inequality among those entitled to equal treatment, which is the essential injustice of that feudalism which was meant to be wholly repudiated and forever banished from this country. Precisely this has been done by the state in the matter of education for women and by the community in copying the example fo the state. Now, the relation between religion and education is that of parent and child. Wrong, then, in a matter of such great importance as the education of one half of the whole people, may well claim the earnest attention of the Christian church, and, therefore, I deem it entirely appropriate to this Sabbath and to this house of worship to argue the following proposition: that while the state, in granting great sums of money in the education of men, and the community, in imitating this, the example of the state, have done well; yet, in so much as both have failed to do so equally for women, this less complete fulfillment of public duty is not only a great wrong to a part of this community, but a great harm to the whole, as it directly fosters an inequality which is repugnant to Christianity and to the best interests of society.

Here we have the opinions of two able men representing widely different classes of thinkers, that girls are excluded from our colleges and universities contrary to law, to the spirit of our Constitution, and to the theory of our government.

The essential demand of Republican government is opposed to all sorts of feudalism, to orders of nobility, to privileged classes, to all discrimination against citizens. Our rulers have come to understand this principle, as applied to men of color. Can nothing but the cannons roar and loud artillery enable them to see its application to women?

To show how unequally women have been treated in this country of equal rights and privileges, contrast the educational advantages of the sexes in the state of New York. The oldest college in the state is Columbia, founded in 1754. It has 15 professors, and its buildings, apparatus, and funds amount to 83 million dollars. Of the two youngest, the Free College of New York has 20 officers in its faculty, its buildings and apparatus amount to 262 thousand dollars, and its yearly appropriations represent a capital of two million 500,000 dollars. Cornell University has 30 on its faculty. It has received a valuable grant of land from the United States as well as a vast sum from private liberality and its endowment is currently estimated at from 2-3 millions. The whole number of colleges and universities in this state is 16, with about 200 professors and 15 million dollars capital invested. It should also be noted that the provision for the education of men in this state, which began at so early a period, has been greatly increased within a few years, as seen in the endowments of Cornell University, the College of New York, the University of Rochester, and the New University of Syracuse, for which a half million of dollars has been subscribed within a few months, besides large sums secretly contributed to other institutions. But from the first settlement of the state down to within a few years, there have been no colleges for women, and there are now but four: Wyham University, Elmira, Vassar and Rutgers College. We may soon add Cornell University as by the munificent gift of the Honorable Henry W. Laye of (?), a building is already being constructed for the accommodation of girls. Rutgers has no endowment. The funds of the other three amount to about 100,000 dollars, their buildings and apparatus to about 1.1 million dollars. More than half of of this is credited to Vassar, the munificent donation of Nathan Vassar.

Now, here we have the estimate in dollars and cents of the popular value placed respectively on the education of men and women. 15 million against 1.1 million dollars. What say the women taxpayers of the state to this inequality? And yet, through all these years, while women, women who believed in women's sphere, who never talked of property rights or the elective franchise did their best to rouse thought to the higher education of girls. Emma Willard, Hannah Upham, Caroline Stanton, Delia Lockett, though they could never get an appropriation from the legislature for their schools, [much] less a bequest from someone of wealth, yet like pillars on high, they have led the way in which Matthew Vassar and Henry W. Sage have followed.

Verily, these men, in founding and fostering Vassar and Cornell, have done more for human advancement than any military chieftain of ancient or modern times. They knew prejudice, and superstition, and that the development of woman's mind will add to the wealth of the state. Let the daughters of New York soon say with united voice, "No more appropriations for the education of boys until the girls have drawn 15 million dollars from the state treasury to endow their institutions of higher learning, or until the leaders of education in this state are nice enough to throw open all institutions of learning to both sexes."

If the daughters of New York or Massachusetts, as Mr. Phillips and President Pierce assert, have the right to enter Harvard and Columbia, why are they denied? One says there is a difference in the sexes, therefore there should be a difference in the education. No doubt there is sex in the mortal and spiritual world, as there is in the vegetable and animal kingdoms. And it is because of this very principle, of this very difference, no man or woman, that they should be educated together. All our systems must be fragmentary or introverted until we have the masculine and feminine elements united; until we have a flow and interflow of brain forces; until man and woman occupy the same plane of thought, man can never reach the divinest heights of which he is capable until woman is ready to meet him there.

And this difference in the sexes is too subtle as yet, too little understood, to attempt to shape all conditions of life with reference to it. Nine faculties and powers of minds only that are common to both sexes are what it is proposed to educate in our schools. We may safely trust the rest to nature; to preserve and educate that subtle difference called sex which she alone understands. We do not find ourselves in human life compelled to spread different tables, to provide apartments at higher or lower degrees of heat for the different sexes. We go to the same churches and lectures, swallow the same theology, to the same theatres, operas, balls and parties, breathing the same carbonic acid gas. We truck in the same streetcars, railroads, and steamboats and are smashed up and blown up in the same way. Though the insurance companies do make a difference, believing that women, like cats, have nine lives, they insure us against death but not accidents. Again, this principle of sex does not affect the common individual manifestation. Behold! Man eats, drinks, sleeps, and so does woman. He loves, is religious, penitent, prayerful, reverent; and so is woman. He hates, is irritable, impatient, unreasonable, tyrannical; so is woman. He is noble, courageous, self-reliant, generous, magnanimous; and so is woman. What virtue or vice, what aspiration or appetite, has ever crowned or clouded the glory of mankind, we have not seen in women too its beauty or its blight? Are not our hopes and fears for time and eternity the same?

In country schools where boys and girls are educated together, sex is lost sight [of] in the playground and in the recitation room. Who has seen a girl smash a boy's face in the snow and carry off a prize in the classics? In studying the classics or reading geometry, in reading Virgil and the Greek testament, who ever found a feminine way? Or of extracting the cube root of XYZ? Or any masculine way of giving through the minds of tenses of the verb "amo"? Let those who quote nature so freely consider her treatment of this principle of sex that pervades all organic life. All living things inhabiting the three elements land, air, and water from the brainless aphids that lives his life upon the tiny leaf to the ichthyrosauraus that crawled among the rushes in the giant times of earth, from the lichen of an Arctic rock to the towering palm of a tropic forest, all have this distinction of sex as clearly or as widely marked as in man, and yet, we find nowhere two systems of administration, two sets of means for the support or increase of this two-fold life. The male and female plant, the male and female animal, through the entire range of animated being, inhale the same vital atmosphere, drink from the same gurgling fountain, bask in the same sunlight, draw all the resources of their existence and growth from one common storehouse. If then it would be ridiculous to talk of male and female atmospheres, springs, rains, or sunshines, how much more ridiculous it is to talk of male and female education, schools, and colleges, seeing that this question of sex is still more subtle in the world of mind than in the world of matter! To quote again from President Pierce's very able address on this point, he says

There is a difference between the sexes that at once raises the question whether there should not be a difference in their education. After the most careful thought that I could give the subject, I am of the opinion that it should be the same to a much greater extent than most persons are willing to concede. Up to a certain point the education of men is much the same; beyond that point comes in a special training. Thus, on leaving college, the young man who is to pursue law receives legal training. But the great fact here to be noticed is that up to a certain point, all liberally educated men are trained much in the same manner. For a long time a liberal education seems to take no notice of specific ends which finally it may be desirable to aim at. It contents itself with enlarging and strengthening the mental powers, it unrolls before the young man the ample page of knowledge, confident that this is the best preparation for any path that he may choose. If then, it is best for the young man that be a

> liberal education, his memory should be
> strengthened, his reasoning powers
> disciplined, his judgement matured, his mind
> enlarged--why is it not the best for the young
> woman also? This is a question for those who
> differ with us to answer. It is a question that
> more would seriously ask were it not that the
> minds of many are unconsciously swayed by
> a belief in the essential inferiority of woman
> and restricting them to the judicious dry toast
> and the enlivening teacup.

Inferiority here is the whole difficulty in a nutshell, judged alone by the comparative advantages we see for the education of the sexes. Men are considered "superior"; hence their education has seemed to all of primal importance; even women of wealth, while making munificent bequests to institutions for boys, have uniformly ignored their own sex.

We may talk of the "angels of society" whose mission is the noblest on earth, "who are the moral powers of the world" but who believes this? Women themselves? Have they shown it in this lack of education? In giving thousands to institutions that forbid a woman to cross their threshold and willing to those that welcome them there? Has one woman yet made a valuable bequest to Vassar College, the best-appointed institution for girls in the world? "Inferiority" is what these gentlemen really mean when they talk of "difference of sex."

If this impeachment of feminine minds has any force instead of repressing their efforts to secure higher education, thus making the inferiority still greater, every encouragement, advantage, and appliance to stimulate women into the right direction or to Cornell University that has offered its doors to all? When women themselves, by their acts and sanctions accept this charge of inferiority, we need not wonder that man acts in the same opinion or should be as freely as put forth as they have been the "superior sex" from the beginning. Were this done, the degrees of "inferiority" might be greatly decreased or the sexes brought into the same balance. In fact, where this has been done, they have been annihilated, the labels completely turned, and the girls proven superior to the boys.[3]

This is the testimony that comes from every college where girls have had fair play. And there is no stronger proof of the natural chivalry of man than the apparent pleasure with which their presidents, professors, and leading educators publish complimentary facts.

When such men in the state of New York as Samuel B. Woolsworth, Secretary of the Board of Regents and for 32 years principal of some of our best academies, Principal House of the State Normal School at Cortland, Dr. Armstrong, Principal of the State Normal School at Freedonia, whose experience extends to colleges also, Principal Sheldon of Oswego and last though not least, President Mark Hopkins of Williams College, when such men all testify in favor of co-education, Columbia College, Union, and New York Free Academy need not longer fear to make the experiment.

Some objectors think it would demoralize young girls to associate with the boys who (?) in college.

Can it be that brothers and sisters who have played together through all the years of childhood, who have shared each other's joys and sorrows, cannot in safety tread the same college walks, study the same books, listen to the same lectures, draw diagrams on the same blackboards, try chemical experiments with the same apparatus, talk lyric on the same subject, under the watchful eyes of teachers, under college rules and discipline? Would our daughters be in greater danger with our neighbors and in such conditions than in taking promenades in crowded cities, in theaters, operas, balls parties, dancing schools, sleigh rides? There is no country in the world where boys and girls, men and women, mingle so freely together as here, and no country can boast as high a standard of morality. Such an objection might do in Turkey, but not in republican America.

But if it be true that the moral atmosphere of our colleges is such that no young lady of refinement could safely enter there, their nice mothers would be unwilling to have their sons subjected to such influences. Might we not find here new fields of effort? The Christian work of devout women has been specially (?) in India and the missionary islands, might it not be equally effective in Harvard, Yale, and Columbia? Remember, these boys are to be our future statesmen, our teachers of law, theology, medicine; the husbands, fathers of the next generation; can the purifying work begin too soon? Are not the best interests of the state, the church, and the home all involved in the moral atmosphere of our college halls? If it were fitting for a Florence Nightingale, amidst the horror of war in a Russian hospital, to minister to the wants of sick and dying soldiers, may not noble girls, with equal propriety and advantage, guard the morals of our future heroes in all these institutions of learning?

I think however that objectors have magnified the dangers in this direction and have done the young gentlemen in our colleges a grave injustice. For the ladies who have entered these temples of learning send back no reports of "hotbeds of vice" or of "human mistreatments". It may be then bugbears disappeared for the coming of the young ladies, as the snakes and frogs of Ireland fled before St. Patrick.

Neither have the young lady students lost their "natural delivery, refinement, and nonmanliness" nor have they "acquired any false ideas of their particular sphere." Nor gone off in balloons in search of new ones. No such predictions have been verified. One might think to hear people talk of woman's "woman beliefs" that it was a kind of amulet made of blown glass which could easily be put on or taken off or dashed to pieces. And yet the daughters of these conservative gentlemen go to balls and parties with bare necks and arms and waltz with gentlemen in the presence of admiring hundreds. Their costume is described in the public journals the next day, and yet their "delicacy, refinement, womanship" is not supposed to suffer.

I have known women to carry great bundles of work from slop shops to their garrets when they supported themselves by the needle, starving on 25 cents a day and yet retain their delicacy. I have known them to live in luxury, with coarse drunken brutal husbands for years and be refined still. So subtle, and imponderable is the quality of womanship. It is remarkable then that President White should be able to report, after his trip of observation, that he "was uniformly impressed with the quiet dignity, modesty, refinement of the young ladies of all the western colleges." And this is the testimony from all quarters.

How much longer will it take the world to learn that the mutual influence of the sexes is to purify, elevate, and dignity each other.[4]

But, says another objector, "it would lower the standard of scholarship to admit young ladies to colleges."

Judge Cooley, one of the professors in Michigan University, says that such has not been the case there. One of the very best mathematicians in that institution for years was a girl. She solved a difficult problem which had been presented to several inventive chaps without finding a solution. One of the best Greek scholars, too, was a girl. How is it possible for students who keep as the head of their class, of all the prizes, to lower the grade of scholarship?

Samuel B. Woolsworth, says on this point, "The co-education of the sexes has been favorable to good order and discipline and exerts a mutual stimulating influence on scholarship."[5]

The general testimony is that girls are more conscientious in study than boys and that this is the main cause of their remarkable success. Another cause may be that girls appreciate more highly advantages so long denied them.

Another fallacy is that women have not the physical health to endure a collegiate education. Any special reform, while all other ends of society remain as they are, seems out of joint with its surroundings, but if one has the faith and patience to survey the future and from the causes at work in the present, realize what the thought and effort of a generation must inevitably accomplish, in all directions, then many things which now seem impractical and dangerous will appear safe and desirable.

Thus, simultaneously with the movement for the higher education of women, reforms in the habits of life, dress, diet and exercise are proffered. Girls now have their boat, ball clubs, running, skating, gymnastics. And in their curriculum are included botany, astronomy and surveying, all compelling outdoor exercise and observation. Thus, the artificial limp-backed, flabby muscled, feeble nerved women of today will soon be unknown forces

But statistics show that, even now, the girls in our colleges enjoy as good health and live as long as the boys.[6]

Simply as a means to this end, there is no greater blessing to the rising generation of young girls than college life, with its years of study, occupation, ambition, and aspiration. We cannot estimate the misery and disease caused by the utter vacuity in the lives of girls, especially in the wealthy classes. The aimless, hopeless, pleasure seekers, for whom good fathers think they have done their utmost, when they have supplied every meal and have left heads and hearts and minds alike unfulfilled. Let the next generation of girls be liberally educated, kept in college until they are 25 years old in the constant society of young men of their own age and attainments, and the health of both sexes would be improved and the tone of society greatly changed for the better.

But another grave objection to co-education is that "attachments would be formed" and "engagements of marriages grown out of them." Thus, the thoughts of both sexes would be drummed from their legitimate studies. Anther class of objections assert that "the higher education of women would open to them so many new and pleasant fields for thought and action that marriage would be indefinitely postponed or ignored all together."

These objections seem to answer each other, if danger lies in one direction, it cannot in the other. And yet, there is some truth in both statements. If we could rouse the ambitions of our daughters to go through a thorough collegiate course, to enter some trade or profession and once enjoy the freedom of self-support and self-dependence, girls would not marry as early in life as they do now. But that, instead of an objection, would be a great blessing to the race, for one object for the higher education for both men and women is the demand for higher types of manhood and womanhood. As girls of twenty, with feeble minds and bodies, make the majority of our mothers, improvement is effectually blocked. Again, when girls are scientifically educated and independent, they will not be governed in marriage by the law of attraction and not by sordid motives of policy. The man will be the central figure, not his bank book or family.

The first step towards higher, purer, more enduring unions is the complete education of woman. Some form of marriage has always existed and will no doubt continue, however the regents of the universities may decide the question of co-education.

Cicero says, "The most important study of man is man." I suppose he used "man" in its comprehensive sense, including woman. And is not such knowledge of each other as important in the scheme of happiness, involving as it does all branches of social science, as is the study of mathematics or the languages? In constant association and active competition for the same prizes, young men and women might bring to this study the same challenge and discrimination as to all other subjects. Our thoughts are not distracted by relations to which we are accustomed. The facts already show that in those colleges where the sexes are educated together, there is less flirting, fewer scandals, less thought of each other than in those monastic institutions where all intercourse is forbidden.[7]

The main objections all summed up against co-education may be correctly stated thus:

1. "The sexes differ, therefore the systems of education should differ."
2. "It would lower the grade of scholarship and morals."
3. "Girls have not sufficient strength of mind to endure the strain of a thorough collegiate course."
4. "It would make boys effeminate, less brave and manly."
5. "Boys and girls cannot study together. They would be continually thinking of each other. Flirtations would take the place of Latin, mathematics, and marriage of graduation and diplomas."

Prove to these objections that the reverse of all of these has proved true, that in those colleges where the experiment has been tried, the grade of scholarship and morals has been elevated; that boys and girls stimulate each other to good lessons and behaviors; that boys have not lost courage; that the colleges sent to us of late a more brave, hearty body of young men than went from Oberlin and Antioch; that such friendships take the place of flirtations. Prove all this and objections will then fly in another direction and maintain that, in this everyday acquaintance in the recitation room, men must lose all their chivalry for women; that the poetry of life would be all gone; forgetting that chivalry and poetry are the essential elements of our being and will ever seek some modes of expression under all circumstances.

In the higher education of the women of the future, vain is the attempt to bend eternal laws to human follies and blunders. With the half-civilized idea of woman's nature, sphere, and duty, every step outside old conventionality seems to imperil the whole social infrastructure. But their ideas are fast passing away. The last type of slavery, that of woman to man, is ended. The hour strikes on the clock, would by no mortal hands, to mark out her own salvation with joy and longing.

"Our Girls," 1872

They are the music, the flowers, the sunshine of our social life. How beautiful they make our homes, churches, schools and festive scenes; how glad and gay they make our streets with their scarlet plumes, bright shawls and tartan plaids. Who can see a bevy of girls tripping home from school without pausing to watch their graceful motions, pretty faces, feet and legs, to listen to their merry words and peals of laughter. See how they romp and play with hoops and balls, with sleds and skates, wash their brothers' faces in the snow and beat them in a race on yonder pond. These boys and girls are one today in school, at play, at home, never dreaming that one sex was foreordained to clutch the stars, the other but to kiss the dust. But watch a while and you will see these dashing, noisy, happy, healthy girls grow calm, pale, and sad and even though lodged in palace homes mid luxury and ease, with all the gorgeous trappings wealth can give, with silks, bright jewels, gilded equippage, music, dancing, books, flowers, they still are listless and unsatisfied. And why? They have awakened to the fact that they belong to a subject, degraded, ostracized class: that to fill their man-appointed sphere, they can have no individual character, no life purpose, personal freedom, aim or ambition. They are simply to revolve around some man, to live only for him, in him, with him; to be fed, clothed, housed, guarded and controlled by him, today by Father or Brother, tomorrow by Husband or Son, no matter how wise or mature they are, never to know the freedom and dignity that are secured in self-dependence and self-support. Girls feel all this though they may never utter it, far more keenly than kind fathers imagine.

Walking in Madison Park one day with my little boy, reading the signs hung in the trees, "No dogs admitted here," he remarked, "It's a good thing, Mother, that dogs cannot read. It would hurt their feelings so to know that they were forbidden to walk in the parks." Yes, we said, the dogs are like the girls seem to be, shut out of the green pastures of life; while both alike are ignorant of the statutes by which it is done. Bruno sleeps on his master's rug in some dark street, pining for the sunshine and the grass and a frolic through the field or forest, without knowing his degradation published in that one invidious announcement, "No dogs admitted here," but if he should try to enter the park, a smart rap on the nose would remind him that he was a dog and not a boy. So our young girls pine and perish for lack of freedom, for the stimulus of work and wages, something to widen their ambitions and love of distinction. They are clothed in purple and fine linen and in their gilded cages fare sumptuously every day, but if by chance, with some new inspiration they awake to life and go forth to claim the place in the world that is by birthright theirs, they find at the very gates of life, at the entrance to every winding path leading to the Temple of Knowledge, wealth, or fame, there self-same little signs hung out, "No girls admitted here." While the dogs and the girls suffer alike the penalty of the law, the degradation of the latter is greatly aggravated by the fact that they can read the signs and what adds to the girl's humiliation is the fact that the boy by her side reads them also and finds out that to him alone the universe is free. The universe of matter and mind is his domain, no constitutions, customs, creeds or codes block his onward way, but all combine to urge him on, his triumphs in science, literature, and art are hailed with loud huzzas. He accepts the homage of the multitude as his sole right and looks with jealous eye at any girl that dares to tread upon his heels. In these artificial distinctions, boys learn their first lessons of contempt for all womankind. They naturally infer that they are endowed with some superior powers to match their superior privileges. But what avails it, that here and there some proud girl repudiates these invidious distinctions, laughs at the supercilious airs these boys affect and braces up her mind to resist this tyranny of sex. She feels she is the peer of any boy she knows. She has measured many a lance on the playground and in the school and now shall custom make her bow to sex, to those inferior to herself. She scorns the thought, but what can one brave girl do against the world. Custom has made this type of boy and soon these grow to perpetuate the custom. Man makes the creeds and the constitutions and codes, while woman is not but a lay figure in the world, a mere appendage to lordly man, a something on which to hang his titles, name and fame. With blighted girlhood, wasted youth and vacant age, the ambition of most women we meet today is simply to be distinguished as the daughter, wife, or mother of General, Honorable, or Judge So-and-so, to shine in their reflected light, to wear their deeds and words of valor and of eloquence as their own bracelet, necklace, or coronal. This should not be. Every girl should be something in and of herself, have an individual aim and purpose in life. As the boy approaches manhood, he gathers up his forces and concentrates them in some definitive work, trade, or profession, as a wish, a will, or way of his own everyone respects.

Hence, he begins life with enthusiasm, early learns the pleasure of self-dependence, growing stronger, braver every day he lives. But alas for the girl; she leaves school with her ambition at white heat; perchance she has outstripped the foremost in sciences and languages, she has her heart ready to carve her way to distinction. She too has a will of her own and desires the dignity of independence and self-support. But any career for a woman is tabooed by the world, and nothing she proposes to do is acceptable to family and friends. If in spite of opposition a woman does step outside all conventional trammels to do something her grandmother did not do, she meets a dozen obstacles where a man does one. Surely the battle of life without any artificial trammels is hard enough, for multitudes of young men even perish in the struggle. But the girl who earns her bread or makes for herself a name has all the boy has to surmount and these artificial barriers of law and custom in addition.

Do you wonder that so few are ready to take their rights? Oh! Men of the Republic! Strike off these chains! The distinctions that God has made he will maintain, he needs none of your puny legislation to vindicate his wisdom or carry out his will. Multitudes of our noblest girls are perishing for want of something to do. The hope of marriage, all we offer girls, is not enough to feed an immortal mind, and if that goal is never reached, what then? The more fiery genius a girl has with no outlets for her powers, the more complete is her misery when all these forces are turned back upon herself. The pent-up fires that might have glowed with living words of eloquence in courts of justice, in the pulpit, or on the stage are today consuming their victims in lunatic asylums, in domestic discontent and disgust, in peevish wailings about trifles and in the vain pursuit of pleasure and fashion longing for that peace that is found only in action. Thus multitudes of girls live and die, unloving and loved, who might have stood high in the shining walks of life as a blessing to themselves and others.

We said to one of the most distinguished men of our day not long since your daughter has a wonderful genius for drawing you should cultivate; it might be a source of great profit as well as great happiness to her. "Ah!" said he, "she is interested in (?) schools now.[2] That fills up her time." "Yes," I replied, "but if you should die and she be thrown on her own resources for bread, she could not live by doing acts of charity, besides it is not wise to fill up one's whole life with benevolence."

All women were not made for sisters of mercy, and it is not best for any to watch the sadness and sorrow of life forever. Charity is a good thing, says Sidney Smith, but it is hard to be pitiful twenty-four hours in the day. I know a beautiful girl just eighteen, full of genius, force and fire, who has had one strong, steadfast desire for years, to be educated for the stage. Her performances in private theatricals are marvelous. She has but little thought of dress, fashion, frivolous pleasures, or matrimony. She lives in the ideal. She can give imitations to the life of Kemball, Charlotte Cushman, Ristore. She reads Shakespeare with sure power and appreciates the wisest shades of his thought. She has a passion for tragedy, all her desires, her longings, her hopes and aspirations center there. She thinks of the stage by day and dreams of it by night and in vain friends try to change the current of her thoughts, her heart's desire, the purpose of her life. They have the power to say her nay, to control her actions, thwart her will, pervert her nature, darken all life, but how can they fill the mighty void that one strong passion unsatisfied makes in the human soul? The weary hours of such a blasted life cannot be cheated with the dull sound of ordinary duties, with the puerile pleasures said to be legitimate to women's sphere. "The stage," they say, "is not respectable," as if a royal soul does not dignify whatever she touches. Have not a Liddons, Kemball, Cushman, Rachel, Ristore made that profession honorable for all times? And what do the guardians of this girl propose for the sacrifice they ask? Can they substitute another strong purpose, will, or wish as they desire? Are human souls like garden beds where passions can be transplanted as easily as flowers? Can these guardians pledge themselves, while they hold this child of genius today in idleness and dependence, that they will surround her with comfort and luxuries her life all through? No. Fathers, Brothers, Husbands die, banks fail, houses are consumed with fire, friends prove treacherous, creditors grasping and debtors dishonest, and the skill and cunning of a girl's own brains and hands are the only friends that are ever with her, the only source of means of protection and support. Give your daughters, then, the best of all fortunes, the full development of their own powers concentrated on some life work.

The cunning girl is to be healthy, wealthy and wise. She is to hold one equal place with her brothers in the world of work, in the colleges, in the state, in the church and in the home. Her sphere is to be no longer bound by the prejudices of a dead past, but by her capacity to go wherever she can stand. The cunning girl is to be an independent, self-supporting being, not as today a helpless victim of fashion, superstition, and absurd conventionalisms.

Let us consider then the reforms in her education necessary to realize the grand result. First, she is to be healthy. As by law of Nature, women mold themselves to man's ideal, she must educate our young men to demand something better than they have yet subsidized. All our customs and fashions, however trivial and transient, are based on the theory that woman was made simply to please man, and to do this not by meeting him on the higher plain of spiritual and intellectual attraction in the world of thought, where, through ages of culture, he is supposed to dwell, and where she, through ignorance and inferiority, is supposed to be unable to go, but by a mere physical (?) such as beauty, manners, and duty can give. Hence, she amuses man by an endless variety in her costume and calls out his chivalry by her seeming helplessness and dependence.

When there is a demand for healthy, happy, vigorous, self-reliant women, they will make their appearance. But with our feeble type of manhood the present supply of vanity and vacuity meets their wants. Woman, as she is today, is men's handiwork. With iron shoes, steel-ribbed corsets, hoops, trains, high heels, chignons, paniers, limping gait, feeble muscles, with her cultivated fears of everything seen and unseen, of snakes, spiders, mice and millers, cows, caterpillars, dogs and drunken men, firecrackers and cannon, thunder and lightning, ghosts and gentlemen, women die ten thousand deaths, when if educated to be brave and self-dependent, they would die but one. This sheer affectation of fear and feebleness men too have become so depraved in their taste as to admire and they really suppose that woman as she is is Nature's work, and when they see a woman with brains and two hands in practical life, capable of standing alone, earning her own bread and thinking her own thoughts, conscious of the true dignity and glory of womanhood, they call her "unsexed." The real facts of life show that man's chivalry and devotion is not manifested in proportion to a girl's need of them, but just the opposite. The beautiful, highly educated, wealthy heiress, who is in no hurry to marry either for a master or a house, calls out ten times the more chivalry than the friendless orphan girl or the penniless widow with half a dozen children. Man's devotion is always in exact proportion to woman's actual independence!

Again, when American women begin to call more for principle than pleasing, more to be than to seem, and understand their true dignity as citizens of a Republic, they will not ape foreign costumes, manners, and fashion all out of joint with our theory of government. Our fashions, as you all know are sent us by the French courtesans, whose life work it is to fascinate man and hold him for their selfish purposes.

I have often wondered in fashionable parties and ball gowns if American girls with bare arms and necks had ever philosophized in the custom that required them to appear there half naked, while their brothers were modestly clothed to the very chin. I have hoped that one of the good results of the late war might be more rational and economical fashion. As the French are to be compelled to pay the Germans $240,000,000, I suppose it would be the height of presumption for American women to invent their own fashions.

An auction block of every drawing room for the exhibition of our daughters' charms and thus unduly stimulating the senses in our sons is demoralizing to the virtue of the Nation, dragging woman and man, too, down to death. It is assuming that the sexes are alike, incapable of the higher and more lasting attractions of character, of moral and spiritual power. God has given you minds, dear girls, as well as bodies, and it is your duty to develop your immortal powers, your life work is not to attract simply man or please anybody, but to mold yourselves into a grand and glorious womanhood.

The world will talk to you of the duties of wives and mothers and housekeepers, but all these incidental relations should ever be subordinate to the greater fact of womanhood. You may never be wives or mothers or housekeepers, but you will be women, therefore labor for the grander and more universal fact of your existence.

Speaking of the common idea that woman was made for man and not for her own happiness and enjoyment, Frances Cobbe, a distinguished English woman says,

> If it be admitted that horses and cows were made first for their own enjoyment, secondly to serve their masters, it is to say the least illogical to suppose that the most stupid of human females has been called into existence by the Almighty principally for man's benefit. Believing that the same woman, a million ages hence, will be a glorious spirit before the Throne of God, filled out with unutterable love and light and joy, we cannot satisfactorily trace the beginning of that eternal and seraphtic [sic] existence to Mr. Smith's want of a wife for a score of years here upon earth or to the necessity Mr. Jones was under to find somebody to cook his food and repair his clothes. If these ideas be absurd, then it follows that we are not arrogating too much in seeking elsewhere than in the interests of man, the ultimate reason of the creation of woman.

It is a great truth to impress on the mind of every girl that she is an independent, creative wildflower, made primarily for her own happiness, making self-development and self-support and the highest good of the race the end of her being. I would have girls regard themselves not as adjectives but nouns, not mere appendages made to qualify somebody else, but independent, responsible workers in carrying forward the grand, eternal plans in the redemption of mankind. There is a very pretty theory extant that every woman has a strong right arm on which to lean until she is safe on the other side of Jordan, but the facts of life conflict with the theory. We see on all sides multitudes of girls and women, maids and maidens alike, thrown on their own resources for their daily bread; hence the importance of educating women for these positions that will secure pecuniary independence. I do not wish to undervalue domestic avocations, but the tasks of women vary as much as the tasks of men, and to educate all women for teachers and seamstresses, cooks and chambermaids is to make the supply in the home sphere greater than the demand, thus permanently to keep down wages and degrade all these branches of labor.

Horace Greeley says what we must want is not women voters but 60,000 good cooks today in our kitchens. Well suppose I educate my two daughters for cooks. The highest wages they could secure is $20 per month, $240 per year. A woman of refined taste cannot live on that. Is there a harder and more monotonous life than [the] revolving 365 days of the year must a cook slave?

The cunning girl is to have health. One of the first needs for every girl who is to be trained for some life work, some trade or profession, is good health. As a sound body is the first step towards a sound mind, food, clothes, exercise, all the conditions of daily life are important in training girls either for high scholarship or practical work. Hence, girls, in all your getting of good health, it is the foundation in every undertaking. Sick men and women always take sickly views of everything and fail in the very hour they are needed. One of the essential elements of health is freedom of thought and action. A right to individual life, opinion, ambition. The problems of body and mind so universal in women may be attributed mainly to their being forever in a condition of tutelage and minority. I am sure, gentlemen, you will all be glad to hear that the millennium is close at hand when you are to hear no more of headaches, earaches, sideaches, and backaches, that your homes are to be changed from the gloomy hospitals of today to abodes of health and happiness, when nerves are to be superseded by muscles. It is as one of the conditions of health that the question of dress becomes one of importance. "There was a time in the history of man," says Carlyle, "when man was primary and his rags secondary, but times have sadly changed, clothes now make the man." I hope we are fast coming to that period in the history of woman when in her dress, health and freedom are to be the first considerations. As women are now rapidly asserting themselves in the world of work, an entire revolution in this respect is inevitable. A physiological need, but look at the forms of all our young girls to appreciate the violence done Nature in the small waists and constrained gait and manners of all we meet. Ordinarily a girl of fourteen is a healthy, happy being in short hair, short dress, in clothes hung loosely on her shoulders. But as soon as her skirts trail and her dressmakers lace and tighten her clothes "to form the waist" as they say, a change takes place at once in her whole manner and appearance. She is moody, listless, weary, strolls when she should run, cries when she should laugh, and this at the very age when she should manifest newfound vigor and enthusiasm. Much of this may be attributed to the many unnatural restraints placed on all girls, the indoor life and sedentary habits, but more to her dress than any one cause. The tight waist prevents a free circulation of the blood and action of the heart and lungs, contracts the ribs and paralyzes a belt of the nerves and muscles at least six inches in width round that part of the body. The long dress prevents all freedom of motion. When we remember that deep breathing has much to do with deep thinking, we see the relation between scholarship and clothes. Girls by the style and material of their dress are practically debarred from outdoor exercise, and yet they need it as much as boys do, and if well trained would enjoy it equally with them. Many a pleasant moonlight walk or sunset from the mountaintop is sacrificed to a clean starched muslin dress or ruffled skirt, the greater often subordinated to the less, the girl forever to her clothes, and the modern idea of what a woman's form should be. In looking at the beautiful paintings and statuary of the old world, I have often wondered where we moderns got our idea of the female form. It is certainly not like anything in heaven above or the earth beneath or the waters under the earth, for even the mermaid is vouchsafed more breathing power than to the woman of the nineteenth century. None of the old artists have immortalized anything of the kind in marble or in canvas and those of our times turn away in disgust from the daughters of Hancock and Adams to copy the Venus and Madonna of the past for the perfection of womanly grace and beauty.

All sensible men laugh at these wasp-like waists of women themselves, affect not to like them, and declare when attacked that their clothes are perfectly loose, that they are small naturally, which is to say that God, by way of making a variety in the human species, thought first to tape the ribs of the American women. I do not like to interfere with the designs of providence, but I should like to see the experiment fairly tried for one generation of hanging all woman's clothes loosely on her shoulders to learn what hand God had in her present weakness and deformity. I do not believe that it is in harmony with God's laws that any woman should move up and down the earth with her ribs lapped.

And the fact that the mass of American women are diseased, old before they are thirty years, proves that some great law is violated.

I conjure every girl in the sound of my voice if she desires, a healthy, happy old age to attend to this question of dress at once, to have her clothes hung loosely on her shoulders and not dragging down as now her vital organs and to have her skirts above her boot tops that she may run up and down stairs with freedom, walk in all kinds of weather, and be ready for any outdoor pleasure that may offer. If a girl must always change her dress for a walk, ten to one she will give up the walk and find some other excuse for doing it. Exercise to be pleasurable and profitable must be regular, and to make it so, one must have a convenient, comfortable dress. Young girls are moved about three times a year to walk five miles to some waterfall or hilltop. From the sense of breathlessness that follows such an effort in long dress and laced boots, they infer that walking does not agree with them. When I was a girl with a short dress, round hat and a pair of light boots made precise by my father, I used to walk five miles before breakfast or ride ten miles on horseback, and to those early habits and the fact that my ribs were not lapped by tight lacing, I am indebted for a life of uninterrupted health and happiness. A man's boot is preferable to those made for women because the pressure is equal on the whole foot and the ankle has free play. Health is the normal condition for all women, weakness, disease, pain and sorrow are the results in all cases of violated law. There is nothing more absurd and untrue of all the talk we hear of the natural weaknesses and disabilities of women and so long as physicians continue to teach this theory women insist on having a feeling of guilt when their children or themselves are always out of health. They will continue to throw all their sins on a mysterious Providence.

With the scientific education of our youth of both sexes and a strict observance of the great immutable laws of life, another generation might show as marked a change in the human family as we have noted in the lower animals, which science has done so much to influence during the last century.

Remember girls you have an inalienable right to be healthy and happy, and it is your duty to secure these blessings. A sound body is to the mind what a good foundation is to a house. Napoleon once said you cannot make a soldier out of a sick man. Neither can you make a wise, kind woman out of a girl whose vital organs have been displaced with lacing and whose feet have been cramped with tight shoes. I have no hope that woman will ever remedy these things herself. I look to Fathers, Husbands, and Brothers to inaugurate some grand reform in this direction, and unless it is done speedily, the higher orders of refined, cultivated American womanhood must give place to the sturdier foreign races. If you appreciate the effect of American institutions on character as highly as I do, you would feel that this would be a great calamity, for I consider the women of this republic, in beauty, intellect, moral power, and true dignity superior to any type of womanhood that the world has ever seen and perhaps it might not be amiss in pausing to say the same of our men also. There was nothing in all Europe that pleased me more than the self-possession of Americans when moving about among the kings, queens, and nobles of the old world. The unconscious way in which Americans ignore all distinctions is a matter of surprise and astonishment to the middle class who always manifest in the presence of the nobility the most pitiful unrest and obsequiousness. Such are the results of our free institutions. We never fully appreciate the beneficent results of our republican theory, "that all men are created equal," until we see our people in contrast with the cringing masses in the old world. It is because I love my country and believe in its free institutions that I desire to see this government maintained and perpetuated as it only can be, by baptizing its women into the spirit of freedom and equality. As I look to the young girls of this nation, the grand work of the future, and as it is impossible to rouse the sick, the weak or the lazy to enthusiasm on any subject, to high purpose or noble action, I urge you one and all to study the laws of health and obey them, that you may bravely do your part in the future in maintaining the strength, virtue, honor, and dignity of this government. Remember woman's sphere is wherever her sires and sons may be summoned to duty.

Another reason why you should observe all the laws of health, is that you may be beautiful. All girls desire to be so, yet they take every means to defeat their desires. I suppose you have all read the recipes for beauty in our daily papers. Here is one I cut from a New York paper, "Beautiful Women." "If you would be beautiful, use Hagan's Magnolia Balm. It gives a pure, blooming complexion and restores youthful beauty. Its effects are gradual, so gradual you never see them. Natural, perfect, it gives the bloom of youth and imparts a fresh plump appearance to the countenance." How, pray, can an external mask make the face plump, and as to the eye, a few ideas on any subject, dear girls, will make your eyes brighter and clearer than a dozen bottles of balm. Again, the recipe says "the magnolia will make a lady of thirty look like a girl of sixteen." Now, what sensible woman of thirty with all the marks of intelligence and cultivation that well-spent years must give would desire to look like an inexperienced girl of sixteen. The papers are full of these quick remedies for wrinkles and gray hairs, old age, disease, and the fact that men can afford to advertise these nostrums everywhere shows that there must be fools enough among womankind to believe them. Pray, waste no money in cosmetics, they are worse than useless, they are positively injurious. White lead enters more or less into the compounding in all of them. Several physicians have told me of young ladies dying in our midst with paralysis from the constant use of cosmetics and hair dyes. Now I think a woman has as good a right as a man has to grow old and have freckles and tan and sunburn if she chooses. When it is only through age that one gathers wisdom and experience, why this endless struggle to seem young? I will give you a recipe, dear girls, for nothing that will prove far more serviceable in preserving your beauty than Hagan's Magnolia Balm at 75 cents a bottle. While his is only skin deep, mine will preserve your beauty of body and soul, until like the old family clock in the corner, the machinery runs down to work no more forever. For the hair, complexion, and clear, bright expression of the eye, there is nothing you can do like preserving your health by exercising regularly, breathing pure air in all your sleeping and waking hours, eating nutritious food, and bathing every day in cold water. Not three times a day as one of the Cincinnati papers reported me, that would wash all the constitution out of you. Don't imitate our financiers who water their stocks so freely as to take all the value out of them. Eat pure roast beef and vegetables, good bread and fruits; do not munch chalk, clay, cloves, india rubber, pine nuts, gum, or slate pencils-- always chewing, chewing, chewing like a cow with her cud.

Remember that beauty works from within, it cannot be put on and off like a garment, and it depends far more on the culture of the intellect, the tastes, sentiment, and affections of the soul than the color of the hair, eyes or complexion. Be kind, noble, generous, well mannered, be true to yourselves and your friends, and the soft lines of these tender graces and noble virtues will reveal themselves in the face, in a halo of glory about the head, in a personal atmosphere of goodness and greatness that none can mistake. To make your beauty lasting when old age with the wrinkles and gray hairs come, and the eyes grow dim and the ears heavy, you must cultivate those immortal powers that gradually unfold and grasp the invisible as from day to day the visible ceases to absorb the soul.

"There is a knowledge of the truth," says Plato, "that gives rest to the soul and thus saves life." But the mere capacity for this knowledge unsatisfied gives the soul not rest but restlessness. Your life work, dear girls, is not simply to eat, drink, dress, be merry, be married, be mothers, but to mold yourselves into a perfect womanhood. Choose then these conditions in life that shall best secure a full symmetrical development. We cannot be one thing and look another. There are indelible marks in every face showing the real life within. One cannot lead a narrow, mean, selfish life, and hide its traces with dye, cosmetics, paint and balm.

Regard yourselves precisely as the artist does his painting or statue, ever stretching forward to some grand ideal. Remember that your duty, every impulse, passion, feeling of your soul, every good action, high resolve, and lofty conception of the good and true, are delicately touched here and there, gradually reminders out of perfecting in yourselves a true womanhood. Oh! Do not mar the pure white canvas or marble statue with dark shadows, coarse lines, and hasty chiseling.

Idleness, frivolity, ill nature, discontent, envy, jealousy, hatred, back biting, and malice, all outburst of ill temper and impatience in low passing, leave their markers and shadows on the face that no balm can chase away, no artifice conceal. What we are is unveiled in the expression and features of the face.

In the second place, the cunning girl is to be wealthy, that is, she is to be a creator of wealth herself. I urge upon the consideration of all parents, guardians, and teachers the necessity of educating girls under their care to some profitable life work, some trade or profession. There cannot be too much said on the helpless condition in which a girl is left when thrown alone on the world without money, without friends, without skill or place in the world of work. One half the stimulus to a girl's education is lost in the fact that she has no aim or ambition in the future. Boys may be doctors, clergymen, lawyers, editors, poets, painters, presidents, congressmen, senators, anything and everything, be what they can, go where they can stand; but girls must be wives and nothing more, or if they are not wives, most people consider their lives failures. Now I want to secure the standard for old maids and teach girls two things, that marriage as a profession nine cases in ten times ends a failure because the wife is pecuniarily dependent. To be independent she must have some trade or profession beside that of the wife, mother, or housekeeper, as only in the happiest and most lasting relations are these offices honored and renumerated. Beside in the most fortunate marriages, women are not secure against want, for good husbands sometimes die bankrupt, leaving a young wife with half a dozen little children to provide for, helpless, friendless, alone, with no trade or profession by which she can gain a livelihood and worse than all with the feeling that labor is a degradation, that it is more honorable for a woman to live on the bounty of another, buy bread or sell herself for a home either in marriage or out of it, than it is to work side by side with her brother anywhere and maintain a lofty independence. A mighty multitude of women find themselves in this position in all our large cities. Over fifty thousand in New York alone earn their daily bread by the needle and below these are deeper depths, where dwell the daughters of vice and folly and want. God only knows how many over whom society draws the veil of forgetfulness or before that sad problem stands hardened or appalled. Full three fourths the girls before me will be called on some period of their lives to support themselves. Shall we prepare them for the facts of life, its real emergencies, or sacrifice them to a theory? Today, perchance, your daughters rest at ease in your palace homes clothed in purple and fine linen or living comfortably. Tomorrow, unfortunate seems as it may to all, your bonds, deeds, mortgages change hands. Your home, furniture, books, pictures, all your household goods are put up at auction to the highest bidder. Sick, sorrowful, disappointed, weary of life, the grave welcomes you to rest, but leaves your helpless wife and daughter to begin alone the hard struggle of life. Go to the departments of Washington and what do you find there, a large majority of the female clerks from the first families in the land. Go to the mercantile establishments, the garrets and cellars of our metropolis, the sinks of iniquity and vice, the busy marts of trade in your own city, and there are the daughters and sisters of Supreme Court judges, presidents, senators, congressmen, priests and bishops.

Remember, vice recruits its ranks not from the children of lust but from the gay, the fashionable, the helpless, those who know not how to work, but yet must eat. The stern question presses itself on our consideration: what can these soft white hands and listless brains do for an honorable support? Make shirts at twelve cents a piece in a New York garret? Teach school at $30 a month and pay $6 a week for board? Go out to service as a waitress or chambermaid at $12 a month and be on the jump 16 hours out of the 24? Or marry a millionaire who drives fast horses, drinks good whiskey, puffs tobacco smoke in her face, and reminds her every day that he married a pauper and expects her to act with becoming humility. "Give a man," says Alexander Hamilton, "a right over any subsistence and he has a power over my whole moral being." When a woman marries a man for a home, for silks, jewels, equippage, she not only degrades herself, but sacrifices him. The sweet incense of love never rises from such attars, and the fruit of such union is blighted ere it blooms.

Instead of this sad picture, we will suppose that your daughters, educated in freedom like your sons, looking forward to some life work or self-support, had each chosen a trade or profession. One is a skillful telegraph operator, making $15 or $20 a week. Another is a notary public or commissioner of deeds with daily fees. Another is a homeopathic physician with an income of $500 a year. Another, having gone through a thorough collegiate and theological course of study is an able Divine preaching in a charming city like San Francisco, a pleasant place like Alfred Center, on $2000 a year. One is in your post office on $3000 a year, and another is President of the United States with $25,000 a year. Are not any of these positions better than teaching a school for a mere pittance, or running a sewing machine in a New York garret with the gilded hands of vice ever beckoning her to ease and plenty in the paths that lead to infamy and death. Oh! Fathers, Husbands, Brothers, Sons, this question of women's work and wages may be nearer to your hearts tomorrow than it is tonight. By some sudden turn in the wheel of fortune, your daughters, sisters, wives may stand face to face with the stern realities of life. If in obedience to the tyrant custom you have left them unprepared for such an emergency, and faced with poverty and temptation they are drawn down the whirlpool of vice, their destruction lies at your door. Today men are ashamed to have the women of their households enter into any kind of profitable labor, because work is supposed to degrade them. This has a depressing influence on all women who are compelled to support themselves. Only when the daughters of the rich are educated to self-support will labor be honorable for all women. Every father has it in his power to educate his daughter in his own trade or profession, and it is his solemn duty to do it be he doctor, lawyer, banker, jeweler, or dentist.

The study of theology is particularly adapted to women, should her tastes draw her to that profession, as its duties are chiefly research, teaching, and sympathy and its pursuit seldom leads one into the public and disagreeable walks of life. After a thorough collegiate course and a few years reading under the care of a judicious father, a gifted and determined woman might stand unrivaled as a preacher of excellence and power. Without preparation, women of all ages have preached the best gospel of their times. It was a woman, Elizabeth Fry, who first went down into that Pandemonium of misery and horrors, Newgate, London, and by her eloquence wrought such changes in the character and surrounding of the unhappy criminals as to fill the wise men of her day with admiration and amazement. The mother of Wesley often preached in the absence of her husband, and Adam Clark says she was "an able Divine." The Methodist Church has long recognized the fact that in the outpouring of God's spirit there is no distinction of sex. At one time a great revival occurred in the church of Wesley in his absence. When he heard that the women as well as the men were all talking in the assembled congregation, he hastened home to stop such irregularities. But his mother told him to wait and watch, for said she, if these women bring sinners to repentance, they are as much called of God as you are. Seeing that Wesley was under great concern of mind on this point, a friend remarked to him one day, if a cock might rouse the slumbering conscience of a Peter, why not a woman reform a man of sin.

Many of our wealthy merchants, too, have daughters suffering for something to occupy their minds, yet their fathers have clerks to do the very things for which their daughters could be easily trained. Most girls could learn the laws of barter, to keep books in a mercantile establishment, and with practice buy and sell with as much skill as their brothers. As to the practice of medicine, the "fair sex" have already taken that by storm. There are medical colleges for girls in most of our great cities; the old established institutions are recently opened to them. Many have graduated and are in a lucrative practice of the healing art. All over the country women are already making from $2000 to $10,000 a year. Is it not better thus to use their brains and secure pecuniary independence, delegating household cares to others, than to be dependent drudges all their days--to have perchance a few hundreds left them by husbands as long as they remain their widows. There too is the legal profession and if the educating, purifying influence of women is needed anywhere, it is in our courts of justice, especially in those cases involving the interests of her own sex. In Shakespeare's "Merry Widow" we see how superior the ready wit, intuition and keen sympathy was to the lumbering logic of the Antonio by her side.

In the life of the present day, with women taking on every subject we look back with wonder that her right was ever doubted. Yet in the time of Shakespeare a woman was not allowed to tread the boards of the stage. All his fine female characters were performed by men: Ophelia, Desdimona, and Juliet. In portraying real sorrows before grave and revered judges, would she be more out of her place than acting imaginary ones on the stage? Would not the study of Blackstone and Kent's commentaries enlarge their minds and be of more practical benefit than the magazine of fashion, the last novel, or hours every day devoted to the needle. Would not daily talks in a lawyer's office, with sensible men, with bankers, merchants, farmers in practical business of life, in statute law, land titles, taxes, bond mortgages, and usury for which they might receive a fee of $25 or $50 be far more suitable than a three hours' unprofitable talk with a dandy in the nothings of fashionable life.

Do you complain of the publicity of such position? Is a lawyer's office with a dozen clients, all sober men engaged in the practical business of life, where your daughters must sit plainly and comfortably dressed, pen and book in hand, as public as a ball room where assembled hundreds may look at her as she minces about, immodestly draped now in the dance taking anybody by the hand, and now in the giddy waltz, whirling about in the arms of some licentious debaucher. Your daughter could attend to all a lawyer's business without taking the hand or whirling the breath of a client, but there is no place where she is subject to such intimate approaches as in fashionable life, and no place where one meets a more sensual type of manhood.

To turn your daughter to a good trade or profession is far better than to leave her an unhappy dependent or a fortune without the necessary knowledge to take care of it.

Every thinking man must see how entirely a woman's virtue and dignity are involved in her pecuniary independence.

Encourage your daughters, sisters, wives to enter into all honest and profitable employment, not only for their own first hand happiness, but for the safety of public morals, for thus only can you strike a blow at licentiousness and excess that shall be seen and felt throughout the land. Girls see all this more readily than their parents. I am in daily receipt of letters from them from all parts of the country expressing the strongest desire for education and profitable work, but unfortunately, these are the very girls who have no means to carry out their desires. Those who have rich parents and who could be thoroughly educated are so enervated by ease and luxury and the firm faith that hardship and trial can never come to them, that they have no motive stimulating them to effort.

But, say some, would not all this conflict with what seems to be the special destiny of girls, marriage and maternity? When women are independent and self-supporting, fewer will enter the marriage relation with the present gross conceptions of its rights and duties, for the cunning girl is to be wise as well as healthy and self-supporting. In the higher civilization now dawning upon us, the love element of pure, refined women guided and controlled by conscience, science, and religion, will find higher, purer outlets for its forces, giving us that glorious period when old maids will be honored and revered. The world has always had its Marys as well as Marthas, women who preferred to sit at the feet of wisdom, to learn science and philosophy rather than to be busy housewives; mothers of ideas, music, poetry and painting rather than of men. All honor to the Mary Carpenters, Florence Nightingales, Maria Mitchells, Harriet Hossners, Louisa Alcotts, Anna Dickensons, Susan B. Anthonys, and the long line of Grimkes, saints and philanthropists, who have directed themselves to act, religion, and reform. It is as absurd to educate all girls for wives and nothing more as it would be to educate all boys for husbands and nothing more.

Again, no girl should marry until she is at least 25 years of age, as she does not reach physical maturity before that time. Thus, many years could be devoted to reading, thought, and study, to a preparation for that higher companioned life of the spirit and intellect with pure, cultivated, scholarly men.

If husbands found this companionship in their wives in science, philosophy, and government, our whole social life would be refined and educated and marriage would be a far more happy and permanent relation than it is today. But marriage has thus far been based wholly on the mass idea, a condition of subjection for women. The Methodist Church has taken the initiative step to the higher idea. I understand by an act in their ecclesiastical councils, they have dropped the word "obey" from their marriage ceremony. All praise to the Methodist Church! When sinners have a proper self-respect, a laudable pride of sex, they will (?) all their old barbarisms of the past that point in any way to the subject condition of woman in either the state, the church, or the home. Until all others follow her example, I hope all girls will insist on being married by the Methodist ceremony and clergymen.

The Episcopal marriage service is more at loggerheads with time than any other now extant in civilized nations. It not only still clings to the word obey, but it has a most humiliating act in giving the bride away. I was never more struck with its odiousness and ludicrous features than in once seeing a tall, queenly looking woman, magnificently arrayed, married by one of the tiniest priests that ever donned a surplice, and given away by the smallest guardian that ever watched a woman's fortunes, to the feeblest, bleariest looking grown man that ever placed a wedding ring on a bridal finger. Seeing those Liliputs surround her, I thought when the little priest said "Who gives this woman to this man" that she would take the responsibility and say "I do," but no, there she stood, calm and serene like an automaton as if it were no affair of hers, while the little guardian, placing her hand in that of the little groom, said, "I do." Thus was this stately woman bandied about by them, by these three puny men all of whom she might have gathered up in her arms and born off to their respective places of abode.

But women are gradually waking up to the degradation of these ceremonies. Not long since, at a wedding, a beautiful girl of eighteen in the response was suddenly struck dumb at the response "obey." Three times the priest pronounced it, with an emphasis and holy emotion, each time slower and louder than before. Father, Mother, and Groom were in agony, the bride with downcast eyes stood speechless; at length the priest slowly closed his book and said the ceremony is at an end.

One imploring word from the groom and a faint "obey" was heard in the solemn stillness. The priest unclasped his books and the knot was tied. The congratulations, feast, and all went on as though there had been no break in the proceedings, but the lesson was remembered and many a rebel made by that short pause.

All these revered gentlemen who insist on the word "obey" in the marriage service should be impeached in the Supreme Court of the United States for a clear violation of the 13th amendment to the federal constitution which says there shall be no slavery or involuntary servitude in the United States. If we would make the home what it should be our first duty is to base it in the republican theory.

An old German proverb says that every girl is born into the world with a stone upon her head. This is just as true now as the day it was first uttered.

Your creeds, codes and conventionalisms have indeed fallen with crunching weight on the head of women in all ages, but Nature is mightier than law and custom, and in spite of the stone on her head, behold her today, close upon the heels of man in the whole world of thought--in art, science, literature, and government. Where has the world produced an orator that could draw such audiences and hold them spellbound as did our own Anna Dickenson at the tender age of seventeen. In science, we have Caroline Lammeulle and Maria Mitchell, in political economy Harriet Martineau, in art Angelica Kaufmann, Harriet Hossner, Rosa Binkeur, who refused admission into the universities of France, studied anatomy of the slaughterhouses of Paris and has given us the most wonderful paintings of animal life that the world has ever seen. In literature we have Elizabeth Barret Browning, the Shakespeare of our age, George Sand, Charlotte Bronte and Harriet Beecher Stowe, who have produced the most popular novels of our century. All these and many more have risen up in spite of the stone on their heads and walk forward as easily as did Sampson.

"The Solitude of Self," *1892*

Mr. Chairman and Gentlemen of the Committee:

We have been speaking before Committees of the Judiciary for the last twenty years, and we have gone over all the arguments in favor of the sixteenth amendment which are familiar to all you gentlemen; therefore, it will not be necessary that I should repeat them again.

The point I wish plainly to bring before you on this occasion is the individuality of each human soul-our Protestant idea, the right of individual conscience and judgment-our republican idea, individual citizenship. In discussing the right of woman, we are to consider, first, what belongs to her as an individual, in a world of her own, the arbiter of her own destiny, an imaginary Robinson Crusoe with her woman Friday on a solitary island. Her rights under such circumstances are to use all her faculties for her own safety and happiness.

Secondly, if we consider her as a citizen, as a member of a great nation, she must have the same rights as all other members, according to the fundamental principles of our government.

Thirdly, viewed as a woman, an equal factor in civilization, her rights and duties are still the same-individual happiness and development.

Fourthly, it is only the incidental relations of life, such as mother, wife, sister, daughter, which may involve some special duties and training. In the usual discussion in regard to woman's sphere, such men as Herbert Spencer, Frederic Harrison, and Grant Allen uniformly subordinate her rights and duties as an individual, as a citizen, as a woman, to the necessities of these incidental relations, some of which a large class of women may never assume. In discussing the sphere of man we do not decide his rights as an individual, as a citizen, as a man, buy his duties as a father, a husband, a brother, or a son, relations some of which he may never fill. Moreover, he would be better fitted for these very relations, and whatever special work he might choose to do to earn his bread, by the complete development of all his faculties as an individual.

Just so with woman. The education that will fit her to discharge the duties in the largest sphere of human usefulness, will best fit her for whatever special work she may be compelled to do.

The isolation of every human soul and the necessity of self-dependence must give each individual the right to choose his own surroundings.

The strongest reason for giving woman all the opportunities for higher education, for the full development of her faculties, her forces of mind and body; for giving her the most enlarged freedom of thought and action; a complete emancipation from all forms of bondage, of custom, dependence, superstition; from all the crippling influences of fear; is the solitude and personal responsibility of her own individual life. The strongest reason why we ask for woman a voice in the government under which she lives; in the religion she is asked to believe; equality in social life, where she is the chief factor; a place in the trades and professions, where she may earn her bread, is because of her birthright to self-sovereignty; because, as an individual, she must rely on herself. No matter how much women prefer to lean, to be protected and supported, nor how much men desire to have them do so, they must make the voyage of life alone, and for safety in an emergency they must know something of the laws of navigation. To guide our own craft, we must be captain, pilot, engineer; with chart and compass to stand at the wheel; to watch the wind and waves and know when to take in the sail, and to read the signs in the firmament over all. It matters not whether the solitary voyager is man or woman.

Nature having endowed them equally, leaves them to their own skill and judgment in the hour of danger, and, if not equal to the occasion, alike they perish.

To appreciate the importance of fitting every human soul for independent action, think for a moment of the immeasurable solitude of self. We come into the world alone, unlike all who have gone before us; we leave it alone under circumstances peculiar to ourselves. No mortal ever has been, no mortal ever will be like the soul just launched on the sea of life. There can never again be just such environments as make up the infancy, youth and manhood of this one. Nature never repeats herself, and the possibilities of one human soul will never be found in another. No one has ever found two blades of ribbon grass alike, and no one will ever find two human beings alike. Seeing, then, what must be the infinite diversity in human character, we can in a measure appreciate the loss to a nation when any large class of the people is uneducated and unrepresented in the government. We ask for the complete development of every individual, first, for his own benefit and happiness. In fitting out an army we give each soldier his own knapsack, arms, powder, his blanket, cup, knife, fork and spoon. We provide alike for all their individual necessities, then each man bears his own burden.

Again we ask complete individual development for the general good; for the consensus of the competent on the whole round of human interest; on all questions of national life, and here each man must bear his share of the general burden. It is sad to see how soon friendless children are left to bear their own burdens before they can analyze their feelings; before they can even tell their joys and sorrows, they are thrown on their own resources. The great lesson that nature seems to teach us at all ages is self-dependence, self-protection, self-support. What a touching instance of a child's solitude; of that hunger of heart for love and recognition, in the case of a little girl who helped to dress a Christmas tree for the children of the family in which she served. On finding there was no present for herself she slipped away in the darkness and spent the night in an open field sitting on a stone, and when found in the morning was weeping as if her heart would break. No mortal will ever know the thought that passed through the mind of the friendless child in the long hours of that cold night, with only the silent stars to keep her company. The mention of her case in the daily papers moved many generous hearts to send her presents, but in the hours of her keenest sufferings she was thrown wholly on herself for consolation.

In youth our most bitter disappointments, our brightest hopes and ambitions are known only to ourselves; even our friendship and love we never fully share with another; there is something of every passion in every situation we conceal. Even so in our triumphs and our defeats.

The successful candidate for Presidency and his opponent each have a solitude peculiarly his own, and good form forbids either to speak of his pleasure or regret. The solitude of the king on his throne and the prisoner in his cell differs in characters and degree, but it is solitude nevertheless.

We ask no sympathy from others in the anxiety and agony of a broken friendship or shattered love. When death sunders our nearest ties, alone we sit in the shadows of our affliction. Alike mid the greatest triumphs and darkest tragedies of life we walk alone. On the divine heights of human attainments, eulogized and worshipped as a hero or a saint, we stand alone. In ignorance, poverty, and vice, as a pauper or criminal, alone we starve or steal; alone we suffer the sneers and rebuffs of our fellows; alone we are hunted and hounded through dark courts and alleys, in by-ways and highways; alone we stand in the judgment seats; alone in the prison cell we lament our crimes and misfortunes; alone we expiate them on the gallows. In hours like these we realize the awful solitude of individual life, its pains, its penalties, its responsibilities; hours in which the youngest and most helpless are thrown on their own resources for guidance and consolation. Seeing then that life must ever be a march and a battle, that each soldier must be equipped for his own protection, it is the height of cruelty to rob the individual of a single natural right.

To throw obstacles in the way of a complete education, is like putting out the eyes; to deny the rights of property, like cutting off the hands. To deny political equality is to rob the ostracized of all self-respect; of credit in the market place; of recompense in the world of work; of a voice among those who make and administer the law; a choice in the jury before whom they are tried, and in the judge who decides their punishment. Shakespeare's play of Titus and Andronicus [sic] contains a terrible satire on woman's position in the nineteenth century-"Rude men" (the play tells us) seize the king's daughter, cut out her tongue, cut off her hands, and then bade her go call for water and wash her hands." What a picture of woman's position. Robbed of her natural rights, handicapped by law and custom at every turn, yet compelled to fight her own battles, and in the emergencies of life to fall back on herself for protection.

The girl of sixteen, thrown on the world to support herself, to make her own place in society, to resist the temptations that surround her and maintain a spotless integrity, must do all this by native force or superior education. She does not acquire this power by being trained to trust others and distrust herself. If she wearies of the struggle, finding it hard work to swim upstream, and allows herself to drift with the current, she will find plenty of company, but not one to share her misery in the hour of her deepest humiliation. If she tries to retrieve her position, to conceal the past, her life is hedged about with fears lest willing hands should tear the veil from what she fain would hide. Young and friendless, she knows the bitter solitude of self.

How the little courtesies of life on the surface of society, deemed so important form man towards woman, fade into utter insignificance in view of the deeper tragedies in which she must play her part alone, where no human aid is possible.

The young wife and mother, at the head of some establishment with a kind husband to shield her from the adverse winds of life, with wealth, fortune, and position, has a certain harbor of safety, secure against the ordinary ills of life. But to manage a household, have a desirable influence in society, keep her friends and the affections of her husband, train her children and servants well, she must have a rare common sense, wisdom, diplomacy, and a knowledge of human nature. To do all this she needs the cardinal virtues and the strong points of character that the most successful statesman possesses.

An uneducated woman, trained to dependence, with no resources in herself must make a failure of any position in life. But society says women do not need a knowledge of the world; the liberal training that experience in public life must give, all the advantages of collegiate education; but when for the lack of all this, the woman's happiness is wrecked, alone she bears her humiliation; and the solitude of the weak and the ignorant is indeed pitiful. In the wild chase for the prizes of life they are ground to powder.

In age, when the pleasures of youth are passed, children grown up, married and gone, the hurry and bustle of life in a measure over, when the hands are weary of active service, when the old armchair and the fireside are the chosen resorts, then men and women alike must fall back on their own resources. If they cannot find companionship in books, if they have no interest in the vital questions of the hour, no interest in watching the consummation of reforms, with which they might have been identified, they soon pass into their dotage. The more fully the faculties of the mind are developed and kept in use, the longer the period of vigor and active interest in all around us continues. If from a lifelong participation in public affairs a woman feels responsible for the laws regulating our system of education, the discipline of our jails and prisons, the sanitary conditions of our private homes, public buildings, and thoroughfares, an interest in commerce, finance, our foreign relations, in any or all of these questions, her solitude will at least be respectable, and she will not be driven to gossip or scandal for entertainment.

The chief reason for opening to every soul the doors to the whole round of human duties and pleasures is the individual development thus attained, the resources thus provided under all circumstances to mitigate the solitude that at times must come to everyone. I once asked Prince Krapotkin, the Russian nihilist, how he endured his long years in prison, deprived of books, pen, ink, and paper. "Ah," he said, "I thought out many questions on which I had a deep interest. In the pursuit of an idea I took no note of time. When tired of solving knotty problems I recited all the beautiful passages in prose or verse I had ever learned. I became acquainted with my self and my own resources. I had a world of my own, a vast empire, that no Russian jailor or Czar could invade." Such is the value of liberal thought and broad culture when shut from all human companionship, bringing comfort and sunshine within even the four walls of a prison cell.

As women ofttimes share a similar fate, should they not have all the consolation that the most liberal education can give? Their suffering in the prisons of St. Petersburg; in the long, weary marches to Siberia, and in the mines, working side by side with men, surely call for all the self-support that the most exalted sentiments of heroism can give. When suddenly roused at midnight, with the startling cry of "Fire! Fire" to find the house over their heads in flames, do women wait for men to point the way to safety? And are the men, equally bewildered and half suffocated with smoke, in a position to more than save themselves?

At such times the most timid women have shown a courage and heroism in saving their husbands and children that has surprised everybody. Inasmuch, then, as woman shares equally the joys and sorrows of time and eternity, is it not the height of presumption in man to propose to represent her at the ballot box and the throne of grace, do her voting in the state, her praying in the church, and to assume the position of priest at the family altar.

Nothing strengthens the judgment and quickens the conscience like individual responsibility. Nothing adds such dignity to character as the recognition of one's self-sovereignty; the right to an equal place, everywhere conceded; a place earned by personal merit, not an artificial attainment by inheritance, wealth, family, and position. Seeing, then that the responsibilities of life rest equally on man and woman, that their destiny is the same, they need the same preparation for time and eternity. The talk of sheltering woman from the fierce storms of life is the sheerest mockery, for they beat on her from every point of the compass, just as they do on man, and with more fatal results, for he has been trained to protect himself, to resist, to conquer. Such are the facts in human experience, the responsibilities of individual sovereignty. Rich and poor, intelligent and ignorant, wise and foolish, virtuous and vicious, man and woman, it is ever the same, each soul must depend wholly on itself.

Whatever the theories may be of woman's dependence on man, in the supreme moments of her life he can not bear her burdens. Alone she goes to the gates of death to give life to every man that is born into the world. No one can share her fears, no one can mitigate her pangs; and if her sorrow is greater than she can bear, alone she passes beyond the gates into the vast unknown.

From the mountain tops of Judea, long ago, a heavenly voice bade His disciples, "Bear ye one another's burdens," but humanity has not yet risen to that point of self-sacrifice, and if ever so willing, how few the burdens are that one soul can bear for another. In the highways of Palestine; in prayer and fasting on the solitary mountain top; in the Garden of Gethsemane; before the judgment seat of Pilate; betrayed by one of His trusted disciples at His last supper; in His agonies on the cross, even Jesus of Nazareth, in these last sad days on earth, felt the awful solitude of self. Deserted by man, in agony he cries, "My God! My God! Why hast Thou forsaken me." And so it ever must be in the conflicting scenes of life, in the long weary march, each one walks alone. We may have many friends, love, kindness, sympathy and charity to smooth our pathway in everyday life, but in the tragedies and triumphs of human experience each mortal stands alone.

But when all artificial trammels are removed, and women are recognized as individuals, responsible for their own environments, thoroughly educated for all positions in life they may be called to fill; with all the resources in themselves that liberal thought and broad culture can give; guided by their own conscience and judgment; trained to self-protection by a healthy development of the muscular system and skill in the use of weapons of defense, and stimulated to self-support by a knowledge of the business world and the pleasure that pecuniary independence must ever give; when women are trained in this way they will, in a measure, be fitted for those years of solitude that come to all, whether prepared or otherwise. As in our extremity we must depend on ourselves, the dictates of wisdom point to complete individual development.

In talking of education how shallow the argument that each class must be educated for the special work it proposes to do, and all those faculties not needed in this special walk must lie dormant and utterly wither for want of use, when perhaps, these will be the very faculties needed in life's greatest emergencies. Some say, "Where is the use of drilling girls in the languages, the sciences, in law, medicine, theology?"

As wives, mothers, housekeepers, cooks, they need a different curriculum from boys who are to fill all positions. The chief cooks in our great hotels and ocean steamers are men. In large cities men run the bakeries; they make our bread, cake and pies. They manage the laundries; they are now considered our best milliners and dressmakers. Because some men fill these departments of usefulness, shall we regulate the curriculum in Harvard and Yale to their present necessities? If not, why this talk in our best colleges of a curriculum for girls who are crowding into the trades and professions; teachers in all our public schools rapidly filling many lucrative and honorable positions in life? They are showing, too, their calmness and courage in the most trying hours of human experience.

You have probably all read in the daily papers of the terrible storm in the Bay of Biscay when a tidal wave made such havoc on the shore, wrecking vessels, unroofing houses and carrying destruction everywhere. Among other buildings the woman's prison was demolished. Those who escaped saw men struggling to reach the shore. They promptly by clasping hands made a chain of themselves and pushed out into the sea, again and again, at the risk of their lives until they had brought six men to shore, carried them to a shelter, and did all in their power for their comfort and protection.

What special school of training could have prepared these women for this sublime moment of their lives? In times like this humanity rises above all college curriculum and recognizes Nature as the greatest of all teachers in the hour of danger and death. Women are already the equals of men in the whole of realm of thought, in art, science, literature, and government. With telescopic vision they explore the starry firmament, and bring back the history of the planetary world. With chart and compass they pilot ships across the mighty deep, and with skillful finger send electric messages around the globe. In galleries of art the beauties of nature and the virtues of humanity are immortalized by them on their canvas and by their inspired touch dull blocks of marble are transformed into angles of light.

In music they speak again the language of Mendelssohn, Beethoven, Chopin, Schumann, and are worthy interpreters of their great thoughts. The poetry and novels of the century are theirs, and they have touched the keynote of reform in religion, politics, and social life. They fill the editor's and professor's chair, and plead at the bar of justice, walk the wards of the hospital, and speak from the pulpit and the platform; such is the type of womanhood that an enlightened public sentiment welcomes today, and such the triumph of the facts of life over the false theories of the past.

Is it, then, consistent to hold the developed woman of this day within the narrow political limits as the dame with the spinning wheel and knitting needle occupied in the past? No! No! Machinery has taken the labors of woman as well as man on its tireless shoulders; the loom and the spinning wheel are but dreams of the past; the pen, the brush, the easel, the chisel, have taken their places, while the hopes and ambitions of women are essentially changed.

We see reason sufficient in the outer conditions of human beings for individual liberty and development, but when we consider the self-dependence of every human soul we see the need of courage, judgment, and the exercise of every faculty of mind and body, strengthened and developed by use, in woman as well as man.

Whatever may be said of man's protecting power in ordinary conditions, mid all the terrible disasters by land and sea, in the supreme moments of danger, alone, woman must ever meet the horrors of the situation; the Angel of Death even makes no royal pathway for her. Man's love and sympathy enter only into the sunshine of our lives. In that solemn solitude of self, that links us with the immeasurable and the eternal, each soul lives alone forever. A recent writer says:

> I remember once, in crossing the Atlantic, to have gone upon the deck of the ship in midnight, when a dense black cloud

enveloped the sky, and the great dep was roaring madly under the lashes of demoniac winds. My feelings was not of danger or fear (which is a base surrender of the immortal soul), but of utter desolation and loneliness; a little speck of life shut in by a tremendous darkness. Again I remember to have climbed on the slopes of the Swiss Alps, up beyond the point where vegetation ceases, and the stunted conifers no longer struggle against the unfeeling blasts. Around me lay a huge confusion of rocks, out of which the gigantic ice peaks shot into the measureless blue of the heavens, and again my only feeling was the awful solitude.

And yet, there is a solitude, which each and every one of us has always carried with him, more inaccessible than the ice-cold mountains, more profound than the midnight sea; the solitude of self. Our inner being, which we call ourself, no eye nor touch of man or angel has ever pierced. It is more hidden than the caves of the gnome; the sacred adytum of the oracle; the hidden chamber of eleusinian mystery, for to it only omniscience is permitted to enter.

Such is individual life. Who, I ask you, can take, dare take, on himself the rights, the duties, the responsibilities of another human soul?

Notes

PART ONE

Chapter 1

1 Theodore Stanton and Harriot Stanton Blatch, eds. *Elizabeth Cady Stanton as Revealed in Her Letters, Diary, and Reminiscences,* vol. 1 (New York: Harper and Brothers, 1922), 1. Hereafter referred to as *ECS Revealed 1.*

2 Stanton and Blatch, *ECS Revealed 1:* 3. She further described her mother as strong-willed and formidable, and as one who expected that people and circumstances could be altered to meet her desires.

3 Stanton and Blatch, *ECS Revealed 1:* 4.

4 Stanton and Blatch, *ECS Revealed 1:* 6. These bells were immutable reminders of an eternal future, and this religious fascination chafed her early in life. She recalled that a nurse challenged her pensive expression as one disguising mischief. Elizabeth replied: "I was wondering why it was that everything we like to do is a sin, and that everything we dislike is commanded by God or some one on earth. I am so tired of that everlasting No! no! no!"

5 Stanton and Blatch, *ECS Revealed 1:* 6.

6 Stanton and Blatch, *ECS Revealed 1:* 22.

7 Stanton and Blatch, *ECS Revealed 1:* 25.

8 Stanton and Blatch, *ECS Revealed 1:* 20.

9 James Parton, et al., eds. *Eminent Women of the Age: Being Narratives of the Lives and Deeds of the Most Prominent Women of the Present Generation* (Hartford, Conn.:1869), 339. Hereafter referred to as *Eminent Women.*

10 Stanton and Blatch, *ECS Revealed 1:* 33.

11 Stanton and Blatch, *ECS Revealed 1:* 35.

12 Lillian O'Connor, *Pioneer Women Orators: Rhetoric in the Ante-Bellum Reform Movement* (New York: Columbia University Press, 1954), 31.

13 Stanton and Blatch, *ECS Revealed 1*: 46.

14 Stanton and Blatch, *ECS Revealed 1*: 46.

15 Stanton and Blatch, *ECS Revealed 1:* 50.

16 Elisabeth Griffith, *In Her Own Right: The Life of Elizabeth Cady Stanton* (New York: Oxford University Press, 1984), 24. Hereafter referred to as *Life of ECS*.

17 Stanton and Blatch, *ECS Revealed 1*: 56.

18 Stanton and Blatch, *ECS Revealed 1*: 59.

19 Carol Hymowitz and Michaele Weissman, *A History of Women in America*. (New York: Bantam Books, 1978), 92.

20 Stanton and Blatch, *ECS Revealed 1*: 77-78.

21 For further reading on Mott, see Otelia Cromwell, *Lucretia Mott* (Cambridge, Mass.: Harvard University Press, 1958) and Margaret Hope Bacon, *Valiant Friend: The Life of Lucretia Mott* (New York: Walker and Company, 1980).

22 Elizabeth Cady Stanton, Susan B. Anthony, and Matilda Jocelyn Gage, eds., *History of Woman Suffrage,* vol. 1. (New York: 1881), 419-421. Hereafter referred to as *HWS 1*.

23 Stanton and Blatch, *ECS Revealed 1*: 75.

24 Stanton and Blatch, *ECS Revealed 1*: 80.

25 Stanton and Blatch, *ECS Revealed 1:* 79.

26 Charles Stewart, Craig Smith, and Robert E. Denton, Jr., *Persuasion and Social Movements* (Prospect Heights, Ill.: Waveland Press, 1984), 39. Hereafter referred to as *Persuasion*.

27 Lloyd F. Bitzer, "Functional Communication : A Situational Perspective," in *Rhetoric in Transition: Studies in the Nature and Uses of Rhetoric*, ed. Eugene E. White (University Park: Pennsylvania State University Press, 1980), 26.

28 Stanton and Blatch, *ECS Revealed 1*: 110.

29 Stanton and Blatch, *ECS Revealed 1*: 117.

30 Stanton and Blatch, *ECS Revealed 1*: 134.

31 Stanton and Blatch, *ECS Revealed 1*: 136.

32 Stanton and Blatch, *ECS Revealed 1*: 144.

33 Stanton and Blatch, *ECS Revealed 1*: 145.

34 Leland M. Griffin, "The Rhetoric of Historical Movements," *Quarterly Journal of Speech* 38 (April 1952): 186.

35 Lloyd Bitzer, "The Rhetorical Situation," *Philosophy and Rhetoric* 1 (1968): 5.

36 *Woman's Rights Conventions: Seneca Falls & Rochester, 1848.* (New York: Arno Press, 1969), 6. Hereafter referred to as *Woman's Rights Conventions.*

37 *Woman's Rights Conventions,* 6.

38 *Woman's Rights Conventions,* 7.

39 *Woman's Rights Conventions,* 4.

40 Alma Lutz, *Created Equal: A Biography of Elizabeth Cady Stanton 1815-1902* (New York: Octagon Books, 1974), 46. Hereafter referred to as *Created Equal.*

41 Stanton and Blatch, *ECS Revealed 1:* 146.

42 Eleanor Flexner, *Century of Struggle: The Woman's Rights Movement in the United States* (Cambridge, Mass.: Belknap Press, 1959), 77. Hereafter referred to as *Century of Struggle.*

43 Stanton and Blatch, *ECS Revealed 1:* 148.

44 Miriam Gurko, *The Ladies of Seneca Falls: The Birth of the Woman's Rights Movement* (New York: Macmillan, 1974), 103.

45 *HWS 1:* 810.

46 Stanton and Blatch, *ECS Revealed 1:* 150.

47 Stewart, et al., *Persuasion,* 39.

48 Lutz, *Created Equal,* 57.

49 For biographical discussion on Anthony, see Katharine Anthony, *Susan B. Anthony: Her Personal History and Her Era* (Garden City, N. Y.: Doubleday, 1954); Ida Usted Harper, *The Life and Work of Susan B. Anthony, 3 vols.* (Indianapolis, In.: Hollenbect Press,1898); or Alma Lutz, *Susan B. Anthony: Rebel, Crusader, Humanitarian* (Boston, Mass.: Houghton Mifflin Company, 1959). For particular insight into the Cady-Stanton and Anthony partnership see Ellen DuBois, ed., *Elizabeth Cady Stanton/Susan B. Anthony: Correspondence, Writings, Speeches* (New York: Schocken Books, 1981).

50 Stewart, et al., *Persuasion,* 40.

51 Stanton and Blatch, *ECS Revealed 1:* 153.

52 Stanton and Blatch, *ECS Revealed 1:* 154.

53 Parton, *Eminent Women,* 361.

54 Stanton and Blatch, *ECS Revealed 2:* 43.

55 Stewart, et al., *Persuasion,* 41.

56 For further information on the location of these speeches, see the Bibliography.

57 Stewart, et al., *Persuasion,* 42.

58 Further discussion on the impact on the women's movement by the amendment may be found in James E. Goodman, "The Origins of the 'Civil War' in the Reform Community: Elizabeth Cady Stanton on Woman's Rights and Reconstruction," *Critical Matrix: Princeton*

Working Papers in Women's Studies 1. 2 (1985): 1-29, and James M. McPherson, "Abolitionists, Woman Suffrage, and the Negro, 1865-1869," *Mid-America* 47 (January 1965): 40-46.

59 Griffith, *Life of ECS*, 128.

60 Further discussion on the impact of *The Revolution* can be found in Lynne Masel-Walters, "Their Rights and Nothing More: A History of *The Revolution*, 1868-1870," *Journalism Quarterly* (Summer 1976): 242-251.

61 *The Revolution*, 19 January 1868, 49.

62 Stanton and Blatch, *ECS Revealed 1*: 123-124.

63 For further discussion of the split, see Robert S. Riegel, "The Split of the Feminist Movement in 1869," *Mississippi Valley Historical Review* 49 (December 1962): 484-496.

64 Alma Lutz papers, Schlesinger Library of Radcliffe College.

65 Stewart, et al., *Persuasion*, 43.

66 Stewart, et al., *Persuasion*, 43.

67 Griffith, *Life of ECS*, 188.

68 For another rhetorical perspective on this speech, see Karlyn K. Campbell, "Stanton's 'The Solitude of Self': A Rationale for Feminism," *Quarterly Journal of Speech* 66 (1980): 304-312.

69 Stewart, et al., *Persuasion*, 44.

70 Stanton and Blatch, *ECS Revealed 1*: 346.

71 Griffin, *Life of ECS*, 207.

72 Many of these published and unpublished articles and addresses are available in the Elizabeth Cady Stanton papers. See the Bibliography for details.

73 Elizabeth Cady Stanton and The Revising Committee, *The Woman's Bible*, vol. 1 (New York: 1895), iv.

Chapter 2

1 I Cor. 14: 34-35.

2 Pastoral Letter of the General Association of Massachusetts (Orthodox) to the Churches under Their Care, 1837; repr. in Elizabeth Cady Stanton, et al., *HWS 1*: 81.

3 Barbara Sinclair Deckard, *The Women's Movement: Political, Socio-economic, and Psychological Issues,* 2nd ed. (New York: Harper and Row, 1979), 226.

4 Alexis de Tocqueville, *Democracy in America,* vol. 3 part 1. trans. Henry Reeve (Boston, 1873): 37.

5 For further insight into the role dichotomies faced by women, see Barbara Welter, "The Cult of True Womanhood: 1820-1860," *American Quarterly*, 18 (Summer 1966): 151-174.

6 For a discussion of female anti-slavery speakers, see Ernest G. Bormann, *Forerunners of Black Power: The Rhetoric of Abolition* (Englewood Cliffs, N.J.: Prentice-Hall, Inc., 1971), chap. 4.

Chapter 3

1 *Woman's Rights Conventions*, 4.

2 The following is a list of addresses on suffrage in the Elizabeth Cady Stanton papers. Container 4: "Speech to Electors of the Eighth Congressional District" (October 10, 1866); "Speech at Judiciary Committee Hearing, New York Senate" (May 1867); "Address on the Rights of Women to Vote for Delegates to the Constitutional Convention" (1867); two untitled speeches from the Kansas suffrage campaign (1867); "Address before the First Convention of the National Woman Suffrage Association" (June 19-20, 1869). Container 6: "Self-Government" (1874); "Speech at the Third Decade Meeting of Women's Rights Conventions" (July 19-20, 1878); "Statement at the U. S. Senate Hearing before the Committee on Woman Suffrage" (April 2, 1888); Statement to the U. S. Senate Special Committee on Woman Suffrage (February 8, 1890). Container 7: "The Degradation of Disfranchisement" (1891); "Suffrage: A National Right" (n. d.); "Is the Bible Opposed to Woman Suffrage?" (May 20, 1883). In addition, the first four volumes of the *History of Woman Suffrage* contain whole texts and excerpts from Cady Stanton's convention and legislative addresses. Other suffrage speech texts or remarks include "Remarks at the Eleventh National Convention" (May 10, 1866; *HWS 2*: 153-54); "Remarks at the New York State Constitutional Convention" (January 23, 1867; *HWS 2*: 271-82); "Remarks at the National Woman's Suffrage Convention" (January 19, 1869; *HWS 2*: 349-55); "Presidential Welcome to the International Council of Women" (March 25, 1888; *HWS 4:* 133-34); "Presidential Welcome at the First National American Woman Suffrage Association Convention" (February 18, 1890; *HWS 4:* 164-66.

3 *HWS 1*: 595-605.

4 *HWS 1*: 679-85.

5 Stanton and Blatch, *ECS Revealed 2*: 54.

6 Stanton and Blatch, *ECS Revealed 2*: 44-45.

7 Cady Stanton remembered presenting the speech to her father quite clearly. She noted in her diary: "On no occasion, before or since, was I ever more embarrassed--an audience of one, and that the one of all others whose approbation I most desired, whose disapproval I

most feared" (Stanton and Blatch, *ECS Revealed 1*: 160). She persevered, detailing the legal disabilities of woman; the speech was carefully documented and eloquently delivered. She said of it: "I threw all the pathos I could into my voice and language at this point, and, to my intense satisfaction, I saw tears filling my father's eyes . . . when I had finished, I saw that he was thoroughly magnetized. He was evidently deeply pondering over all he had heard, and did not speak for a long time. I believed I had opened to him a new world of thought. (Stanton and Blatch, *ECS Revealed 1*: 161).

[8] *HWS 1*: 595.

[9] There is some historical confusion about the exact date of the speech; the *History of Woman Suffrage*, from which this copy was transcribed, gives the date as February 18; however, both Lutz (*Created Equal*) and Griffith (*Life of ECS*) cite the date as March 19.

[10] *HWS 1*: 686.

Chapter 4

[1] The Elizabeth Cady Stanton papers contain the following manuscripts. In Container 4: "Education" (1850s); "Anti-Slavery" (1860); "Free Speech" (February 4, 1861); "Address on Divorce" (February 8, 1861); "Slavery" (1861). In Container 5: "Speech on Marriage and Divorce" (1869); "Address on the Divorce Bill" (February 8, 1881). In Container 7: "Are Homogeneous Divorce Laws in All the States Desirable?" (February 24, 1902); and sermons, including "The Ultimate Religion" (September 1893); "Woman's Position in the Christian Church" (September 1882); "Is the Bible Opposed to Woman Suffrage?" (May 20, 1883); "Genesis" (n. d. and incomplete). The various volumes of *History of Woman Suffrage* also include texts and excerpts of some speeches, including an excerpt from Cady Stanton's presidential address to the New York State Temperance Convention (April 20, 1852. *HWS 1:* 481-82). A lengthy excerpt from her address at the Decade Meeting on Marriage and Divorce (October 20, 1870) is available in Paulina W. Davis, *A History of the National Women's Rights Movement for Twenty Years.* (New York, 1871), 60-83.

[2] Part II contains an excerpt from "The Limitations of Sex" as it appears in full in *HWS 4:* 57-58.

[3] *HWS 4:* 460-61.

[4] *HWS 1*: 716-17.

[5] *HWS 1*: 718.

[6] *HWS 1:* 721.

7 This speech was transcribed from the manuscript in Container 5 of the Elizabeth Cady Stanton papers. While the speech may appear to be unfinished, this is the complete version, according to notes in the file.

8 The note attached to the manuscript says: "from 1868-1880, Elizabeth Cady Stanton was increasingly occupied in the Lyceum; she usually engaged in this work 8-9 months per year. A lecture to meet one such occasion was written on the wing on the back of a former lecture often on odd sheets of paper from a small hotel. The date on the following lecture was 1872." Elizabeth Cady Stanton Papers, Container 5.

Chapter 5

1 There are many examples of Cady Stanton's vision of the true nature and position of womanhood. Among addresses available in the Elizabeth Cady Stanton papers are the following: in Container 4, "Woman" (1856); "What Can Woman Do for the War?" (1861); in container 6, "Home Life" (August 1878); "The Pleasures of Age" (November 12, 1885); in container 7, "Woman in the Bible" (n. d.); "Woman's Position in the Christian Church" (September 1893).

2 A typical lyceum tour would find Cady Stanton in more than two dozen cities and small towns during a six-week period. She crossed the Mississippi several times each season, traveling by day or through the night to speak in the evening. Travel was often undependable because of missed trains, poor weather, and the like. According to Elisabeth Griffith, "Our Girls" was so popular that Cady Stanton's daughter claimed she earned $30,000 from that speech alone. Griffith, *Life of ECS*, 165.

3 An interesting side note is that Cady Stanton's campaign against quack medicine and false cures was perhaps one of the causes of *The Revolution's* financial woes: she refused to allow patent medicine ads in the paper (Griffith, *Life of ECS*, 133). Cady Stanton herself recalled one confrontation with a "bread powder advertiser" whose ad had been published without her permission. She wrote an editorial condemning it in *The Revolution's* next issue. The advertiser, who then withdrew his ad, said, "I prophesy a short life for this paper; the business world is based on quackery, and you cannot live without it." Cady Stanton replied, "I fear you are right." Elizabeth Cady Stanton, *Eighty Years and More: Reminiscences 1815-1897* (1898 repr. New York: Schocken Books, 1971), 257-58.

4 Lutz, *Created Equal*, 290.

5 For an analysis of these speeches, see chapter 3. These addresses focused upon detailed descriptions of the legal and political disabilities suffered by women.

6 Karlyn Kohrs Campbell, "Stanton's 'The Solitude of Self': A Rationale for Feminism," *Quarterly Journal of Speech* 66 (1980): 304.

Conclusion

1 Judith Nies, *Seven Women: Portraits from the American Radical Tradition.* (New York: Viking Press, 1977), 67.

PART II

Address to the New York Legislature, 1854

1 Here, Cady Stanton referred to the Constitution of New York, Article 2, Section 2.

2 Cady Stanton read a short poem from Petruchio, herein omitted.

3 Cady Stanton read a passage from Howard's Practice Reports, 105, detailing the rights of husbands over wives' possessions. *HWS 1*: 600.

4 Cady Stanton presented a passage from the section 1, page 150 of the Second Revised Statutes of New York, herein omitted. *HWS 1*: 602.

"The Limitations of Sex," 1885

1 These excerpts from Elizabeth Cady Stanton's presidential remarks at the Seventeenth National Suffrage Convention of 1885 were apparently taken from her principle address of the evening, "The Limitations of Sex." This is the only record of that speech. *HWS 4*: 57-58.

Speech on Marriage and Divorce, 1869

1 Neither the date nor the first location of this address's presentation are noted in the Cady Stanton papers. It is likely that this was one of her lyceum addresses. ECS papers, Container 5.

2 Because this speech was transcribed from Cady Stanton's handwritten manuscripts, there are occasional places where words or phrases were unclear. I have noted such illegible areas with (?).

"Co-Education," 1872

[1] Neither the full date nor the first location of this address's presentation are noted in the Cady Stanton papers. It is likely that this was one of her lyceum addresses. ECS papers, Container 5.

[2] Because this speech was transcribed from Cady Stanton's handwritten manuscripts, there are occasional places where words or phrases were unclear. I have noted such illegible areas with (?).

[3] Cady Stanton presented a lengthy quotation from T. W. Hugson, herein omitted.

[4] Cady Stanton presented a lengthy quotation from President Pierce, herein omitted.

[5] Cady Stanton presented lengthy quotations from Principal Sheldon, President White of Cornell, President Fairchild of Oberlin, and Dr. Winchell of Michigan State University, herein omitted.

[6] Cady Stanton presented lengthy quotations from Oberlin's President Fairchild and President Raymond of Vassar, herein omitted.

[7] Cady Stanton presented lengthy quotations from Oberlin's President
Fairchild and President White of Cornell, herein omitted.

"Our Girls," 1872

[1] Neither the full date nor the first location of this address's presentation are noted in the Cady Stanton papers. This was reportedly the most popular of her lyceum addresses. ECS papers, Container 5.

[2] Because this speech was transcribed from Cady Stanton's handwritten manuscripts, there are occasional places where words or phrases were unclear. I have noted such illegible areas with (?).

Chronology of Speeches

Declaration of Women's Rights and Sentiments at the First Women's
    Rights Convention, Seneca Falls, New York, July 19-20, 1848.
Education, 1850's.
Presidential Address, Women's State Temperance Association
    Convention, Corinthian Hall, Albany, New York, April 20, 1852.
Presidential Address, New York State Woman's Rights Convention,
    Association Hall, Albany, New York, February 14, 1854.
Address Before the New York Legislature Joint Judiciary Committees,
    Senate Chambers, Albany, New York, February 20, 1854.
Woman, 1856.
Address on Married Women's Property Rights (also known as A
    Slave's Appeal), Judiciary Committee of New York Senate,
    Albany, New York, March 19, 1860.
Suffrage Address, American Anti-Slavery Society, New York, New
    York, May 8, 1860.
Address on Marriage and Divorce, Tenth National Women's Rights
    Convention, Cooper Institute, New York, May 10, 1860.
Slavery, 1861.
What Can Woman Do for the War? 1861.
Free Speech, February 4, 1861.
Address on Divorce Before the New York Legislature Judiciary
    Committee, Albany, New York, February 8, 1861.
Address to Congress, Eleventh National Woman's Rights Convention,
    Washington, D.C., May 10, 1866.
Speech to the Electors of Eighth Congressional District, New York, New
    York, October 10, 1866.
Address in Assembly Chamber of the New York Senate Judiciary
    Committee, Albany, New York, January 23, 1867.
Speech at Judiciary Committee Hearing, New York Senate, Albany,
    New York, May 1867.

Address on the Right of Women to Vote for Delegates to the
    Constitutional Convention, Suffrage Subcommittee of the New
    York Constitutional Convention, Albany, New York, June 27,
    1867.
Untitled Addresses (two) from Kansas Suffrage Campaign, 1867.
Address before the First Convention of the National Woman Suffrage
    Association, Washington, D.C., January 19, 1869.
Lyceum Bureau tours. Speech titles include Our Young Girls, Our Boys,
    Co-Education, Marriage and Divorce, The True Republic,
    Marriage and Maternity, Prison Life, Thurlow Weed, William
    Seward, and Horace Greeley, Famous Women in the Bible, and
    The Bible and Women's Rights, 1869-1881.
Speech in Favor of Woman Suffrage in the District of Columbia,
    United States Senate Judiciary Committee, Washington, D.C.,
    January 12, 1870.
Speech to the United States Senate Judiciary Committee, Washington,
    D.C., January 10, 1872.
Self-Government, 1874.
Home Life, August 1878.
National Protections for National Citizens, United States Senate
    Committee on Privileges and Elections, Washington, D.C.,
    January 11, 1878.
Speech at the Third Decade Meeting of Women's Rights Conventions,
    Washington, D.C., July 19-20, 1878.
Address on the Divorce Bill, February 8, 1881.
Is the Bible Opposed to Woman Suffrage? May 20, 1883.
Address, United States Senate Committee on Woman Suffrage,
    Washington, D.C., March 7, 1884.
The Limitations of Sex, National Woman Suffrage Association,
    Washington, D.C., January 20, 1885.
The Pleasures of Old Age, New York, New York , November 1885.
Address of Welcome to International Council of Women, Washington,
    D.C., March 25, 1887.
Address to the United States Senate Committee on Woman Suffrage,
    Washington, D.C., April 2, 1887.
Statement at the U.S. Senate Hearing before the Committee on
    Woman Suffrage, Washington D.C., April 2, 1888.
Address to the United States Senate Committee on Woman Suffrage,
    Washington, D.C., February 8, 1890.
The Friendship of Women, Washington, D.C., February 15, 1890.
Presidential Opening Address, National American Woman Suffrage
    Association, Washington, D.C., February 18,1890.
The Degradation of Disfranchisement, National American Woman
    Suffrage Association Convention, Washington, D.C., January
    1891.
The Matriarchate, National Council of Women, February 1891.

The Solitude of Self, Judiciary Committee of United States House of
    Representatives, Washington, D.C., January 18, 1892. Also
    delivered January 18 to National American Woman Suffrage
    Association and on January 20 to Senate Committee on Woman
    Suffrage.
Woman's Position in the Christian Church, September 1893.
The Ultimate Religion, September 1893.
Are Homogeneous Divorce Laws in All the States Desirable? February
    24, 1902.

Bibliography

Successful research into Cady Stanton's varied feminist activities requires a patient disposition, determined optimism, and (in many cases) the reconstruction skills of an archaeologist. Impairing the researcher is the clouded state of the primary sources, which includes a diary, an autobiography, the *History of Woman Suffrage,* letters, *The Woman's Bible,* newspaper columns, and unpublished manuscripts of essays, letters, and speeches. Also available are correspondence of family and friends, newspaper reports, and the archives of the National and National American Woman Suffrage Associations. However, while it might appear that there is a wealth of material available, its functional accessibility is limited by many factors.

Elizabeth Cady Stanton was an unorganized and haphazard keeper of her own records. In a letter dated October 1, 1896, she confessed:

> Since I got back to town, my chief occupation has been looking over my papers, destroying many, and putting the rest in order. As from day to day I have worked alone at the monotonous task, I have felt that perhaps this is the last time I shall ever handle them, and that I should make the work of destruction easier for my children. How we dislike to burn what we once deemed valuable, and yet what a nuisance to those who come after us are bushels of old papers. Well, I have thinned mine out and may try it again should I remain on this planet half a dozen years longer. (*ECS Revealed*, 321)

In addition, research into unpublished speech manuscripts and drafts, assorted essays and letters, and other written material available on microfilm such as the Elizabeth Cady Stanton papers in the Library of Congress, is made challenging due to Cady Stanton's often illegible handwriting. Many of the entries were left unfinished and others are undated. The microfilm, which consists of over 1,000 catalogued items available at the Library of Congress (Shelf Accession Number MSS 17,781), does include an index to the materials, which aids in its use.

Elizabeth Cady Stanton was not alone in the responsibility for clouding her record. After Cady Stanton's 1902 death, two of her children, Harriot Stanton Blatch and Theodore Stanton, began collecting her papers for publication. *Elizabeth Cady Stanton as Revealed in Her Letters, Diary, and Reminiscences* is an edited, altered biography, as Blatch and Stanton refashioned some of the primary sources, destroyed Cady Stanton's diary, rewrote some of the letters, and then eliminated many of the primary documents. While they might have considered their motives to be pure (a familial desire to illuminate the record of their mother's life), the damage they did to primary documents makes many of the documents suspect.

The remaining primary sources are scattered throughout several research library collections. The broadest and most valuable research collections may be found at the Library of Congress, Douglass College, and Vassar College. Letters exist in various forms in different places, for after the originals had been located, the Blatch and Stanton both typed copies with carbons; unfortunately, they also deleted and altered many of the letters. Harriot Blatch's originals and copies were divided into scrapbooks and then donated to the Library of Congress and Vassar College. Theodore Stanton's copies were left to Rutgers University and later deposited at Douglass College. According to Griffith, family members say that after copies were made, Mrs. Blatch burned the remnants. (*Life of ECS,* xvi) Another collection of letters were made available to Alma Lutz, who was writing a biography of Cady Stanton in 1939. Thus, Lutz's biographies of Cady Stanton and Blatch quote letters that are unavailable elsewhere.

Cady Stanton's children also altered their mother's autobiography, *Eighty Years and More*, by deleting whole sections of the original and adding pages. In painting a sanitized version of their mother's life, they deleted any reference to marital friction, domestic discord, or political conflict (Griffith, *Life of ECS*, xvii). Even without her children's interference, Cady Stanton's autobiography should be viewed with skepticism, for in it she represented herself as an ardent, steadfast, and scrupulous heroine with few serious deficiencies; she also rarely mentioned her mother, husband, or any scandals, in addition to furnishing incorrect dates and incidents. All of these factors muddle the historical accuracy of the record.

The public life of Elizabeth Cady Stanton offers the researcher a broader, more accurate, and more illuminating picture. The first four volumes of the *History of Woman Suffrage* present the reader with a record of her suffrage work as well as reprints of whole and excerpted speeches. Since the *HWS* was edited by so many people and was essentially a collaborative scrapbook of events, it contains data about meetings, speech texts, clippings, essays by participants, portraits, and other miscellaneous writings. It is not a complete record of the suffrage movement, nor indeed a chronicle of feminists and their contributions to the issues they addressed. For instance, Lucy Stone refused to honor Cady Stanton's request for materials, so the record of her speeches and contributions is very limited in the *HWS*. In addition, because it has no thorough index, the order is often confusing.

Researchers will also find these related manuscript collections:

Susan B. Anthony Papers, Library of Congress.

Susan B. Anthony, Matilda Joslyn Gage, Blackwell Family, Woman's Rights, and Alma Lutz Papers, Schlesinger Library of Radcliffe College.

Susan B. Anthony, Garrison Family, Woman's Rights Papers, Sophia Smith Collection of Smith College.

Susan B. Anthony Papers, University of Rochester.

Elizabeth Smith Miller and Susan B. Anthony Papers, New York Public Library.

National American Woman Suffrage Association Papers, Library of Congress.

Gerrit Smith Papers, University of Syracuse.

Elizabeth Cady Stanton Papers, Library of Congress.

Elizabeth Cady Stanton Commonplace book, Boston Public Library.

Elizabeth Cady Stanton and Alma Lutz Papers, Vassar College.

Theodore Stanton Collection of Elizabeth Cady Stanton Papers, Douglass College of Rutgers University.

Stanton clippings at Seneca Falls New York Historical Society.

Periodicals, journals, and newspaper collections (available in microfilm) that contain Cady Stanton's writings include:

The Lily, 1849-1858.

The Una, 1853-1855.

The Revolution, 1868-1872.

The National Citizen and Ballot Box, 1876-1881.

ANNOTATED BIBLIOGRAPHY

Primary Sources

DuBois, Ellen, ed. *Elizabeth Cady Stanton/Susan B. Anthony: Correspondence, Writings, Speeches*. New York: Schocken Books, 1981.
DuBois has selected documents that reveal the dimensions of the relationship between Cady Stanton and Anthony, whose advocacy partnership lasted for over fifty years. In addition, the selections aptly demonstrate the impact each advocate had on the women's movement during its initial growth period and maintenance phase. The critical commentary DuBois provides is insightful, vivid, and interesting, illuminating the historical, social, and political context for the reader. DuBois's interpretations of events and circumstances highlight the chronology of the movement; but more important, her lively, intelligent style provides an important character study. Her carefully selected examples enable the reader to peruse rhetorical artifacts that shed light on the personality and character of two leading feminists.

Elizabeth Cady Stanton papers, Library of Congress. MSS 17,781.
The greater part of the Elizabeth Cady Stanton papers collection in the Library of Congress was acquired through donations from Susan B. Anthony in 1903 and Harriot Stanton Blatch in 1927-1928. There are approximately 1,000 items catalogued and stored. Most of the material concentrates on Cady Stanton's life from 1840-1902. The material is also available on five microfilm reels. Included in the collection are handwritten drafts of speeches, books, and articles; copies of printed materials such as newspaper editorials, essays, and letters; and miscellaneous printed matter such as certificates, scrapbooks, other people's speeches; and correspondence. Cady Stanton's correspondence collection contains letters to and from such diverse people as Susan B. Anthony, Daniel Cady, William H. Channing, Lydia Marie Child, Frances Power Cobbe, Paulina Wright Davis, Fredrick Douglass, William Lloyd Garrison, Thomas W. Higginson, Julia Ward Howe, Lucretia Mott, Emiline Pankhurst, Wendell Phillips, Elizabeth Pike, John Sargent, Elizabeth D. Smith, Gerrit Smith, Henry B. Stanton, Lucy Stone, Edith Roosevelt, John Swinton, Theodore Tilton, Thurlow Weed, and John Greenleaf Whittier.
The containers of documents (and corresponding microfilm reels) contain the following materials:

Container   Reel   Contents

1   1   General Correspondence, 1814-1928, and undated
                  material.

2 - 8   1 - 2 Speeches and Writings, 1848-1902 and
                  undated material: drafts of books, articles and
                  speeches, published letters, miscellaneous.

8 - 10   3 - 5 Miscellaneous material, 1840-1946, and undated
                  material: biographical data, certificates, printed
                  matter, other people's speeches, scrapbooks,
                  miscellaneous.

The following is a detailed list of the contents of the collection.
   Container   1: Register of the five microfilm reels and ten
containers;   general   correspondence   1814-1928   and   undated;
handwritten draft of *Reminiscences*, chapters 7-10.
   Container 2: Handwritten draft of *Reminiscences* chapters 11-
12, 16-17, 19, 21-22, 26, 30-32, 34-36, 41-44, 47-48, 50-51, 56-57,
60-64, 66, 68, 70; handwritten draft of a chapter entitled "Marriage
and Divorce"; miscellaneous other pieces.
   Container 3: Handwritten draft of *The Woman's Bible*, chapters
on Genesis, Exodus, Numbers, and Matthew. Articles include "The
Man Marriage" (*The Revolution*, 8 April 1869); "Religion for Women
and Children" (*The Index*, 11 March 1886); "The Bycicle (sic) Era"
(*The Index*, undated 1890's); "Wyoming" (*The Index*, 4 July 1890);
"What Woman Suffrage Means" (*Woman's Tribune*, 30 August 1890);
"Shall the World's Fair Be Open on Sunday?" (*National Bulletin*,
February 1893); "An Appeal to Women of New York (*National
Bulletin*, January 1894); "Women Do not Wish To Vote: (*National
Bulletin*, April 1894); "Educated Suffrage" (*The Independent*, 14
February 1895); "The Woman's Bible" (1895); "Great Men's Wives"
(*Omaha Republican*, 1899); "Are Homogeneous Divorce Laws
Desirable" (*National American*, 1898); "Self-Government" (June 24,
1902); "Home Life a Century Ago" (*Philadelphia Sunday Press*, 8
December 1901); "Honored Place for the Bible" (*New York American
and Journal*, 5 October 1902); "How Shall We Solve the Divorce
Problem" (*New York American and Journal*, 13 October 1902); "Home
Patriotism (n.d.); "Jails and Jubilees" (*The Open Court*, n.d.); "Shall
Women Ride the Bicycle" (n.d.); "What Should Be Our Attitude
Towards Political Parties." (*The Women's Tribune*, n.d.); "The Worship
of God in Man" (*The Open Court*, n.d.); "The Women's Bible" (n.d.);
miscellaneous articles.
   Container 4: assorted speeches, including: untitled speech 1848
(?); "Education" (1850s); "Woman" (1856); "Anti-Slavery" (1860);

"Free Speech" (February 4-5, 1861); "Address on Divorce" (February 8, 1861); untitled speech (1861); "Slavery" (1861); "What Can Woman Do for the War?" (1861); "The Future of the Republic (1860s); "Speech to the Woman's Loyal League" (1863); untitled speech on religion (1863); untitled speech (1865-1869?); Speech to Electors of Eighth Congressional District (October 10, 1866); speech at Judiciary Committee Hearing, New York Senate (May 1867); "Address on the Right of Women to Vote for Delegates to the Constitutional Convention" (1867); two speeches from Kansas Suffrage Campaign (1867); labor speech (1868); "Address before the First Convention of the National Woman Suffrage Association" (June 19-20,1869).

Container 5: "Speech on Marriage and Divorce" (1869); speech on the McFarland Trial (1870); "The True Republic" (June 1870); speech to the Young Men's Suffrage Association (1870); extract from speech (1870s); Speech to the Judiciary Committee (January 12,1872); "Co-Education" (1872); "Our Young Girls" (n.d., assumed 1872); "Presidents and Parties" (n.d.).

Container 6: "Self-Government" (1874); "Our Boys" (1876); "Prison Life" (1876); "The Subjection of Woman" (1876); "National Protection for National Citizens" (1878); speech at the Third Decade Meeting of Women's Rights Conventions (July 19-20, 1878); "Home Life" (August 1878); "Address on the Divorce Bill" (February 8, 1881); "The Pleasures of Age" (November 12, 1885); "Taxation" (1880); untitled speech (June 25, 1883); untitled speech at the opening of the NWSA convention (1884); "Welcome at the International Conference of Women" (1888); statement at the U. S. Senate Hearing before the Committee on Woman Suffrage (April 2, 1888); address to the NWSA (January 21, 1889); statement to the U. S. Senate Special Committee on Woman Suffrage (February 8, 1890).

Container 7: "Change is the Law of Progress" (February 23, 1890); speech at the NAWSA Convention (December 4, 1890); "The Degradation of Disfranchisement" (1891); "The Solitude of Self" (1892); speech at the First Foremothers Celebration (December 1892); "Christmas on the Mayflower" (December 22, 1893); "New York Constitutional Convention of 1867"; untitled speech on her eightieth birthday (November 12, 1895); "Woman Suffrage" (February 13, 1900); "Are Homogeneous Divorce Laws in all the States Desirable?" (February 24, 1902); "Fear" (n.d. but assumed 1840s); "Reconstruction"(n.d.); "Suffrage: A National Right" (n.d.); "Woman in the Bible" (n.d.); miscellaneous undated speech notes; "The Antagonism of Sex" (May 16, 1893); "Emma Willard, Pioneer in the Higher Education of Women" (July 19, 1893). Sermons: "The Ultimate Religion" (September 1893); "Woman's Position in the Christian Church" (September 1882); "Is the Bible Opposed to Woman Suffrage?" (May 20, 1883); "Genesis" (n.d., unfinished).

Container 8: other written material, including: an account of Cady Stanton's attempts to vote (1880); "An Interpolation" (n.d.); "Annie Besant" (n.d.), Pamphlet entitled "Bible and Church Degrade Women"; "Clerical Assumptions" (n.d.); drafts of Resolutions for Suffrage Convention of 1875, "My Creed"; published letters; suggestions for the NWSA in Spring 1872; untitled essay (1876); address by Caroline Severance at Cady Stanton's memorial service (Los Angeles, November 15, 1902); address by Moncure D. Conway at Cady Stanton's funeral service (New York 1902); biographical data, certificates, clippings, memorials, and tributes; 1922 reviews of Blatch and Stanton's *Elizabeth Cady Stanton as Revealed*; Hearing for the NAWSA by the US House of Representatives Judiciary Committee (January 28, 1896); Daniel Cady's legal papers (1840 and 1854); *The Lily* (May 1852).

Container 9: miscellaneous materials; a report on the National Womens Party 1923 Celebration of the 1848 Seneca Falls Convention; a protest by the NWSA Officers (September 17, 1887); Elizabeth Cady Stanton's 1848 scrapbook on the first Women's Rights Convention; Susan B. Anthony's scrapbook no. 1.

Container 10: Susan B. Anthony's scrapbooks nos. 2 and 3; 1915 speech "Elizabeth Cady Stanton" by Harriot Stanton Blatch; speeches by Nora Stanton Barney (1944, 1946); *The Una* (January 1855); article "Woman's Half-Century of Evolution" by Susan B. Anthony (*North American Review*, December 1902).

Stanton, Elizabeth Cady, Susan B. Anthony, and Matilda Jocelyn Gage, eds. *History of Woman Suffrage*, vols. 1-3.   Susan B. Anthony and Ida H. Harper, eds., v. 4.   Ida H. Harper, ed., vols. 5-6. New York: Fowler and Wells, 1881-1922.
The first three volumes were collected with the purpose of "putting into permanent shape the few scattered reports of the Woman Suffrage Movment . . . and to make it an arsenal of facts for those who were begining to inquire into the demands and arguments of the leaders of this reform." (1:8).   The final three volumes became necessary after it was apparent that the movement needed further documentation until suffrage was achieved. The historical record includes newspaper reprints, speech manuscripts, copies of letters and essays, reports of conventions and legal proceedings, engravings, and editorials, all interwoven with personal reminiscences and biographical sketches. The editors acknowledge that some people active in the movement refused to contribute any material, "through ill-timed humility"; they also confess to some chagrin at being both the tactical and philosophical leaders of the reform movement as well as its historians.   However, they assert that history allowed them to describe their impelling motives and the struggles they overcame, and thus they feel the *HWS* gets near the "soul of the

subject." In fact, volume 3's preface refers to the series as being missionary-like, as it "bear(s) the glad gospel of woman's emancipation to all civilized nations. (3: iv). Although only the first three volumes had Cady Stanton's direct editorial input, the reader might find it interesting to see the progression of ideas and arguments as the movement began, developed, suffered splits, and rejoined before triumphing with the Federal Woman Suffrage Amendment in 1920.

Volume 1 covers the period 1848-1861, including a historical review dating to the beginnings of civilization and the subjugation of women. Topics covered include woman in newspapers, a report on the 1840 London World's Anti-Slavery Convention; the Seneca Falls convention; women's rights meetings in New York, Ohio, Massachusetts, Indiana, Wisconsin, Pennsylvania, and New Jersey; and the relationship between woman, Church, and State.

Volume 2 covers 1861-1876; its focus is on the achievements and setbacks the movement made during and after the war. Topics represented include women during the Civil War, Congressional action on women's rights, conventions, the Kansas campaign for suffrage, Reconstruction, legal cases, and the birth of the American Woman Suffrage Association. This last section, written by Harriot Stanton, was included upon her insistence; because of the controversial schism, no mention of that group had been included by the editors in their initial planning.

Volume 3 extends from 1876-1885; its preface says that this volume's special interest lies in the international contributions from women reporting on experiences and legislative progress. Its coverage includes Centennial celebrations (1876); convention and congressional reports, debates, and hearings; reports from a majority of the states and territories; and reports from Canada, Great Britain, and Continental Europe. The volume ends with excerpts from Cady Stanton's autobiography, here entitled "Reminiscences" and covering the period in 1882 when she visited Great Britain. This volume does offer an abbreviated index to the first three volumes.

Volume 4, edited by Anthony and Ida Husted Harper, covers 1883-1900. Its materials include a review of the movement's progress; arguments on the constitutional right of women to vote; convention and congressional hearing reports; reports on the various rights granted to women in different states; women's rights efforts in Great Britain (including the British Empire) and other foreign countries; and a discussion of national organizations of women. The index in volume 4 is more extensive than the one in Volume 3, especially in the indexing of speeches.

Volume 5, edited by Harper, covers 1900-1920, with its primary focus on the history of the attempts made to secure state-by-state suffrage. In addition to accounts of annual conventions of the NAWSA, this volume presents the "story of the federal suffrage amendment" by reviewing various hearings and depicting attempts to get a woman suffrage plank into the platforms of the national political parties. Finally, several chapters are devoted to other women's organizations, such as the League of Woman Voters. Additional material included involves the war service of women and miscellaneous speeches, including addresses at Cady Stanton's funeral.

Volume 6, edited by Harper, concludes the account of 1900-1920, with its coverage including state reports on the work for woman suffrage, including attempts for ratification of the Suffrage Amendment. In addition, there are chapters on the effort in the Territories and internationally.

Stanton, Theodore, and Harriot Stanton Blatch, eds. *Elizabeth Cady Stanton As Revealed in Her Letters, Diary, and Reminiscences.* 2 Vols. New York: Harper and Brothers, 1922.

Volume 1 presents Cady Stanton's revision of *Eighty Years and More,* which the editors claim she had begun prior to her death. Volume 2 includes letters from 1839-1880, plus selections from Cady Stanton's diary, which she began in 1880. Because of the extensive editing (including changes in content, deletion of entire passages, and addition of other material), the two volumes are of dubious merit for the researcher. An appendix at the end of volume 1 provides a list of Cady Stanton's addresses and other written or spoken appeals, which might prove useful for chronology.

Woman's Rights Conventions: Seneca Falls & Rochester, 1848. New York: Arno Press, 1969.

This brief book reprints the reports of the proceedings of the woman's rights conventions held at Seneca Falls (July 1848) and Rochester (August 1848). The first report presents the resolutions and the Declaration of Sentiments, while the second report summarizes various positions taken by the key speakers. This book supplements the material found in volume 1 of the *History of Woman Suffrage.*

Biographies

Banner, Lois W. *Elizabeth Cady Stanton: A Radical for Woman's Rights.* Boston: Little, Brown and Company, 1980.

This brief biography, part of the *Library of American Biography* series, presents the fundamental details of Cady Stanton's private and public life. Due to its brevity, it can serve as a basic source to get the essential facts. Unfortunately, there is no documentation of material; thus, the uninformed reader might assume that some of the interpretations Banner puts forth are historical fact. For instance, Banner discusses the sexual relationship between Cady Stanton and her husband and infers that "(it) also was probably a source of frustration" (35); this conclusion is apparently based upon the 1853 phrenological analysis of Elizabeth that said she was able to enjoy the connubial relationship to a high degree, in contrast with what she often wrote publically about the unregulated male sexual drives. But because the biography was written to introduce the uninformed to the chronology of Cady Stanton's major events, crises, and activities and not as a comprehensive evaluation and interpretation of all her impact, Banner's book can serve to initiate the reader into key events.

Clarke, Mary Stetson. *Bloomers & Ballots: Elizabeth Cady Stanton and Women's Rights.* New York: Viking Press, 1972.
Clarke's fictional biography is intended to introduce younger readers to Elizabeth Cady Stanton. As such, it is an enthusiastically written chronology, admiring Cady Stanton's accomplishments, dramatizing many of her life events, and painting a picture of a spirited, tireless fighter for women's rights. Because of the juvenile and dramatic tone, the lack of cited scholarship, and the glossing over of many details, the book is unsuitable for the researcher.

Faber, Doris. *Oh, Lizzie! The Life of Elizabeth Cady Stanton.* New York: Lothrop, Lee & Shepard Company, 1972.
Faber's biography, written for juvenile readers, dramatizes selected events in Cady Stanton's life. The sensational tone, imaginary dialogue, and glossing over of details provides the adult reader little useful material.

Griffith, Elisabeth. *In Her Own Right: The Life of Elizabeth Cady Stanton.* New York: Oxford University Press, 1984.
This comprehensive, thoroughly documented scholarly work is the most outstanding of all the Cady Stanton biographies. The book grew from the author's dissertation, and as such provides extensive research via the methodology of social learning theory. This method allowed Griffith to view Cady Stanton's life as a progression of behavior patterns based upon successive role models. The method is not intrusive in depicting the range of events and personalities that influenced Cady Stanton's character. Indeed, the book depicts Cady Stanton's life as a series of calculated choices, in which she learned, selected, practised, and maintained different roles and strategies to portray her ideal vision. Griffith presents the reader with the "complete" Cady Stanton by investigating her childhood, recalling her contributions, and analyzing her character and motives. The overall theme of the psychobiography is that Cady Stanton's life was unified

by a feminist ethic of independence, which she then articulated as an "ideology of autonomy for other women" throughout her public career.

While the author admits that this is a "great woman biography," she presents a balanced view of Cady Stanton, who carefully constructed the public image by which she wanted to be remembered. The biography also provides family trees of the Livingston-Cady family and the Cady-Stanton family, an account of a phrenological reading done in 1853 of Cady Stanton, a well-documented set of notes, and sixteen pages of photographs of Cady Stanton, members of her family, and important other figures. Griffith's style is both inspiring and authoritative; she portrays Cady Stanton's imperfections as well as triumphs. This work should be the biographical benchmark for the researcher interested in the multi-faceted dimensions of Cady Stanton's personality, character, and public and personal life.

Lutz, Alma. *Created Equal: A Biography of Elizabeth Cady Stanton 1815-1902*. New York: Octagon Books, 1974.
Lutz depicts Cady Stanton as the torchbearer who predicted changes in the roles and duties of women. Harriot Stanton Blatch granted Lutz permission to use much of Cady Stanton's private papers, but because it lacks any reference notes or other citation forms, the book's scholarly usefulness is limited. Lutz presents the basic familial and historical contexts that Cady Stanton had covered in her autobiography and other published materials: here are the narratives about the death of her brother, the Bloomer costume, and various campaigns. The narrative style is picturesque, the tone reverent. Lutz does not characterize Cady Stanton in a negative fashion, and scandals (such as the love between her and Bayard or the Beecher-Tilton case) are described with a more positive than objective slant. While for many years, this biography was the standard source by which to learn about Cady Stanton, it suffers in comparison with the outstanding scholarship of the Griffith text; therefore, its primary usefulness probably lies in its general faithfulness to the Cady Stanton story rather than in its scholarly approach.

Oakley, Mary Ann B. *Elizabeth Cady Stanton*. New York: The Feminist Press, 1972.
This brief paperback biography, written in a conversational style, presents the essential data about Cady Stanton: her childhood, marriage, introduction to reform causes, and presence in the women's rights movement. The book mixes historical material with fictionalized conversation, which the author defends because, she asserts, "I tried to follow what I feel would have been said" based upon conversation or narrative from *Eighty Years and More* and

HWS.   The simplicity of the chronology may be useful for the unfamiliar reader who is searching for a quick summary of the major facts and accomplishments of Cady Stanton's life.   However, it is not recommended for research purposes other than to gain the broadest historical background.

Stanton, Elizabeth Cady. *Eighty Years and More: Reminiscences 1815-1897.* 1898; repr.   New York: Schocken Books, 1971.
The autobiography presents Cady Stanton as she wanted others to remember her: a heroic and undaunted figure,   an "enthusiastic housekeeper and mother of seven children," and a woman possessing few flaws.   As a research source, its accuracy is questionable, for Cady Stanton's memory for dates and occurrences was often inexact, her descriptions of the people in her life were incomplete, and her involvement in various crises and scandals was often ignored. In addition, Cady Stanton's children altered the manuscript as originally published; they deleted sections that referred to domestic problems or scandals and added material in other areas.   This 1971 edition, however, presents Cady Stanton's original version.   Cady Stanton does present her perceptions covering her astounding career, which had a major impact on vast areas of social, political, and legal life. She briefly reviews the "mistakes" she was accused of (including demands for the vote, divorce, and on the Church) and justifies her actions on all accounts. Thus, the reader gets a sense of the private Cady Stanton (if there were such a person) to a limited degree, for she depicts her life as one where she generally filled many roles with ease, where "right" generally won, and where "common sense" prevailed. The reader must keep in mind the imperfections of this work in assessing its significant usefulness; however, it can serve as an introduction to Cady Stanton's critical thinking process, style and tone, which might serve well once the reader pursues the more accurate historical record of Cady Stanton's public life.

SELECT BIBLIOGRAPHY

Books

Adams, Elmer C., and Warren D. Foster. *Heroines of Modern Progress.* New York: Macmillan, 1926.
Altback, Edith, ed. *From Feminism to Liberation.* Cambridge, Mass.: Schenkman, 1971.
Anderson, Judith, ed. *Outspoken Women: Speeches by American Women Reformers, 1635-1935.* Dubuque, Iowa: Kendall/Hunt, 1984.

Anthony, Katharine. *Susan B. Anthony: Her Personal History and Her Era.* Garden City, New York: Doubleday, 1954.

Bacon, Margaret Hope. *Valiant Friend: The Life of Lucretia Mott.* New York: Walker and Company, 1980.

Ballard, Laura C. "Elizabeth Cady Stanton" In*Our Famous Women: An Authoritative Record of the Lives and Deeds of Distinguished American Women of Our Times.* Hartford, Conn.1886.

Beard, Mary R. *Woman as Force in History: A Study in Traditions and Realities.* New York: Octagon Books, 1967.

Blackwell, Alice Stone. *Lucy Stone, Pioneer of Woman's Rights.* Boston: Little, Brown, and Company,1930.

Blatch, Harriot Stanton, and Alma Lutz. *Challenging Years: The Memoirs of Harriot Stanton Blatch.* New York: G. P. Putnam's Sons, 1940.

Bloomer, Amelia. *The Life and Writings of Amelia Bloomer.* Ed. Dexter C. Bloomer. Boston: 1895; repr. New York: Schocken Books, 1974.

Bode, Carl. *The American Lyceum.* New York: Oxford University Press, 1956.

Bormann, Ernest G. *Forerunners of Black Power: The Rhetoric of Abolition* Englewood Cliffs, N.J.: Prentice-Hall, Inc., 1971.

Bowers, John W. and Donovan Ochs. *The Rhetoric of Agitation and Control.* Reading, Mass.: Addison-Wesley, 1971.

Burnap, George W. *The Sphere and Duties of Woman.* Baltimore,1848.

Buhle, Paul, and Mari Jo Buhle, eds. *The Concise History of Woman Suffrage: Selections from the Classic Work of Stanton, Anthony, Gage, and Harper.* Urbana: University of Illinois Press, 1978.

Catt, Carrie Chapman, and Nettie Shuler. *Woman Suffrage and Politics: The Inner Story of the Suffrage Movement.* New York: Scribner's Sons, 1926.

Cott, Nancy F. *The Bonds of Womanhood; "Woman's Sphere" in New England 1780-1835.* New Haven, Conn.: Yale University Press, 1977.

Cromwell, Otelia. *Lucretia Mott.* Cambridge, Mass.: Harvard University Press, 1958.

Davis, Paulina W. *A History of the National Women's Rights Movement for Twenty Years.* New York: 1871.

Deckard, Barbara Sinclair. *The Women's Movement: Political, Socio-economic, and Psychological Issues.* 2nd ed. New York: Harper and Row, 1979.

Delamont, Sara, and Lorna Duffin, eds. *The Nineteenth-Century Woman: Her Cultural and Physical World.* New York: Harper and Row, 1978.

DuBois, Ellen. *Feminism and Suffrage: the Emergence of an Independent Women's Movement in America, 1848-1869*. Ithaca, N.Y.: Cornell University Press, 1978.

Earhart, Mary. *Frances Willard: From Prayers to Politics*. Chicago: University of Chicago Press, 1944.

Flexner, Eleanor. *Century of Struggle: The Woman's Rights Movement in the United States*. Cambridge, Mass.: Belknap Press, 1959.

Foster, G. Allen. *Votes for Women*. New York: Criterion Books, 1966.

Gluck, Sherna. *From Parlor to Prison: Five American Suffragists Talk About Their Lives*. New York: Octagon Books, 1976.

Graham, Abbie. *Ladies in Revolt*. New York: Woman's Press, 1934.

Grimes, Allen. *The Puritan Ethic and Woman Suffrage*. New York: Oxford University Press, 1967.

Gurko, Miriam. *The Ladies of Seneca Falls: The Birth of the Woman's Rights Movement*. New York: MacMillan, 1974.

Hahn, Emily. *Once Upon a Pedestal*. New York: Thomas Y. Crowell Company, 1974.

Hallowell, J., ed. *James and Lucretia Mott: Life and Letters*. Boston, 1884.

Harper, Ida Usted. *The Life and Work of Susan B. Anthony*, 3 vols. Indianapolis, In., 1898.

Hays, Elinor Rice. *Morning Star: Biography of Lucy Stone, 1818-1893*. New York: Harcourt, Brace, 1961.

Hersh, Blanche Glassman. *The Slavery of Sex: Feminist-Abolitionist in America*. Urbana: University of Illinois Press, 1978.

Hymowitz, Carol, and Michaele Weissman. *A History of Women in America.* New York: Bantam Books, 1978.

Irwin, Inez Haynes. *Angels and Amazons: A Hundred Years of American Women*. Garden City, N.J.: Doubleday, Doran, and Company, 1934.

Kraditor, Aileen S., ed. *Up From the Pedestal; Selected Writings in the History of American Feminism*. Chicago,: Quadrangle Books, 1968.

---. *The Ideas of the Woman Suffrage Movement, 1890-1920*. New York: Columbia University Press, 1965.

Kennedy, Patricia S., and Gloria H. O'Shields. *We Shall Be Heard: Women Speakers in America*. Dubuque, Iowa: Kendall/Hunt, 1983.

Lerner, Gerda. *The Grimke Sisters from South Carolina: Pioneers for Woman's Rights and Abolition*. Boston: Houghton Mifflin, 1967.

Lutz, Alma. *Emma Willard, Daughter of Democracy*. Boston: Houghton Mifflin, 1929.

---. *Susan B. Anthony: Rebel, Crusader, Humanitarian*. Boston,: Beacon, 1959.

McPherson, James. *The Struggle for Equality: Abolitionists and the Negro in the Civil War and Reconstruction*. Princeton: Princeton University Press, 1964.

Melder, Keith. *Beginnings of Sisterhood: The American Woman's Rights Movement, 1800-1850*. New York: Schocken Books, 1977.

Morgan, David. *Suffragists and Democrats; The Politics of Woman Suffrage in America*. Ann Arbor: Michigan State University Press, 1972.

Nies, Judith. *Seven Women: Portraits from the American Radical Tradition*. New York: Viking Press, 1977.

O'Connor, Lillian. *Pioneer Women Orators: Rhetoric in the Ante-Bellum Reform Movement*. New York: Columbia University Press, 1954.

O'Neill, William L. *Everyone Was Brave; The Rise and Fall of Feminism in America*. Chicago: Quadrangle Books, 1969.

Parker, Edward G. *The Golden Age of American Oratory*. Boston: 1857.

Parton, James, Horace Greeley, et al., eds. *Eminent Women of the Age: Being Narratives of the Lives and Deeds of the Most Prominent Women of the Present Generation*. Hartford, Conn., 1869.

Phelps, Elizabeth S., ed. *Our Famous Women*. Hartford, Conn., 1888.

Paulson, Ross E. *Women's Suffrage and Prohibition: A Comparative Study of Equality and Social Control*. Glenview, Ill.: Scott, Foresman, 1973.

Ramelson, Marian. *The Petticoat Rebellion: A Century of Struggle for Women's Rights*. 3rd ed. London: Lawrence and Wishart, 1976.

Rice, Arthur. "Henry B. Stanton as a Political Abolitionist." Ph.D. diss. Columbia Teachers College, 1968.

Riegel, Robert. *American Feminists*. Lawrence: University of Kansas Press, 1963.

Ross, Isabel. *Ladies of the Press*. New York: Harper and Brothers, 1936.

Rossi, Alice S., ed. *The Feminist Papers: From Adams to Beauvoir*. New York, New York: Columbia University Press, 1973.

Schlipp, Madelon, and Sharon M. Murphy. *Great Women of the Press*. Carbondale: Southern Illinois University Press, 1983.

Schneir, Miriam, ed. *Feminism: The Essential Historical Writings*. New York: Vintage Press, 1972.

Stanton, Elizabeth Cady, and the Revising Committee. *The Woman's Bible.*(2 vols.) New York:1895-1898.

Stanton, Henry B. *Random Recollections*. New York: 1887.

Stewart, Charles, Craig Smith, and Robert E. Denton, Jr. *Persuasion and Social Movements*. Prospect Heights, Ill.: Waveland Press, 1984.

Thompson, Eleanor Wolf. *Education for Ladies 1830-1860; Ideas on Education in Magazines for Women.* Morningside Heights, N. Y.: King's Crown Press, 1947.

VanVuuren, Nancy. *The Subversion of Women as Practiced by Churches, Witch-Hunters, and Other Sexists.* Philadelphia: Westminster Press, 1973.

Waggenspack, Beth M. "Elizabeth Cady Stanton's Reform Rhetoric 1848-1854." Ph.D. diss. The Ohio State University, 1982.

Articles

Andrews, James R. "Reflections of the National Character in American Rhetoric." *Quarterly Journal of Speech* 57 (April 1970): 316-24.

---. "History and Theory in the Study of the Rhetoric of Social Movements." *Central States Speech Journal* 31 (Winter 1980): 274-81.

---."An Historical Perspective on the Study of Social Movements." *Central States Speech Journal* 34 (Spring 1983): 67-69.

Bitzer, Lloyd. "The Rhetorical Situation." *Philosophy and Rhetoric* 1 (1968): 1-14.

---. "Functional Communication: A Situational Perspective." In *Rhetoric in Transition: Studies in the Nature and Uses of Rhetoric*, ed. Eugene E. White. University Park: Pennsylvania State University Press, 1980.

Blackwell, Alice Stone. "Woman's 75 Year Fight." *Nation* (18 July 1923): 53-54.

Bormann, Ernest G. "Fantasy and Rhetorical Vision: The Rhetorical Criticism of Social Reality." *Quarterly Journal of Speech* 58 (December 1972): 396-407.

Bosmajian, Haig A. "The Abrogation of the Suffragists' First Amendment Rights." *Western Speech*,38 (Fall 1974): 318-22.

Campbell, Karlyn Kohrs. "Stanton's 'The Solitude of Self': A Rationale for Feminism." *Quarterly Journal of Speech* 66 (1980): 304-12.

---. "Elizabeth Cady Stanton." In Duffy, Bernard K. and Halford R. Ryan, eds. *American Orators Before 1900: Critical Studies and Sources.* Westport, Conn.: Greenwood Press, 1987.

Cathcart, Robert S. "New Approaches to the Study of Movements: Defining Movements Rhetorically." *Western Speech* 36 (Spring 1972): 82-88.

---. "A Confrontation Perspective on the Study of Social Movements." *Central States Speech Journal* 34 (Spring 1983): 69-74.

Conrad, Charles. "Agon and Rhetorical Form: The Essence of 'Old Feminist' Rhetoric." *Central States Speech Journal* 32 (Spring 1981): 45-53.

Coughlin, Elizabeth Myette and Charles E. Coughlin. "Convention in Petticoats: the Seneca Falls Declaration of Woman's Rights." *Today's Speech* 21. 4(Fall 1973): 17-23.

DuBois, Ellen. "The Radicalism of the Woman Suffrage Movement." *Feminist Studies* 3 (Fall 1975): 61-71.

Galpin, W. Freeman, ed. "Elizabeth Cady Stanton and Gerrit Smith: Excerpts from Their Correspondence between 1856 and 1875, Pertaining to Abolition and Women's Rights." *New York History* 16 (1935): 323.

Goodman, James E. "The Origins of the 'Civil War' in the Reform Community: Elizabeth Cady Stanton on Woman's Rights and Reconstruction." *Critical Matrix: Princeton Working Papers in Women's Studies* 1. 2 (1985): 1-29.

Griffin, Leland M. "The Rhetoric of Historical Movements." *Quarterly Journal of Speech* 38 (April 1952): 184-88.

Hahn, Dan F. and Ruth M. Gonchar. "Studying Social Movements: A Rhetorical Methodology." *Speech Teacher* 20 (January 1971): 44-52.

Hancock, Brenda R. "Affirmation by Negation in the Women's Liberation Movement." *Quarterly Journal of Speech* 58 (October 1972): 264-71.

Harper, Ida Husted. "Elizabeth Cady Stanton." *American Monthly Review of Reviews* (December 1902): 715-19.

Hart, Roderick P. "The Rhetoric of the True Believer." *Speech Monographs* 38 (November 1971): 249-61.

Hope, Diana Schaich. "Redefinition of Self: A Comparison of the Rhetoric of the Women's Liberation and the Black Liberation Movements." *Today's Speech* 23 (Winter 1975): 17-25.

Kroll, Becky Swanson. "From Small Group to Public View: Mainstreaming the Women's Movement." *Communication Quarterly* 31 (Spring 1983): 139-47.

Lerner, Gerda. "The Lady and the Mill Girl: Changes in the Status of Women in the Age of Jackson." *Mid-Continent Studies Journal* 10 (1969): 5-15.

---. "The Political Activites of Antislavery Women." In *The Majority Finds Its Past: Placing Women in History*. Oxford University Press, 1979.

Lomas, Charles W. "The Agitator in American Society." *Western Speech* 24 (Spring 1960): 76-83.

Marzolf, Marion. "The Feminist Press Then and Now." In *Up From the Footnote: A History of Women Journalists*. New York: Hastings House, 1977.

Masel-Walters, Lynne. "Their Rights and Nothing More: A History of *The Revolution*, 1868-1870." *Journalism Quarterly* (Summer 1976): 242-51.

McPherson, James M. "Abolitionists, Woman Suffrage, and the Negro, 1865-1869." *Mid-America* 47 (January 1965): 40-46.

Riegel, Robert S. "The Split of the Feminist Movement in 1869." *Mississippi Valley Historical Review* 49 (December 1962): 484-96.

Simons, Herbert W. "Requirements, Problems, and Strategies: A Theory of Persuasion for Social Movements." *Quarterly Journal of Speech* 56 (February 1970): 1-11.

Smith-Rosenberg, Carroll. "The Female World of Love and Ritual: Relations Between Women in Nineteenth-Century America." *Signs* 1 (Autumn 1975): 1-29.

Smith, Ralph, and Russell Windes. "The Rhetoric of Mobilization: Implications for the Study of Movements." *Southern Speech Communication Journal* 42 (Fall 1976): 1-19.

Smith, Ralph R. "The Historical Criticism of Social Movments." *Central States Speech Journal* 31 (Winter 1980): 290-97.

Stearns, Bertha-Monica. "Reform Periodicals and Female Reformers 1830-1860." *The American Historical Review* 37. 1 (October 1973): 678-99.

Welter, Barbara. "The Cult of True Womanhood, 1820-1860." *American Quarterly* 18 (Summer1966): 151-74.

Wilkinson, Charles A. "A Rhetorical Definition of Movements." Central States Speech Journal 27 (Summer 1976): 84-94.

Index